Dotawo ▸
A Journal of Nubian Studies

2020 #7

Comparative Northern East Sudanic Linguistics

Edited by
Vincent W.J. van Gerven Oei

p.

Dotawo ▸ A Journal of Nubian Studies

Design
Vincent W.J. van Gerven Oei and Marcell Mars.

Cover image
Wrestlers from the Nuba Mountains. Photo by Vincent W.J. van Gerven Oei.

For submission guidelines please see our website,
https://escholarship.org/uc/dotawo
dotawo@unionfornubianstudies.org

ISBN-13: 978-1-953035-39-4 (print); 978-1-953035-40-0 (ePDF)
ISSN: 2373-2571 (online)
LCCN: 2021933400

Dotawo ▸

1. A medieval Nubian kingdom controlling the central Nile Valley, best known from Old Nubian documents excavated at Qasr Ibrim and other sites in Lower Nubia.
2. An open-access journal of Nubian studies, providing a cross-disciplinary platform for historians, linguists, anthropologists, archaeologists, and other scholars interested in all periods and aspects of Nubian civilization.

1. ⲟⲩⲛⲇⲉ̄ⲛⲛⲁ, ⲇⲟⲧⲁⳣⳣⲟ ⲛⲟⲡⲁⲛ ϩⲓⲣⲓⲥⲧⲓ̈ⲁⲛⲟⲥⲛ ⲟⲣⲕⲓ ⳣⲉ̄ⲣⲁ ⲙⲉⲛⲟ. ⲧⲁⲣ ⲁⲙⲁⲛ-ⲓⲣⲕⲓⲛ ⲅⲁⲥⲕⲟⲕⲕⲁ ⲙⲟⲩⲣⲧⲁ ⲇⲁ̄ⲅⲓ ⲕⲉⲛⲟ. ⲇⲟⲧⲁⳣⳣⲟⲅ ⲁϣⲣⲓ̄ⲕⲓⲣ ⲓⲣⲡⲉⲥⲁ ⲟⲩⲛⲇⲉ̄ⲛ ⲛⲟⲡⲁⲛ ⲫⲁ̄ⲓ̈ⲧⲧⲓ ⳣⲉ̄ⲕⲕⲟⲩⲗⲟⲅⲟ, ⲙⲁⲛ ⲓⲡⲣⲓⲙⲓⲛ ⲕⲁⲥⲁⲗⲗⲁ ⲉⲗⲇⲁⳝⳝⲟⲗⲗⲁⲧⲟ̄ⲛⲁ, ⲓ̈ⲁ̄ⲛ ⲁⲅⲁⲣ ⲓϭϭⲓⲕⲕⲟ̄ⲩ̄ⲗⲗⲁ, ⲙⲁⲛ ⲛⲟ̄ⲩ̄ⲡⲁⲛ ⲧⲁⳣⳣⲟ ⲉⲗⲇⲁⳝⳝⲟⲗⲗⲁⲧⲟ̄ⲛⲁ.
2. ⲓⲥⲁⲕⲕⲁ, ⲇⲟⲧⲁⳣⳣⲟ ϣⲟ̄ⲡ ϣⲟ̄ⲡⲓⲛ ⲕⲓ̄ⲛ ⲥⲓⲅⲉⲣⲓⲛ ⲉⲣⲣⲓ ⳣⲉ̄ⲣⲁ ⲁⳝⳝⲟ. ⲇⲟⲧⲁⳣⳣⲟ, ⲛⲟⲡⲁⲛ ⲕⲟⲩⲗⲗⲓⲧⲧⲓ ⲙⲁⲗⲗⲉ̄ⲗⲗⲉⲕⲓⲛ ⲕⲁⳣⳣⲁⲫⲓ. ⲇⲟⲧⲁⳣⳣⲟ, ⲥⲁⲙ ⳣⲉ̄ⲕⲕⲁ ⲡⲁ̄ⲥⲕⲉ, ⲕⲟⲩⲗⲗⲓⲧⲧⲓ ⲓϭϭⲓⲕⲕⲟ̄ⲩ̄ ⳁⲁⲙⲙⲓⲕⲁϭϭⲁⲗⲓ̈ⲁ. ⲓⲛ ⲥⲁⲙⲓⲕⲕⲟⲛⲓ, ⲟⲩⲛⲇⲉ̄ⲛ ⲕⲟⲩⲗⲗⲉⲕⲁⲧⲧⲓ̄ⲕⲕⲟ, ⲧⲁⲙⲉⲛ ⲕⲟⲩⲗⲗⲉⲕⲁⲧⲧⲓ̄ⲕⲕⲟ, ⲡⲓⲣⲡⲉ̄ⲛ ⲕⲟⲩⲗⲗⲉⲕⲁⲧⲧⲓ̄ⲕⲕⲟ, ⲙⲟⲩⲅⲙⲁⲣⲓⲛ ⲕⲟⲩⲗⲗⲉⲕⲁⲧⲧⲓ̄ⲕⲕⲟⲛⲁ ⲁⳝⳝⲓ. ⳣⲓ̄ⲇⲁⲅⲟ̄ⲛⲓ, ⲇⲟⲧⲁⳣⳣⲟ, ⲥⲁⲙ ⲇⲁⳣⳣⲓ ⳣⲉ̄ ⲫⲁ ⲁⳝⳝⲓ, ⲕⲟⲩⲗⲗⲉⲕⲁⲧⲧⲓ ⲓϭϭⲓ ⲙⲁⲗⲗⲉ̄ⲛⲁ. ⲙⲁⲛ ⲕⲟⲩⲗⲗⲉⲕⲁⲧⲧⲓ ⲙⲁⲗⲗⲉ̄, ⲛⲟⲡⲁⲛ ⲇⲓⲫⲫⲓⲕⲕⲓⲛ ⲕⲓⲛⲛⲓⲅⲟ̄ⲩ̄ⲕⲕⲟⲛ, ⲅⲁ̄ⲣⲕⲟ̄ⲩ̄ⲅⲟ̄ⲛ ⲕⲟⲩⲗⲗⲓⲛⲛⲁⲛⳝⲁ ⲫⲓⲣⲅⲓ.*

1. Ammiki Nuba-n sirki Tungula-n Bahar aal poccika anda kannim, ne poccika an ammikin Nuba-n kitaaba an Kasr Ibrimiro poon isshi Nuba aro-n ammiki ir kar əəl koran əəllooyanero poccikare əəl oddnooyim.
2. Ele ne Nuba poccikan muɟallayane, aal poccika yaa əərngaanyatn, taariikiro, aallo, elekon poon ammik(i) ir ayin ir kanniyam pirro, poon ammik(i) aallo, elek(i) aallo poccikaa yaa əərngaanyatn.**

* Translation into Nobiin courtesy of Mohamed K. Khalil.
** Translation into Midob Nubian courtesy of Ishag A. Hassan.

issue/ *Dotawo 7: Comparative Northern East Sudanic Linguistics*

editor/ *Vincent W.J. van Gerven Oei*

has articles/

1. Preface by the Editor

1.1. A New Platform

Since its inception, the *www/*Union for Nubian Studies has been committed to opening up Nubiological research to a wider audience and broadening access to source materials. *Dotawo: A Journal of Nubian Studies* was launched in 2014 as an open-access journal, with free access for both authors and readers. It has been hosted by www/DigitalCommons@Fairfield of Fairfield University and since 2019 by University of California's www/eScholarship platform.

Both digital platforms allowed *Dotawo* to grow, expanding its reach by means of the creation of persistent digital identifiers and membership of the www/Directory of Open Access Journals. The content of *Dotawo,* however, remained essentially tailored to human — rather than machine — readers because it was only available in PDF or printed form, and to privileged readers with access to institutional libraries because the references it included were often difficult to access for members of the public without such access, even though most if not all of this research was produced with the aid of public funds. This state of affairs presented a challenge in terms of the accessibility and discoverability of the journal as well as the long-term preservation and openness of the scholarship presented and referenced.

Starting with the present issue, *Dotawo* will design and publish its content via the www/Sandpoints platform. *Dotawo* contributions are formatted in www/Markdown syntax, thus moving away from proprietary software such as Microsoft Word and Adobe InDesign. For collaboration and version-control we employ www/Git rather than Google Drive or Dropbox. The online issue is created via www/Gitea and www/Hugo, which take the Markdown files from the Git repository and generate a static website from them. The result is a compact and fast website, which moreover can also be used offline. Also the typography of *Dotawo* is now based on open fonts. The journal is typeset in www/Gentium, which is released under an www/SIL Open Font License. The PDF output is generated by www/PagedJS, and will continue to be hosted on the eScholarship platform, while the printed book will remain available through scholar-led open access press www/punctum books. In short, all of the software used in the creation of *Dotawo* is now open source. Although this process demands a certain amount of flexibility of the editors, it also shows that transitioning an open access journal to open infrastructure is not only possible but also feasible.

The plundering and destruction of the University of Khartoum by forces allied with the former dictator during the 2019 Sudanese Revolution[1] has once again impressed upon us the precarity of the research environment in which many scholars of Nubia operate and thus the necessity and moral obligation of creating open and resistant scholarly infrastructures. To improve the long-term preservation of and access to the scholarship contained and referenced in

Dotawo, all sources mentioned in contributions to the journal will henceforth be linked, as much as possible, to records deposited in a public library using the open infrastructure of www/Memory of the World.[2] This will allow for easy storage and dissemination of both content and context of the research presented in *Dotawo* to those scholars of Nubia — and there are many — who are not institutionally privileged, including many who live in the Global South.

A recent, bleak assessment by Richard Poynder of the goals set by the www/ Budapest Open Access Initiative (BOAI) Declaration in 2002, and the open access movement more broadly, states that "it now seems unlikely that the *affordability* and *equity* problems will be resolved, which will impact disproportionately negatively on those in the Global South":[3]

> OA advocates failed to anticipate — and then for too long ignored — how their advocacy was allowing legacy publishers to co-opt open access, and in ways that work as much against the goals of BOAI as for them. And they have often downplayed the negative consequences that OA policies and initiatives developed in the Global North will have for those in the Global South.[4]

Furthermore, it appears that the turn toward open access in the scholarly communications landscape is increasingly facilitating the agendas of an oligopoly of for-profit data analytics companies. Perhaps realizing that "they've found something that is even more profitable than selling back to us academics the content that we have produced,"[5] they venture ever further up the research stream, with every intent to colonize and canalize its entire flow.[6] This poses a severe threat to the independence and quality of scholarly inquiry.[7]

In the light of these troubling developments, the expansion from *Dotawo* as a "diamond" open access to a *common access* journal represents a strong reaffirmation of the call that the late Aaron Swartz succinctly formulated in his "Guerilla Open Access Manifesto":

> Those with access to these resources — students, librarians, scientists — you have been given a privilege. You get to feed at this banquet of knowledge while the rest of the world is locked out. But you need not — indeed, morally, you cannot — keep this privilege for yourselves. You have a duty to share it with the world.[8]

Swartz's is a call to action that transcends the limitations of the open access movement as construed by the BOAI Declaration by plainly affirming that knowledge is a common good. His call goes beyond open access, because it specifically targets materials that linger on a paper or silicon substrate in academic libraries and digital repositories without being accessible to "fair use." The deposition of the references from *Dotawo* contributions in a public library is a first and limited attempt to offer a remedy, heeding the "Code of Best Practices in Fair Use" of the www/Association of Research Libraries, which approvingly cites the late Supreme Court Justice Brandeis that "the noblest of human productions — knowledge, truths ascertained, conceptions, and ideas — become, after voluntary communication to others, free as the air to common use."[9] This approach also dovetails the interpretation of "folk law" recently propounded by Kenneth Goldsmith, the founder of public library www/Ubuweb.[10]

I strongly believe that it is in the interest of Nubian Studies and its stakeholders, especially scholars in adjunct or para-academic positions without access to institutional repositories, and the Nubian people who are actively denied knowledge of their own culture, to enable the *widest possible* dissemination of scholarship. In this enterprise, striving for common access and relying on open source software are merely a first step.

1.2. About This Issue

The seventh issue of *Dotawo* is dedicated to Comparative Northern East Sudanic (NES) linguistics, offering new insights in the historical connections between the Nubian languages and other members of the NES family such as Nyima, Taman, Nara, and Meroitic. A special focus is placed on comparative morphology.

The Nilo-Saharan phylum was first proposed by Joseph Greenberg as a linguistic remainder grouping whose internal affiliations remained unclear.[11] The Nilo-Saharan phylum contained what Greenberg then called Chari-Nile languages, which in turn included the Eastern Sudanic family. The coherence of this larger linguistic grouping will be investigated in the contribution by Roger Blench, *article/*"Morphological Evidence for the Coherence of East Sudanic."

Within Eastern Sudanic,[12] there is a further subdivision between what Lionel Bender referred to as the Ek- and En-branch, based on the shape of the 1SG pronoun.[13] Bender's Ek-branch contains the Nubian language, Nara, as well as the Nyima and Taman languages. This group of languages is now commonly referred to as Northern East Sudanic.

Although the contours of NES are relatively well established, much of the details of its linguistic development and relations remain the subject of ongoing research and debate. There are three particular issues within NES linguistics to which the articles in the present issue make a contribution:

- The coherence of Nile Nubian
- The inclusion of Nyima
- The inclusion of Meroitic

1.2.1. The Coherence of Nile Nubian

Robin Thelwall proposed that the apparent proximity between Nile Nubian languages Nobiin and Mattokki–Andaandi was not the result of their belonging to the same branch within the Nubian language family, but due to prolonged language contact.[14] In other words, he proposed that there was no such thing as "Nile Nubian." This proposal was further developed by Marianne Bechhaus-Gerst using lexicostatistical methods.[15]

Based on comparative NES phonology, Claude Rilly concluded on the contrary that Nobiin and Mattokki–Andaandi were closely related, and that the divergence between the two in terms of vocabulary was due to the influence of a substrate language underneath Nobiin.[16] Rilly's arguments are supported independently by lexicostatistical evidence presented by George Starostin in his contribution *article/*"Restoring 'Nile Nubian': How to Balance Lexicostatistics and

Etymology in Historical Research on Nubian Languages." Angelika Jakobi's article/ "Nubian Verb Extensions and Some Nyima Correspondences" provides further morphological evidence for the coherence of Nile Nubian.[17]

1.2.2. The Inclusion of Nyima

Although Bender, Rilly, and Dimmendaal include the Nyima languages within NES,[18] these are excluded by Christopher Ehret in his *Historical-Comparative Reconstruction of Nilo-Saharan.*[19] Rejecting Ehret's proposition, Russell Norton's contribution article/"Ama Verbs in Comparative Perspective" provides morphological evidence for inclusion of Nyima in NES. This is reinforced by several correspondences discussed in Jakobi's contribution between Nubian and Nyima.

1.2.3. The Inclusion of Meroitic

Finally, the inclusion of Meroitic in NES has long been a point of contention owing to our fragmentary comprehension of the language.[20] In this respect, the work of Claude Rilly represents an enormous leap forward in our understanding, which can now with relatively strong certainty be classified as Nilo-Saharan, in particular Northern East Sudanic.[21] His contribution article/"Personal Markers and Verbal Number in Meroitic" provides for the first time a systematic overview of person marking in Meroitic, no doubt opening up further avenues in comparative Northern East Sudanic linguistics.

2. Bibliography

Aguado-López, Eduardo & Arianna Becerril-Garcia, *bib/*"The Commercial Model of Academic Publishing Underscoring Plan S Weakens the Existing Open Access Ecosystem in Latin America." *LSE Impact Blog,* May 20, 2020. *www/* https://blogs.lse.ac.uk/impactofsocialsciences/2020/05/20/the-commercial-model-of-academic-publishing-underscoring-plan-s-weakens-the-existing-open-access-ecosystem-in-latin-america/.

Anon. *bib/*"Designing the Public Domain." *Harvard Law Review* 122, no. 5 (2009): pp. 1489–1510.

Bechhaus-Gerst, Marianne. *bib/*"'Nile-Nubian' Reconsidered." In *Topics in Nilo-Saharan Linguistics,* edited by M. Lionel Bender. Hamburg: Helmut Buske, 1989: pp. 85–96.

Bender, M. Lionel. *bib/The East Sudanic Languages: Lexicon and Phonology.* Carbondale: Southern Illinois University, 2005.

Bodó, Balázs. *bib/*"Own Nothing." In *Guerrilla Open Access,* ed. Memory of the World. Coventry: Post Office Press, Rope Press, and Memory of the World, 2018: pp. 16–24.

Dimmendaal, Gerrit J. *bib/*"Nilo-Saharan." In *The Oxford Handbook of Derivational Morphology,* edited by Rochelle Lieber & Pavol Štekauer. Oxford: Oxford University Press, 2014: pp. 591–607.

Ehret, Christopher. *bib/A Historical-Comparative Reconstruction of Nilo-Saharan.* Cologne: Rudiger Köppe, 2001.

Goldsmith, Kenneth. *bib/Duchamp Is My Lawyer: The Polemics, Pragmatics, and Poetics of Ubuweb.* New York: Columbia University Press, 2020.

Greenberg, Joseph H. *bib/The Languages of Africa.* The Hague: Mouton, 1963.

Güldemann, Tom. *bib/*"Historical Linguistics and Genealogical Language Classification in Africa." In *The Languages and Linguistics of Africa,* edited by Tom Güldemann. Berlin: Mouton de Gruyter, 2018: pp. 58–444.

Kelty, Christopher. bib/"Recursive Publics and Open Access." In *Guerrilla Open Access,* ed. Memory of the World. Coventry: Post Office Press, Rope Press, and Memory of the World, 2018: pp. 6–15.

Mars, Marcell, Manar Zarroug & Tomislav Medak. bib/"Public Library." In *Javna knjižnica – Public Library,* edited by Marcell Mars, Tomislav Medak, and WHW. Zagreb: WHW/Multimedijalni Institut, 2015: pp. 75–85.

Moore, Samuel. bib/"The Datafication in Transformative Agreements for Open Access Publishing." July 3, 2020. www/ https://www.samuelmoore.org/2020/07/03/the-datafication-in-transformative-agreements-for-open-access-publishing/

bib/"Report: Large Parts of University of Khartoum Destroyed on June 3." *Dabanga,* August 7, 2019. www/https://www.dabangasudan.org/en/all-news/article/report-large-parts-of-university-of-khartoum-destroyed-on-june-3.

Rilly, Claude. bib/*Le méroïtique et sa famille linguistique.* Leuven: Peeters, 2010.

Swartz, Aaron. bib/"Guerrilla Open Access Manifesto." July 2008. www/ https://archive.org/details/GuerillaOpenAccessManifesto/page/n1/mode/2up.

Thelwall, Robin. bib/"Linguistic Aspects of Greater Nubian History." In *The Archaeological and Linguistic Reconstruction of African History,* edited by Christopher Ehret and Merrick Posnansky, pp. 39–56. Berkeley: University of California Press, 1982.

Endnotes

1. "Report: Large Parts of University of Khartoum Destroyed on June 3." ↩

2. A public library is defined as follows: "[A] public library is: free access to books for every member of society; library catalog; librarian" (Mars, Zarroug & Medak, "Public Library," p. 85). ↩

3. Poynder, "Open access: 'Information wants to be free'?" p. 2. ↩

4. Ibid., p. 22. ↩

5. Bodó, "Own Nothing," p. 23. ↩

6. See, e.g., Moore, "The Datafication in Transformative Agreements for Open Access Publishing." ↩

7. The reduction in agency of academics as a result of the implementation of open access schemes has been widely recognized. As Christopher Kelty put it succinctly: "OA has come to exist and scholarship is more available and more widely distributed than ever before. But, scholars now have less control, and have taken less responsibility for the means of production of scientific research, its circulation, and perhaps even the content of that science" ("Recursive Publics and Open Access," p. 7). These problems are exacerbated in the Global South, as the financial models for OA funding developed in the Global North threaten local public infrastructures managed by academics (Aguado-López & Becerril-Garcia, "The Commercial Model of Academic Publishing Underscoring Plan S Weakens the Existing Open Access Ecosystem in Latin America"). ↩

8. Swartz, "Guerilla Open Access Manifesto." ↩

9. *Int'l News Serv. v. Associated Press,* 248 U.S. 215, 250 (1918) (Brandeis, J., dissenting), cited in Anon., "Designing the Public Domain," p. 1494. ↩

10. Goldsmith, *Duchamp Is My Lawyer.* ↩

11. Greenberg, *The Languages of Africa,* p. 130. ↩

12. See, for a recent overview, Güldemann, "Historical Linguistics and Genealogical Language Classification in Africa," pp. 299–309. ↩

13. Bender, *The East Sudanic Languages,* p. 1. ↩

14. Thelwall, "Linguistic Aspects of a Greater Nubian History," pp. 47–48. ↩

15. See, in particular, Bechhaus-Gerst, "'Nile Nubian' Reconsidered." ↩

16. Rilly, *Le méroïtique et sa famille linguistique,* pp. 274–288. ↩

17. Perhaps it is now time for www/Glottolog to update its entry on Nubian. ↩

18. Bender, *The East Sudanic Languages,* p. 1; Rilly, *Le méroïtique et sa famille linguistique,* pp. 181–183; Dimmendaal, "Nilo-Saharan," p. 593. ↩

19. Ehret, *A Historical-Comparative Reconstruction of Nilo-Saharan,* p. 88. Ehret refers to NES as "Astaboran." ↩

20. See, for an overview, Rilly, *Le méroïtique et sa famille linguistique,* pp. 25–36. ↩

21. Dimmendaal, "Nilo-Saharan," p. 593. ↩

article/ *Personal Markers and Verbal Number in Meroitic*

author/ Claude Rilly

abstract/ *Thanks to the use of linguistic comparison and analyses of new inscriptions, Meroitic, the extinct language of the kingdom of Meroe, Sudan, has become increasingly well known. The present article deals with the identification of personal markers and verbal number. It shows how Meroitic, like many other languages, used a former demonstrative, qo, as a 3rd person independent pronoun. An in-depth analysis of the royal chronicles of the kings and princes of Meroe, compared with their Napatan counterparts written in Egyptian, further yields the 1st person singular dependent pronoun e- (later variant ye-), which can be compared with 1st person singular pronoun found in related languages. A stela of Candace Amanishakheto found in Naga is the starting point for identifying the 2nd person singular and plural independent pronouns are and deb. These two morphemes are linked with the most recent reconstructions of Proto-Nubian pronouns and confirm the narrow genetic relation between Nubian and Meroitic. Finally, the reassessment of the so-called "verbal dative" -xe/-bxe shows that this morpheme is simply a former verbal number marker with integrated case endings. This makes it a rare instance of transcategorisation in the cross-linguistic typology of verbal number.*

keywords/ Meroitic, Meroe, Kush, Napata, pronouns, Egyptian, decipherment, verbal morphology, pronominal morphology, person, comparative linguistics, Old Nubian, Nobiin, Andaandi, Ama, Nara, Taman, Mattokki, Karko

1. Introduction

Meroitic was the language spoken by the elite of the successive kingdoms of Ancient Sudan since at least the second millennium BCE.[1] Only from the third century BCE was it written with a script borrowed from Demotic. Later, a second script, using the same writing system but with hieroglyphic signs, was created for the sacred texts, particularly the wall inscriptions of the temples. The two scripts were deciphered in 1911.[2] Approximately 2,000 texts have been published so far. The main issue with regard to Meroitic inscriptions is the understanding of their content. The language disappeared in the early Middle Ages without descendants.

Internal methods have been used since 1911 to investigate the meaning of the texts, with remarkable success in the realm of the funerary inscriptions, which are many and highly stereotypical. In addition to these philological methods, a comparative approach has become possible now that the linguistic affiliation of Meroitic, a hotly debated issue for decades, was settled by the present author.[3] Meroitic belongs to the Northern East Sudanic (NES) language family, a branch of the Nilo-Saharan phylum. This family further includes:

- Nubian–Nara
    - Nubian, comprising Nobiin, Andaandi (Dongolawi), and Mattokki (Kenzi) spoken in Egypt in Sudan; Midob, (nearly) extinct Birgid, and the Kordofan Nubian (Ajang) languages in Sudan;
    - Nara, a small language spoken in Western Eritrea;
- Taman, comprising Tama and Mararit, in Darfur and Chad;
- Nyima, comprising Ama and Afitti in the Nuba Mountains in central Sudan.

Nubian and Nara are closest to Meroitic, yet unfortunately neither is close enough to allow for a quick and straightforward comparison of vocabulary and morphology. The split between the different branches of NES is supposed to have occurred in early third millennium BCE,[4] so that the chronological depth between the NES sister-languages is comparable to the time gap that separates Indo-European languages. For that reason, the comparative method must not be used alone, but in combination with internal methods.

The present paper deals with personal markers that can be identified in Meroitic inscriptions. This topic was not investigated until now, mainly because the Meroitic morphology was — and mostly remains — a *terra incognita.* The texts that have been found so far rarely offer a situation of uttering[5] in which the subject can be easily identified. For example, the royal chronicles include reports of military campaigns where the verb *ked* "cut in pieces, kill" frequently occurs. However, in most cases, the verbal form is simply *ked,* without any pronoun or affix that could indicate which person is the subject.

In addition, when the situation of uttering is clear and verbal affixes are present, they often vary from one text to another and are distorted by assimilative phenomena, so that it is extremely difficult to isolate the personal markers and assign them an accurate value. For example, in funerary inscriptions, a textual category that makes up a third of the corpus, the situation of uttering is clear: These texts are prayers to the gods of the afterlife, uttered by a fictive enunciator who probably represents the funerary priest or the family of the deceased. He invokes the gods at the beginning and beseeches them in the last sentences to provide the deceased with water and food. The final verb is expectedly an optative or imperative form. It is not preceded by a 2nd person plural pronoun, but it includes a prefixed element *pso-, psi-* (or many other variants) and two suffixes. The first is *-x* or *-xe* ("verbal dative") and is located immediately after the verbal stem. The second suffix is a compound *-kte, -kete, -ketese, -kese,* which can be reduced to *-te* as a result of assimilation with the first suffix. Until Fritz Hintze published his *Beiträge zur meroitischen Grammatik,* no scholar managed to find which of these complex affixes marked the person of the verb. Thanks to his morphological study of the verb in funerary benedictions,[6] it is now clear that the final compound suffix is the marker of the 2nd person plural on the verb. Further analyses of old data can provide better insights into other personal markers, particularly the 3rd person singular and plural pronouns and possibly the first person singular subject marker, as can be seen in the following sections. Furthermore, some textual material recently discovered can be used to identify new personal markers, namely the 2nd person singular and plural possessive pronouns and the 2nd person singular subject pronoun.

2. Preliminary Remarks about the Conventions of the Meroitic Writing System

Morphological issues in Meroitic cannot be addressed without taking into account the conventions of the writing system, because this is the only way we have to reconstruct the actual pronunciation of the words. The traditional transliteration of the texts, which follows the rules established by Griffith in 1911, is convenient because it is a direct reflection of the Meroitic signs (the default vowel /a/ is not written), but it is not a faithful rendering of the pronunciation. For instance, the Meroitic transcription of Greek Καῖσαρ (Latin *Caesar*) is written *kisri* but was pronounced /kaisari/. The Meroitic script is an alphasyllabary (**Fig. 1**), like Indic scripts or the Ethiopian abugida.[7] There were actually two scripts, the cursive script and the hieroglyphic script, but they followed the same principles and differ only by the forms of the signs, like capital and lowercase letters in Latin script, with the difference that the two registers are never mixed in the same text.

Meroitic alphasyllabary

hieroglyphic	cursive	transliteration	values
		a	initial /a/ or /u/
		b	/ba/
		d	/da/
		e	/e/, /ə/, or no vowel
		h	/xʷa/ and /ŋʷa/ (?)
		i	modifier /i/
		k	/ka/
		l	/la/
		m	/ma/
		n	/na/
		ne	/ne/, /nə/ or /n/
		o	modifier /u/
		p	/pa/ (Egypt.) ; /ba/
		q	/kʷa/
		r	/ra/
		s	/sa/
		se	/se/, /sə/ or /s/
		t	/ta/
		te	/te/, /tə/ or /t/
		to	/tu/
		w	/wa/
		x	/xa/ and /ŋa/ (?)
		y	/ya/ (?)
⁝	:	:	word-divider

Figure 1. The Meroitic alphasyllabary

The script includes nineteen syllabic signs. Fifteen of them have the value "consonant + /a/." The default vowel /a/ can be modified by adding one of the three vocalic signs *e, i,* and *o*. Like in English, the sign *e* has three values: /e/, /ə/ (schwa), and zero. The zero value is used to write consonant clusters or final consonants, for instance *qore* "ruler," pronounced /kʷur/. The sign *o* is used for

/u/ and /o/. Four additional syllabic signs have a fixed vocalic value: three of them represent "consonant + *e*" (*ne, se, te,* with the three values of *e*), one represents "consonant + *o*" (*to*). For initial vowels, there is a single sign transliterated *a,* which represents /a/, /u/, and probably /o/ and /ə/. Initial /e/ and /i/ were written *e* and *i* until the first century CE. In later times, they were written *ye* and *yi* with a dummy *y,* which was not pronounced. Finally, the texts include a word-divider, made of two dots like our modern colon, which is used (more or less regularly) between words or more commonly between the different clauses of a sentence.

The sound values of the Meroitic signs are generally known,[8] but there remains a few unclear points. Until recently, it was supposed that the sign ⊏, transliterated formerly *ḫ,* and *x* according to the revised conventions,[9] had only the value [χ], a velar fricative like Egyptian *ḫ.* A second sign, which can replace *x* in several variant spellings, is *h,* formerly *ẖ.* I suggested that *h* was a labialized version of *x,* in IPA [χʷ], because it mainly occurs before or after labiovelar vowels [o] or [u]. These two values [χ] and [χʷ] are evidenced by the use of *x* and *h* in Meroitic transcriptions of Egyptian words. The same distribution can be observed between *k* and *q,* the latter being a labialized velar consonant [kʷ]. However, in the Old Nubian alphabet, the Meroitic sign ⊏ *x* was borrowed, not for the velar fricative consonant [χ], for which the Coptic sign ϩ was used, but for the velar nasal consonant /ŋ/, written ⲅ̄. Furthermore, in several Egyptian transcriptions of Meroitic royal names that include *x* or *h,* the scribes used a digraph *nḫ.*[10] My impression is therefore that the signs *x* and *h* had a double set of values: [χ] and [χʷ] in loanwords from Egyptian and [ŋ], and [ŋʷ] in native words. This assumption is supported by strong arguments but still needs to be checked word by word.

A last peculiarity, pertaining rather to phonetic changes than to spelling conventions, needs to be mentioned here because it will be found in some of the following quotations from Meroitic texts. From the first century CE onwards, the sequence /s/ + /l/ (written *se* + *l*), which was frequent in Meroitic due to the use of the article *-l* at the end of noun phrases, merged into /t/. For example, the sentence written *kdise-l-o* "she is the daughter" became *kdit-o.* This phonetic development is known as "Griffith's law."[11]

3. The Third Person Markers

Among the possible markers of the third person, only pronouns are known so far, namely *qo/qe* and variants for singular and *qoleb* for plural. No verbal ending that could be connected with the third person, such as Latin *-t/-nt* or Egyptian *=f/=sn*, has been spotted in the texts. The case of the "verbal dative" will be later investigated, but this morpheme is probably to be classified as a clitic pronoun.

In the paradigm of personal pronouns, the 3rd person has a special place. Whereas the 1st and 2nd persons refer to the protagonists of the uttering situation (see n. 6), the 3rd person refers to people and things that are outside this situation. According to the relevant categorization of Arab grammarians, the 3rd person is "the absentee."[12] From this perspective, 3rd person pronouns are close to demonstratives. This is particularly obvious when it comes to morphology. In many languages, these pronouns are derived from demonstratives. In Romance languages for example, they stem from the Latin distal demonstrative *ille* "that," for instance French *il* "he," Spanish *él,* Romanian *el.* Some languages even use the same word for the demonstrative and the 3rd person pronoun.[13] In Latin, the proximal demonstrative *is, ea, id* "this" was used as a 3rd person pronoun. In Turkish, a language that displays a full range of typological similarities with Meroitic,[14] the same demonstrative *o* is used as a demonstrative adjective, a demonstrative pronoun and a 3rd person pronoun.[15] This seems also to be the case in Meroitic, which has apparently the same word, *qo/qe,* for "this" (adjective), "this" (pronoun), and "he," "she," "it."[16]

3.1. Demonstrative Pronoun or Independent Third Person Pronoun Object?

(1) **Meroitic**
Arilnemkse ***q(o)****-o*
Arilanemakas this-COP
"This is Arilanemakas." (REM 0239A, epitaph)

(2) *Mloton* **q(o)**-*o-wi* :
Malutuna this-COP-EMP
"This is Malutuna." (REM 0277, epitaph)

(3) **qo:** *Atqo* **q(o)**-*o-wi* :
this Ataqu this-COP-EMP
"This (one), this is Ataqu." (REM 1057, epitaph)

The pronoun *qo* was among the first elements that Griffith singled out in the funerary inscriptions after his decipherment of the script.[17] The word occurred in final position in the "nomination" of the deceased, either bare (1) or followed by an optional particle -*wi* "for emphasis" (2).[18] Quite often, another *qo* preceded the name of the deceased (3). Griffith suggested that this first *qo* was an epithet meaning "honorable" or "noble" and the final *qo* was a grammatical tool "to introduce the name of the deceased." In his *Beiträge zur meroitischen Grammatik,* Hintze was the first to regard *qo* as a demonstrative pronoun.[19] According to him, the original form of this word was *qe* and the predicative compound *qo(wi)* was composed of *qe* + copula -*o* ± particle -*wi.* Actually, *qe* is a variant spelling of *qo* and the two forms were pronounced /ku/,[20] so that *qo(wi)* can be analysed also as *qo* + copula -*o* ± particle -*wi* with a merger of the two consecutive *o*'s. The additional *qo* at the beginning (3), found in 10% of the epitaphs, is used as a topic "this one, this is…."[21] It emphasizes the deixis that connects the inscription and the deceased, since these texts were inscribed on offering-tables or stelae that were placed at the entrance and inside the funerary chapels respectively.

(4) *kdi* **qo**: *Mitslbe* *q(o)-o-wi* :
woman this Mitasalabe this-COP-EMP
"This woman, this is Mitasalabe." (REM 0087, epitaph)

(5) *wle* **qo** *p-xn* *tlt* 3
dog this CAUS-yield(?) talent 3
Netror-se-l-o
Natarura-GEN-DET-COP
"May this dog yield(?) three talents, it is Natarura's." (REM 1165, beside graffito of a greyhound)

Another function of *qo,* which confirms the demonstrative status of this word, is adjectival. Like in English or German, the same word is used for the adjective and the pronoun. In (4), also drawn from a funerary text, the topic found in (3) is extended: *qo* "this one" becomes *kdi qo* "this woman," "this lady." This interpretation, which I first advanced with some reservations,[22] was since then confirmed: (5), (6), and (7) are captions of pictures, respectively the graffito of a dog hunting a hare in the Great Enclosure of Musawwarat, the drawing of a gazelle on a wooden board found in the temple of Amun in Qasr Ibrim and a pair of feet engraved in the temple of Isis in Philae. The deictic nature of *qo* is perfectly obvious here. Its use as a 3rd person pronoun in Meroitic is therefore an extension of his function, because the other way round, namely that a personal pronoun could become a demonstrative, is cross-linguistically highly improbable.

> (6) *abese* **qo-li**
> gazelle this-DET
> "This gazelle..." (REM 1198 and 1199) The rest of the sentence cannot yet be translated.

> (7) *ste* **qo-leb** *Addo[.]-se*
> foot this-DET.PL Adadu[.]-GEN
> "These feet (are) Adadu[.]'s." (REM 0113)

Examples (6) and (7) show that the demonstrative adjective *qo* is compatible with the use of the determiner (article), singular *-l(i),* plural *-leb,* unlike English or French, but like Greek[23] or Hungarian. It is, however, absent in some instances, such as (5) above.

In these examples, the determiner is apparently attached, not to the demonstrative, but to the noun phrase as a whole, as is normal in Meroitic.[24] However, a plural form *qoleb*[25] can be found independently as a pronominal object, but, from the instances found so far, it is difficult to decide if it is a demonstrative or a personal pronoun. This form is particularly attested in royal chronicles.[26]

(8) *Atnene :* *ssmrte-l :* *Imlotror :* *wtotrse-l :* ***qoleb:***
Atanene (title)-DET Imalutarura (title)-DET 3PL
Amnp : *i-de-bx :*
(to) Amanap 1SG.S-give(?)-VNM.PL
"Atanene, the *ssmrte* (and) Imalutarura, the *wtotrse*, I gave(?) them to Amanap." (REM 1044/25–26)

Example (8) is quoted from the great stela of king Taneyidamani kept in Boston. Engraved around 150 BCE, it is the earliest royal chronicle written in Meroitic. The excerpt deals with the assignment to the temple of Amanap (Amun of Napata) of two officials, Atanene and Imalutarura. Their names and titles are enumerated and followed by *qoleb*. The context is utterly different from (7), where the deixis is obvious, since it is engraved beside the image of two feet. As in (3) and (4), we are doubtlessly dealing with a topicalized construction. The topic is formed by the names and the description of the two officials, whereas *qoleb* is an anaphoric pronoun that refers to these two persons, but operates as the actual object of the verb.[27] In anaphoras referring to animate antecedents as shown in (8), most languages where demonstratives and 3rd person pronouns are clearly distinct, a personal pronoun is used. In Meroitic, it seems that *qoleb*, at least when it is the object of the verb, can function as a personal pronoun. Unfortunately, there are no similar instances, namely in sentences with verbs, with the singular *qo*, but the non-verbal sentence in (3) suggests that it would function similarly. In the latter example, the first *qo* plays the role of a deictic whereas the second *qo* assumes the function of an anaphoric.

3.2. The Third Person Possessive Pronoun

Whereas Hintze regarded *qe/qo* as a demonstrative, Hofmann held it as a personal pronoun because it is the basis of the 3rd person possessive marker, *qese* and variants.[28] It is found mainly after the kinship terms, as in (9) below, drawn from a funerary stela where two brothers are commemorated.[29]

(9) *Qoreqore-l-o-wi* [: *y*]*etmde* ***qese:*** *Qoretkr*
Qurqurla-COP-EMP relative 3SG.GEN Qurtakara
q(o)-o-wi :
this-COP-EMP
"(This) is Qurqurla; this is his elder Qurtakara." (REM 0273/2–4, funerary stela)

The possessive of the 3rd person singular includes the pronoun *qo/qe,* followed by the genitival postposition *-se* and means literally "of him/her."[30] Once again, it can be compared with Latin demonstrative *is, ea, id,* whose genitive *eius* is also used as a 3rd person singular possessive. Three variants are known: *qose,* very rare, *eqese* in REM 1003, and *aqese,* much more common.[31] Unexpectedly, the 3rd person plural possessive is not **qolebse,* but *qebese,* as can be seen in (10), drawn from an epitaph from Gebel Adda that was written for a deceased whose relatives were administrators and scribes from the temple of Isis. Like (3) and (4) above, the sentence includes a topicalized constituent. The genitival phrase (i.e., the officials of the temple) is the topic and is referred to in the predication by the anaphoric possessive *qebese* (their nephew).

(10) *perite :* *Wos-se-leb :* *qorene* *Wos-se-leb :*
agent Isis-GEN-DET.PL royal scribe Isis-GEN-DET.PL
yetmde ***qebese****-l-o-wi :*
nephew 3PL.GEN-DET-COP-EMP
"He was the nephew of agents of Isis and royal scribes (?) of Isis." (GA. 04, epitaph)

The possessive *qebe-se* includes *qebe-,* a plural form of *qo* that is more conservative than *qoleb,* but is, unlike the latter, never attested in isolation. It includes the plural suffix *-b* that can also be found on the plural determiner:[32]

› Determiner: singular *-l* → plural *-le**b***
› Pronoun: singular *qo-/qe-* → plural *qe**b**e-*

Qebese has several variants, *aqebese, aqobese* (see n. 32) *eqebese,* and especially *bese,* which is frequent. This last form, in all likelihood, is not an abbreviated variant but is based on a still earlier form of the 3rd person pronoun, *-b,* which will be considered below § 3.3.6.

3.3. The "Verbal Dative" as Possible Enclitic Pronoun or Verbal Number Marker

The funerary inscriptions from the Karanog and Shablul cemeteries were the first texts published by Griffith, after his decipherment of the script. He was able to get a rough understanding of their content, but could not yet deliver a detailed analysis of the verbal compounds that end the benedictions. The first two benediction formulae, commonly named A and B, are prayers to Isis and Osiris, asking them to provide the deceased with water and bread respectively, as can be seen in (11)–(14).[33]

(11) Formula A, singular beneficiary

ato	*mhe*	*pso-he-(xe)-k(e)te*
water	plentiful	CAUS-drink-VNM.SG-OPT.2PL

"May you cause him/her to drink plentiful water!"

(12) Formula A, plural beneficiary

ato	*mhe*	*pso-he-bxe-k(e)te*
water	plentiful	CAUS-drink-VNM.PL-OPT.2PL

"May you cause them to drink plentiful water!"

(13) Formula B, singular beneficiary

at	*mhe*	*psi-xr-(xe)-k(e)te*
bread	plentiful	CAUS-eat-VNM.SG-OPT.2PL

"May you cause him/her to eat plentiful bread!"

(14) Formula B, plural beneficiary

at	*mhe*	*psi-xr-bxe-k(e)te*
bread	plentiful	CAUS-eat-VNM.PL-OPT.2PL

"May you cause them to eat plentiful bread!"

Meroitic is an agglutinative language, but it has a strong propensity to assimilative processes that blur the boundaries between successive morphemes.[34] However, Griffith managed to identify the element *-bx* or *-bxe* as a "plural ending in the funerary formulae," which appeared each time several individuals were commemorated in the same epitaph.[35] In his *Beiträge,* Hintze was the first to suggest a plausible segmentation of these verbal compounds.[36] He showed that -*bxe* (which, meanwhile, had been termed "dative infix") had a singular counterpart -*x* or -*xe*[37] that was theoretically present in the verbal compound, but concealed by a nearly systematic assimilation to the following suffix.[38] Only in the archaic versions of formulae A and B (15)–(16) was this singular "infix" visible.

(15) Formula A (archaic)
ato *mlo* *el-x-te*
water good give-VNM.SG-OPT.2SG
"May you give him/her plentiful water!" (REM 0427)

(16) Formula B (archaic)
at *mlo* *el-x-te*
bread good give-VNM.SG-OPT.2SG
"May you give him/her plentiful bread!" (REM 0427)

The same wording occurs in the prayers to the gods that were engraved near their figures in votive stelae (17) or in Meroitic temples (18). In the latter example, cited from the Lion temple in Naga, the beneficiaries are the king, his mother, and the prince.

(17) *A[pe]dem[k-i]* *Tneyidmni* *pwrite*
Apedemak-VOC Taneyidamani life
el-x-te
give-VNM.SG-OPT
"O Apedemak! May you give life to Taneyidamani!" (REM 0405)

(18) *Apedemk-i* *pwrite :* *l-bx-te*
Apedemak-VOC life give-VNM.PL-OPT
"O Apedemak! May you give life to them!" (REM 0018)

3.3.1. Earlier Hypotheses

In an early analysis of these sentences,[39] I interpreted this "dative infix" as an applicative suffix, with reference to Kanuri, a Saharan language. Applicatives are used to encode a beneficiary of the action in the verb, instead of adding an adposition or a case ending to the noun. They are quite common among African languages and are for example found in Nubian.[40] However, this can hardly apply to the Meroitic construction. The applicative is a voice, such as passive and causative, and the affixes it uses cannot convey the notions of singular or plural. Example (19) from a Bantu language, Tswana, shows that the same applicative suffix *-el* is used regardless of the beneficiaries' number.[41]

(19a) **Tswana**

ke	*rek-a*	*ditlhako*
1SG.S	buy-FIN	shoes

"I am buying shoes."

(19b)

ke	*rek-el-a*	*bana*	*ditlhako*
1SG.S	buy-APPL-FIN	children	shoes

"I am buying shoes for the children."

(19c)

Lorato	*o*	*tlaa*	*kwal-el-a*	*Kitso*	*lokwalo*
Lorato	3:1.S	FUT	write-APPL-FIN	Kitso	letter

"Lorato writes a letter to Kitso."

In (19b), the beneficiary is plural (*bana* "children," SG *ngwana*), whereas in (19c), *lokwalo* "letter" is singular. In both cases, the applicative suffix is *-el.* The Meroitic suffixes *-x* and *-bx,* by contrast, agree in number with the beneficiary.

In addition, this morpheme was first identified as a beneficiary marker from the instances found in the benedictions of the epitaphs, hence its name "dative infix." However, in royal chronicles and biographical passages of several funerary texts — which have been little studied to date — the suffix obviously refers to a direct object, as can be seen in (20) drawn from the funerary stela of viceroy of Nubia Abratoye.[42]

(20) **Meroitic**

kdi mdxe 35 anese 25 : kelw :
woman virgin 35 donkey 25 also
Ø-arohe-bx
1SG.S-take.control-VNM.PL
"I took control of 35 virgins and 25 donkeys." (REM 1333/16)

For these two reasons, in a later analysis,[21] I considered *-x(e)* and *-bx(e)* to be object personal pronouns that had been incorporated into the verbal compound as clitics. A similar enclisis can be found, for instance, in the imperative forms of Romance languages,[43] especially in Spanish: *dámelo* "give it to me," *presentémonos* "let us introduce ourselves."

This analysis, however, does not account for the location of these so-called clitic personal markers inside the verbal compound. In the examples from Spanish above, they occur in final position, as is expected for external elements that were later added to a fully inflected form. In Meroitic, as can be seen in (11)–(18), they are directly attached to the verbal stem and followed by the subject person marker and tense–aspect–mood (TAM) endings. For that reason it was termed "infix" and not "suffix."

3.3.2. Verbal Number Markers in Northern East Sudanic

The unexpected location of *-x(e)* and *-bx(e)* in the verbal complex can be compared with that of the verbal number marker in two groups of the NES linguistic family, Nyima and Nubian. In these languages, the plurality of the subject in intransitive constructions and of the object in transitive constructions ("ergative pattern") is realized by the same verbal suffix which is added directly to the verbal stem, before the TAM suffixes. The clearest instances of this construction are found in the Nyima language Ama and involve an ergative-pattern verbal plural marker[44] *-(ì)d̪ì* as shown in (21)–(22).

(21a) **Ama**

kùd̪ū t̪èbīò bà nɛ̀
goat black ASP be.IMPFV
"The goat is black."

(21b) *kùd̪ū t̪èbīò bà nè-d̪ì*
goat black ASP be.IPFV-VNM
"The goats are black."

(22a) *á bá dámì-ō tàm*
1SG ASP egg-ACC eat.IPFV
"I am eating an egg."

(22b) *á bá dámì-ō tàm-īd̪ì*
1SG ASP egg-ACC eat.IPFV-VNM
"I am eating eggs."

In Old Nubian and Nobiin, this suffix is *-(i)j.* A related marker *-j-* is found in Midob.[45] In Kordofan Nubian, a similar suffix *-c* is attested along with others suffixes, such as *-Vr,* which is much more frequent. Recent publications showed that the Nubian suffixes function according to the same ergative pattern as the Ama suffix.[46] Example (23) illustrates the use of the suffix to mark subject plurality with intransitive verbs, whereas examples (24)–(25) show the suffix marking object plurality with transitive verbs.[47]

(23) **Nobiin**
ter balee-la kar-j-is-an [kaccisan]
3PL wedding-LOC came-VNM-PRT1-3PL
"They came to the wedding."

(24) *ay tii-ga aag jurr-il*
1SG COW-ACC PROG milk-PRS.1SG
"I am milking the cow."

(25) *ay tii-guu-ga aag jurr-ij-il*
1SG COW-PL-ACC PROG milk-VNM-PRS.1SG
"I am milking the cows."

It is noteworthy that, unlike in the Ama examples above, the plural marking operated by the suffix *-(i)j* is redundant, since plurality is already marked by the subject pronoun *ter* "they" in (23) and the plural nominal suffix *-guu* in (25). In

Ama, apart from rare instances of replacive patterns such as *wīd̪ɛ́ŋ* "child"/*dŕīŋ* "children," and a plural suffix *-gí/-ŋì* which can be attached to kinship terms, plurality is unmarked in nouns. This makes it necessary, either to mark it by determiners ("several," "many," etc.) or to encode it in the verb by a specific marker, as showed in (20b) and (21b) above.

Considering that the nominal plural suffixes that can be found in the NES languages are so diverse that no protoform can be reconstructed, it is plausible that Proto-NES had no plural nominal markers, but only a few replacive patterns and collective nouns with singulatives forms marked by a suffix **-tV*.[48] It was therefore necessary to encode the plurals of the participants in the verbal compound. Proto-Nubian seems to have been in this regard close to its ancestor Proto-NES.[49] Later on, for unknown reasons — but areal influence probably played a major role in it — each Nubian group worked out its own plural markers for all the nouns. This novelty of course competed with the earlier plural marking by verbal suffixes. However, both of them survived to this day, but they often follow economy principles. Khalil notes that "the *j*-suffix appears sporadically in the intransitive clause" and that "[i]n the transitive clause [...], when the object noun phrase is modified by a numeral or a quantifier such as *mallee* [many] or *minkellee* [how many], the plural marker on the object noun phrase becomes optional and subsequently the suffixation of *-j* becomes optional, too."[50]

A third use of verbal plural markers in NES languages is to encode in ditransitive verbs the plurality of the indirect object, i.e., the beneficiary or recipient of the action. In this construction, the plural verbal suffix refers to the indirect object and not to the object in Old Nubian[51] and Nobiin[52] and probably in Ama. For the latter language, I have unfortunately no clear example of this point in my limited fieldwork data, but an example provided by Norton illustrates this point for dual, which operates exactly like plural, but with the suffix *-ɛ̄n/-ēn* (the macron stands for mid tone).[53]

(26) **Ama**

àì	*bā*	*ə̄mōr-ì*	*āmīɛ̄r*	*t̪ɛ̄g-ɛ̄nì*
1SG	VER	friend-DAT	pen	give-DU

"I gave a pen to two friends."

Here, the verbal number marker refers to the beneficiary ("friend") and not to the object ("pen"), as it does in monotransitive constructions, although this beneficiary is already marked as a dative by the case ending -ì. The same feature is observed in Nobiin as shown in (27) and (28).[54]

(27) **Nobiin**

ay	*torbar-ka*	*aŋŋaree-nci-ga*
1SG	farmer-ACC	bed-PL-ACC

kaay-a-tis
make-*a*-APPL.PRT1.1SG
"I made the farmer beds."

(28)

ay	*torbar-ii-ga*	*aŋŋaree-g*
1SG	farmer-PL-ACC	bed-ACC

kaay-a-tic-c-is
make-*a*-APPL-VNM-PRT1.1SG
"I made the farmers a bed."

3.3.3. Plural Object Marking in Meroitic

The verbal number marking in these languages follows a syntactic hierarchy: it refers to the subject if there is no object, to the object if there is no beneficiary and to the beneficiary if there is one. This brings us back to Meroitic, in which the so-called "verbal dative" again has close parallels with the Ama and Nobiin verbal number marker. Unfortunately, no clear instance of *-x(e)/-bx(e)* can be found with intransitive verbs, mainly because none has been so far translated with certainty. Unlike Ama (21a–b), Meroitic does not use a real verb "to be," but a copula which is inflected for plural with a different suffix. Nonetheless, transitive and ditransitive constructions display the same hierarchy for the use of the verbal plural suffix as Ama and Nobiin.

Examples (29) and (30) are prayers to Amun, said by a fictive enunciator, in favour of king Amanakhareqerema (end of 1st c. CE). The first is engraved upon the base of ram statues from the entrance of the king's temple in El-Hassa (REM 0001 and 1151[55]) and the second is a wall inscription from Temple 200 in Naga.[56] The long epithet of Amun, which is irrelevant to the present discussion, is omitted. Example (31) is one of the four columns of text engraved on the shaft of each of the sandstone columns in the Amun Temple in Naga (REM 0034A).[57] Each of these inscriptions is a prayer to Amun, that he may give to the royal family the cardinal point it is facing (here "north"). The three members of the royal family are King Natakamani, Queen-Mother Amanitore, and Prince Arakakhataror. The epithet of Amun is again omitted here for convenience.

(29) **Meroitic**

Amni (...)	*Mnxreqerem*	*qore :*	*Mni*
Amun	Amanakhareqerema	ruler	Amun.GEN

tke-l :	*pwrite :*	*l-x-te :*
beloved-DET	life	give-VNM.SG-OPT.2SG

"O Amun (...), to Amanakhareqerema, ruler beloved of Amun, may you give life!"

(30)

Amni (...)	*Mnxreqerem*	*qore :*	*Mni*
Amun	Amanakhareqerema	ruler	Amun.GEN

tke-l :	*pwrite :*	*ntke :*	*kesekene*
beloved-DET	life	strength	also

l-x-te :
give-VNM.SG-OPT.2SG

"O Amun (...), to Amanakhareqerema, ruler beloved of Amun, may you give life and strength!"

(31)

Amni (...)	*Ntkmni*	*Amni*	*mdese-l :*
Amun	Natakamani	Amun.GEN	descendant-DET

Mnitore	*Aritene-l*	*mdese-l*
Amanitore	Aritene-DET.GEN	descendant-DET

Arkxtror	*Mke-deke-l*	*mdese-l :*
Arakakhataror	God-great-DET.GEN	descendant-DET

hr-l :	*alose :*	*l-bx-Ø-te :*
north-DET	entirely	give-VNM.PL-2SG-OPT

"O Amun (...), to Natakamani, the descendant of Amun, to Amanitore, the descendant of (the) Aritene,
to Arakakhataror, the descendant of the Great God, may you give the north entirely!"

In (29), the singular suffix *-x* is added to the stem *l-* "give." It refers to a single beneficiary, king Amanakhareqerema. Admittedly, the object, namely *pwrite* "life, vital strength," is also singular, so that evidence of the agreement with the beneficiary is to be sought in examples (30) and (31). In (30), the object is plural, *pwrite ntke* "life and strength," since there is no dual in Meroitic. However, the suffix remains in the singular. In (31), the object is again singular, *hrl alose* "the north entirely," but the beneficiary is now a plural, namely the three members of the royal family. In this case, the plural form *-bx* of the suffix is used,[58] just as we have seen in Ama and Nobiin.

3.3.4. The Verbal Plural Marker in NES Languages and in Meroitic

The Meroitic plural suffix *-bx(e)* shares three significant features with the verbal number markers in Ama and Nobiin: its direct adjunction to the stem within the verbal compound; its function as a plural marker of direct/indirect object; and its dependency on the hierarchy between participants of the action (cf. n. 59). Nonetheless, some important divergences can be observed. First of all, the Meroitic plural suffix is not a single morpheme like Ama *-(ī)d̪ì* and Nobiin *-(i)j* (where /i/ is a epenthetic vowel) but the plural form of a singular suffix *-x(e)*. In languages where verbal number is an operative category, the most frequent situation contrasts unmarked singular and marked plural. Nonetheless, the growing literature on verbal number/pluractionality records some languages where there is an opposition between marked verbal singular and marked or unmarked verbal plural. In her study of verbal number in Karko, a Kordofan Nubian language, Jakobi gives some instances of such verbs (**Table 1**).

Gloss	Sg. Object	Pl. Object
hang up	*kúʃ-ɛ́ɛ́r*	*kùj-ùk*
split wood	*kák-ɛ̀ɛ́r*	*kàk*
pull out	*ɖúʃ-ɛ̀ɛ́r*	*ɖùj*
kindle	*ʃíl-ɛ̀ɛ́r*	*ʃìl-ìk*
wake up	*fɛ́ʃ-ɛ̀ɛ́r*	*fɛ̀j-ɛ̀k*

Table 1. Transitive verbs in Karko, singular stems marked by *-ɛɛr*, plural stems either unmarked or extended by *-Vk*.[59]

In Maba, a language of Ouaddai (Eastern Chad) belonging to the Nilo-Saharan phylum, Weiss recorded instances of singular verbal suffix *-n* versus plural verbal suffix *-k*.[60]

> (32a) **Maba**
> *ɛ́njì:* *à-wá:-**k**-ì*
> water 1SG-pour-VNM.PL-DECL
> "I pour out a lot of water, I pour out water regularly."

> (32b) *ɛ́njì:* *à-wá:-**n**-ì*
> water 1SG-pour-VNM.SG-DECL
> "I pour out a bit of water."

However, these examples are utterly different from the Meroitic verbal number system. In each case, the singular and plural verbal suffixes are independent. In Meroitic, the plural marker *-b-x(e)* is morphologically the plural of the singular marker *-x(e),* which might be termed not the "dative" suffix, because it also encodes the direct object, but the "objective" verbal suffix. As in the related language groups Nubian and Taman, Meroitic merges the accusative and the dative nominal cases in an "objective" case marked by the same case endings.

The second discrepancy between the Meroitic plural suffix and "canonical" number markers such as the Nubian plural suffix *-(i)j* is the range of their functions. Unlike Western European languages, where plurality of events is conveyed by lexical derivation (Latin *sal-t-a-re* "dance" from *sal-i-re* "jump") or adverbs ("repeatedly," "often," "again and again," etc.), with plurality of participants being encoded by verbal agreement and nominal or pronominal plural markers, verbal number is a category that includes equally all these pluralities. As this category falls between stem derivation and aspect, it is morphologically marked, either by modification of the verbal stem (syllable reduplication, vocalic or tonal change, etc.) or by affixes directly appended to the verbal stem. Consequently, in languages such as Nubian, where verbs are inflected by suffixation, verbal number markers are directly appended to the stem, before TAM or person markers.

3.3.5. Plural Object Marker or Plural Event Marker

The Meroitic suffix *-bx(e)* is therefore located in the right place, but, contrary to its Nubian counterparts, its use, as much as we can judge in the limited corpus available, seems restricted to plural object marking and does not extend to the plurality of events. The following examples of frequentative forms are attested in Nobiin (33) and Karko (34).[61]

(33) **Nobiin**

ay *neer-j-ir*

1SG sleep-VNM-1SG

"I sleep several times."

(34) **Karko**

súk *ʃɛ̀-ṭɛ̀g*

market.LOC go.VNM-FRQ.IMP

"Go PL to the market frequently!"

It may, however, be mentioned that in Nubian languages, few instances of the use of the same morpheme for the frequentative (plurality of events) and the verbal number (plurality of participants) are attested. Nobiin and Old Nubian are the only Nubian languages where *-(i)j* is attested as both a plural event and participant marker, as shown in (33).[62] Still, it is uncertain whether this was also the case in Proto-Nubian. In (34) from Karko, the plurality of participants is indicated by the vowel *ɛ̀* in the verbal stem *ʃɛ̀-* (the singular stem is *ʃù-*), whereas the plurality of events is marked independently by the suffix *-ṭɛ̀g*. It may happen that a verb exhibits three different stems in Karko: one for a singular participant, one for a plural participant, and one for plurality of action.[63] A conspicuous instance is the verb "call," which is *òg-* with singular object, *ògór* for plural object, and *òʃór* for plural action, i.e., a distributive meaning "call one by one." The suffix *-(V)ʃ* is a frequent number marker in Karko[64] and other Kordofan Nubian languages, and is doubtlessly a reflex of Proto-Nubian suffix **-(i)j*. Another verbal number marker, the most frequent, is *-Vr*, with a vowel that is subject to vowel harmony. It is obvious that *òʃór* is an assimilated compound derived from **og-ʃ-Vr*. The two verbal plural suffixes *-(V)ʃ* and *-Vr* are used successively in the same stem to express plurality of object and plurality of events respectively. A similar distribution of these two verbal extensions is paralleled in Andaandi, where *-(i)j* is used for frequentatives, whereas the suffix *-ir* is used to mark the plurality of participants (only objects in this language).[65] The markers *-(i)j* and *-ir* are clearly the Mattokki–Andaandi cognates of Kordofan Nubian *-(V)j* and *-Vr,* so that their use as specialized verbal plural markers might go back to Proto-Nubian.

A distinct marker *-k* is found in Nubian for the plurality of events,[66] e.g., Nobiin *jòog* "grind" → **joog-k > jòkk* "chew." This suffix dates back to Proto-NES, or at least to its eastern branch, because it is also found in Nara and Meroitic.[67] In Nara, it differentiates verbal forms such as *ishayto* (< **ishag-to*) "he asked" from *ishakkito* (< **ishag-k-i-to*) "he asked them" or "he asked several questions," but is rarely used.[68] This suffix is also attested in Meroitic,[69] as shown in the following example:

> (35) **Meroitic**
> *abr-se-l :* *e-ked :* *kdi-se-l :*
> man-each-DET 1SG.S-kill woman-each-DET
> *e-(e)r-k :*
> 1SG.S-take-PLC
> "I killed each man; I (repeatedly) took each woman." (REM 1044/4–5)

Although it encodes the plurality of events, it seems that this suffix cannot be used in combination with the plural object marker *-bx(e),* unlike the verbal form *ɔ̀ʃór* in Karko, where the plural event suffix is combined with the plural object suffix. Examples (36) and (37) are drawn from Queen Amanirenas and Prince Akinidad's stela REM 1003 and describe military campaigns against two different tribes in nearly identical terms. The first uses the pluractional suffix *-k,* but no plural object marker is present, probably because the distributive value of *tk-k* "seize one by one" implies the plurality of the object. Conversely, in the second sentence, the verbal plural marker *-bx* is present, but not the pluractional suffix -*k.*[70]

> (36) *abr :* *100 :* *kdi* *1[.]2 :* *qo-leb :* *apote*
> man 100 woman 1[.]2 this-DET.PL envoy
> *be-se :* *tk-k :*
> 3PL-GEN seize-PLC
> "(I) seized 100 men, 1[.]2 women (and) their envoy." (REM 1003/10)

(37) *abr :* *58 :* *kdi* *223 :* *qo-leb :* *apote*
man 58 woman 223 this-DET.PL envoy
qebe-se : *ye-tk-bx-i :*
3PL-GEN 1SG.S-seize-VNM.PL-TAM
"I seized 58 men, 223 women (and) their envoy." (REM 1003/12–13)

The difference between Meroitic, where the pleonastic use of the two plurality markers is avoided and Karko, where it is allowed, shows how verbal number marking can vary within the same language family. This flexibility may be due to the rivalry between these markers and other ways to express plurality, according to Gerrit Dimmendaal:

> These typological properties suggest that such systems are subject to a considerable degree of communicative dynamism, and hence to historical change or reinterpretation. There may be a number of reasons for the relative instability of such systems, compared to some other grammatical domains in these languages, such as noun-class systems in Niger-Congo languages, or gender marking in Afroasiatic languages. One reason, as argued in the present contribution, may derive from construction-level effects of number marking across categories. As shown below, pluractional marking, as a derivational phenomenon describing event structure, interacts with plural argument marking.[71]

3.3.6. A New Hypothesis Concerning the Origin of *-bx(e)*

The plural object marker *-bx(e)* displays an astonishing feature, which has yet to be noted. One may expect the plural of *-x(e)* to be **-x(e)b,* with a suffixed plural marker *-b,* as is the cases with other morphemes. The plural of the article *-l* is *-leb* and the possessive *qe-se* "his/her" (lit. "of him/her") becomes *qe-be-se* "their" (lit. "of them") when the possessor is in the plural (see §3.2). The unexpected initial location of the plural marker in the compound *-b-x(e)* is best explained by supposing that the plural morpheme *-b* was the basic element of this group. The object marker *-x(e)* was later added to it, and not the opposite. In this case, we can surmise that, originally, the verbal plural marker was simply *-b*. As is obvious from comparative pairs such as Proto-Nubian **nogu* ~ Meroitic *nob* /nuba/ "slave"; Proto-Nubian **aŋgur* ~ Meroitic *abore* /abur/ "elephant," the Meroitic reflex of Proto-NES **g* followed or preceded by a labiovelar vowel is /b/.[72] The original verbal plural marker was therefore **gu*. In Old Nubian and Nobiin, this element is preserved as a nominal and pronominal plural marker: ⲙⲁⲛ /man/ "that," ⲙⲁⲛⲛ̄-ⲅⲟⲩ /manin-gu/ "those."

It is nevertheless unclear whether the Old Nubian and Nobiin verbal plural marker *-(i)j* (see §/3.3.2) is a cognate of **gu*. The Proto-Nubian phoneme **ɟ* cannot be reconstructed in Proto-NES, but principally derived from **g*, when followed or preceded by the palatal vowels **i* and **e*.[73] The Nubian verbal plural marker might accordingly result from a protoform **-ig*. Similarly, its Ama counterpart -*(ī)d̪ì* probably derived from **(-i)gi*. The Ama dental stops *t̪* and *d̪* are the regular reflexes of Proto-NES **k* and **g* with back vowels,[74] but there are some instances of the same development with palatal vowels, such as *kwɔ̀dŕ* "strong" < Proto-NES **kugir*[75] or *tɛd̪i-ŋ* "under" < Proto-NES **tago-* "belly."[76] To sum it up, the Meroitic suffix derives from **gu*, whereas the Ama and Nubian suffixes derive from **(i-)gi*. Because Ama and Nubian belong to two separate groups within the NES languages, it is plausible that **(i-)gi* is the Proto-NES etymon, whereas **gu* is a secondary protoform restricted to the eastern branch of NES (Nubian/Meroitic and Nara).

Like *-(i)j* in Old Nubian and Nobiin, the verbal plural marker *-b* was once used for plurality of events or plurality of object. The name of the Napatan king Amani-nataki-lebte,[77] who ruled during the second half of the 6th century BCE, does not make sense if the suffix *-b* marks the plurality of object. It would mean "Amun, give them strength," with no clue as to who these multiple beneficiaries could be. Actually, the suffix marked the plurality of events and emphasised the repetition of the gift: "give again and again," "give continuously," or "keep giving."[78]

(38) **Egyptian transcription** *Jmn-* *ntk-*
Meroitic (reconstituted) *Amni-* *ntki-*
Gloss Amun strength
lbt
l-b-te
give-VNM-OPT.2SG
"Amun, may you keep giving strength!"

At first sight, the addition of the object marker *-x(e)* to the verbal plural suffix *-b*, i.e., the suffixation to a suffix, makes no sense grammatically. This would be only possible if this suffix, at a moment in the history of the Meroitic language, was interpreted as a pronoun. The following example from the Old Nubian legend of Saint Mina can illustrate how this transcategorization of the verbal plural marker occurred.[79]

(39) **Old Nubian**
ⳟⲥ̄ⲥⲟⲩ ⲙⲏⲛⲁ-ⲛ ⲕⲥ̄ⲥⲉⲗⲁ ⲧ̄ϭϭⲁⲛⲁⲥⲁ
ŋissou *mēna-n* *kisse-la*
holy Mina-GEN church-DAT
tij-j-ana-sa
give>2/3-O.PL-IMP.2/3PL-PURP
"So that we give it to them in the church of Saint Mina." (M 9.3–4)

In his analysis of the text, Van Gerven Oei notes that the "plural object marker -ϭ [is] referring to the recipients of the egg, which remain unexpressed."[80] Nevertheless, even if the plural object marker is not *stricto sensu* a pronoun, it operates in this sentence as an anaphoric element and is accordingly translated "to them" by the editor of the text. It is probably via a similar process that its Meroitic counterpart *-b* became a 3rd person plural enclitic pronoun. This explains the strange location of this morpheme, which is directly appended to the stem, before the TAM suffixes.

Once it was considered to be a pronominal marker, *-b* was inflected by the objective case ending. This morpheme is attested after noun phrases in two variants; *-xe* (40) and *-w* (41).

(40) **Meroitic**
atepoke : *dot-l-**xe***
offering(?) large(?)-DET-OBJ1
pisi-tk-bxe-kese (< *-kete-se*)
CAUS-offer-VNM.PL-OPT.2PL.IMPP
"May you PL present them with a large(?) offering(?)" (REM 1063)

(41) *x(re)* *mlo-l-**w*** *hol-kete*
food good-DET-OBJ2 serve-OPT.2PL
"May you PL serve him a good meal" (REM 0059)

The difference between the two suffixes is unclear. The previous examples are drawn from benediction formulae used at the end of the funerary texts, formula J in (40) and formula C' in (41).[81] They can co-occur in the same text.[82] The Proto-NES ending for the objective case can be reconstructed as **-gV,*[83] which is preserved in Nubian and vestigially in Nara. In the Taman language group and in Ama, the vowel *V* was dropped and the final **-g* became *-ŋ*. We have seen in §2 that the value of the grapheme *-x* in local words was most likely /ŋ/. The following *e* probably had a zero value, so that *-xe* was simply a final /ŋ/ like the Taman and Ama marker.

This "objective case" in Nubian and in Tama undergoes some restrictions governed by economy principles. In his analysis of Tama, Dimmendaal speaks of "differential object marking."[84] In Meroitic, the objective case has become so rarely marked that the absence of case ending was more a rule than an exception. Example (41) is the benediction formula C'. It is the royal and princely counterpart of formula C which is used for private people. The only difference was the presence of the objective case-ending in C', whereas it was missing in the C formula.[85] It probably gave the royal benediction a more formal wording, worthy of the lofty position of the deceased.

Similarly, the objective case ending may be omitted, as can be seen in the second of two consecutive sentences from King Taneyidamani's stela. In (43), the expected verbal compound, parallel to the singular form *ekedeto* in (42), should be *ekedbxto.* However, maybe because of the presence of the object pronoun *qoleb,* the objective case ending *-x* is absent.

(42)

Nhror	*wide-l :*	*e-kede-to :*
Nakharura	brother-DET	1SG.S-kill-TAM

"I killed the brother, Nakharura" (REM 1044/143–144)

(43)

qoleb :	*axro*	*tewideb-wit*	*e-ked-b-to*
3PL	?	?	1SG.S-kill-VNM-TAM

"I killed them, ???" (REM 1044/148–150)

In conclusion, the suffixes *-x(e)* and *-bx(e)* operate in the verbal compound as enclitic object pronouns. It originally consisted of a verbal plural marker *-b,* similar to its counterparts in Nubian and Ama. Between the 6th and the 2nd century BCE, this suffix underwent a transcategorization and became an enclitic object pronoun inflected with the objective case ending *-x(e).* In parallel, a singular counterpart, *-x(e),* without the plural marker *-b,* was created. However, they cannot be termed "personal pronouns" unless different forms for the 1st and the 2nd persons are identified, so as to constitute a full paradigm. Considering the formation of this morpheme, it is altogether unlikely that it also marked person.

4. The First Person Singular Marker

If the wording of the Meroitic inscriptions was identical to the Egyptian texts of the same genre, we should expect to find first person singular markers in the captions accompanying the divine figures in the temples and in the royal chronicles. However, the Meroitic culture, though deeply influenced by the Egyptian civilisation, still preserved many of its own peculiarities. The gods, for instance, never speak for themselves in religious texts. In an Egyptian or a Napatan temple, the caption inscribed beside an image of Amun would begin with the sentence: "Utterance of Amun. I have given all life and all power to you."[86] In the Meroitic texts of the temples of Naga, Meroe, Amara, and others, the god is not speaking himself. Rather, a fictive enunciator is inviting him to shower his blessings upon the ruler and his family: "O Amun! May you give X life and strength," as shown in (17)–(18) and (29)–(31). For that reason, no first person marker can be expected in these inscriptions.

4.1. Person in Egyptian Royal Texts

The Egyptian royal chronicles, the so-called *Königsnovellen,*[87] alternatively use the first person pronoun and the phrase *ḥm=f* "his Majesty" to designate the king – the hero of the narrative. This is for instance the case in the famous poem of Kadesh, where passages in the first person and the third person freely intertwine to describe the battle that Ramesses II fought against the Hittites. In Kush, the earliest and the most sophisticated *Königsnovelle* is the Victory Stela of King Piankhy (*FHN* I: pp. 62–118), engraved around 720 BCE and erected in the dynastic temple of Amun in Jebel Barkal. Apart from the passages including the king's speech, which are in the first person, the narrative uses *ḥm=f* "his Majesty" to refer to Piankhy. The same usage is found in the stelae erected in the temple of Kawa by king Taharqo and, later, in the inscriptions of the early Napatan kings Anlamani and Aspelta.[88]

In the mid-5th c. BCE, a dramatic shift occurred. The inscriptions of the late Napatan king Amannote-erike (*FHN* II: pp. 400–428) still use the time-honored phrase *ḥm=f,* but the two subsequent royal stelae, erected in the temple of Amun in Jebel Barkal by kings Harsiotef (*FHN* II: pp. 438–464) and Nastasen (*FHN* II: pp. 471–501), are written in the first person, even in the reports of military campaigns in which the ruler did not take part in person. This shift was not an isolated novelty, but took place among several divergences from the Egyptian/Early Napatan pattern. In Nastasen's inscription, for example, the time scale by regnal years is replaced by vague adverbial phrases such as *kt ʿn* "another matter again" in the war reports.[89] This chronological vagueness was to become systematic in the royal stelae written in Meroitic, where no regnal year is ever mentioned. The reasons for these changes are unclear but the influence of local oral epics may have played a role.

In Harsiotef's stela, after the titles and the eulogy, where the king is referred to in the third person, the text abruptly shifts to the first person, without any kind of transition (*FHN* II: p. 441, l. 4). In Nastasen's stela, the main text similarly begins with the titles of the king and a long eulogy, after which the narrative is introduced by the clause *dd=f* "he says," referring, of course, to the king. This addition, lacking in Harsiotef's stela, makes clear that, from this point on, the narrator is the ruler.[90] The following passage from Nastasen's chronicle (ll. 54–

56) illustrates this novel use of the first person in Napatan war reports.[91] Conspicuously, the monarch is not acting in person, but through his warriors, hence the use of the factitive verb *dj* "make, cause to."

(44) **Egyptian**
k.t ꜥn
"And another thing again.
dj=ỉ sj=f pd.t ḥr sby.t Mḫ Šrḫrtj
I had a battalion of archers to go against the enemy tribe of the Makho of Sharakharti.
dj=j ḫꜣy ꜥꜣ
I caused a great bloodbath.
dj=j ṯꜣ pꜣ wr pꜣ nty jw=f r s.ꜥnḫ jr.t n-jm=f nb ḥmt nb.t
I had the chief seized, (together with) all that on which he [= they] would feed, and all the women.
dj=j <s>w ẖr=j x[ꜥ]q jwꜣ 203,146 mnmn 33,050
I put in my possession a booty (of) 203,146 oxen and 33,050 head of livestock."

The first preserved royal text in Meroitic, namely the great stela of king Taneyidamani from the temple of Amun in Jebel Barkal, was inscribed a century and a half later. In the meantime, the Egyptian-language donation stelae of king Aryamani, Kawa XIV and XV, are admittedly written in the first person, but the texts — at least what is left of them — are speeches to Amun and contain no narrative.[92] On the other end of the Meroitic period, a century after the fall of Meroe, the wall inscription of the Nobadian ruler Silko in Kalabsha, though written in Greek, also is in the first person.[93] It is therefore highly probable that the Meroitic royal chronicles fall in this long-lasting tradition and include events and war reports narrated by the ruler in the first person, like the late Napatan royal stelae and the post-Meroitic inscription of king Silko.

4.2. The Verbal Affix *(y)e-* in Meroitic Royal Texts

Although the major part of the Meroitic royal inscriptions remains untranslatable, the passages that enumerate the spoils of war are now fairly well understood.[94] They include, on the one hand, verbs such as *ked* "kill"; *are* and *er* "take hold of"; *tk* "seize"; and *kb* "seize, plunder," sometimes followed by the pluractional marker *-k* (*er-k, tk-k*), and, on the other hand, nouns such as *abr* "man"; *kdi* "woman"; *ar* "boy"; *anese* "donkey"; *mreke* "horse"; and *d* "house,"[95] all of them being parts of the booty and therefore, cited with figures or more summarily followed by *-se-l* "each." Examples (20), (35), (36), (37), (42), and (43) above are instances of booty lists from royal inscriptions.

In his publication of the so-called Akinidad stela from Hamadab (REM 1003), Griffith was the first to deal with these passages. Thanks to his then recent translation of *kdi* "woman" and *abr* "man," he correctly identified the first two clauses (*abrsel yekedi: kdisel: arseli: tkk*) as the outcome of military campaigns and tentatively translated them as "slaying men, enslaving women."[96] By using participles, he eluded the thorny issue of the subject of the verbs. After Griffith, few scholars addressed this particular question. In her analysis of the same passages, Inge Hofmann dealt with the meaning of the verb *ked,* but ignored the problem of its subject.[97] As for Millet, in a first study of Kharamadoye's royal inscription REM 0094, he suggested that *ked* was a noun meaning "slayer."[98] Later, in a revised analysis of the same article, he assumed that *ked* was a verb in the third person singular,[99] but did not explain how this third person was morphologically expressed.

It is necessary first to summarize the different forms that the verbs "kill" and "seize" (*vel sim.*) can take in different royal, princely, and viceregal inscriptions. **Table 2** includes a list of these forms with reference to the texts which are quoted in chronological order:

- Great stela of king Taneyidamani from Barkal (REM 1044, ca. 150 BCE);
- Graffito of prince Akinidad in the temple of Dakka (REM 0092, ca. 25 BCE);
- Stela of Amanirenas and Akinidad from Hamadab (REM 1003, ca. 20 BCE);
- Funerary stela of viceroy Abratoye from Tomas (originally Karanog, REM 1333, ca. 270 CE);
- Late inscription of the Blemmyan kinglet Kharamadoye from the temple of Kalabsha (REM 0094, ca. 420 CE).

Note that only the passages where at least the verb *ked* is present are taken into consideration here.

Text	Lines	Example	"kill"	"seize" (*vel sim.*)
REM 1044	5		*e-ked*	*erk* (< *e-* + *er-k*)
	130–131		*e-ked-td*	*er-td* (< *e-* + *er-td*)
	143	(42)	*e-kede-to*	
	144		*e-kede-to*	
	149–151	(43)	*e-kede-b-to*	
REM 0092	6–8		*kede-to*	*are-de-to*
	12–14		*kede-to*	*are-de-to*
REM 1003	4–5	(35)	*ye-ked-i*	*tk-k; yerki* (< *ye-* + *er-k-i*)
	9		*ye-ked-i*	*erk* (< *e-* + *er-k*)
	11	(36)	*ye-ked*	*tk-k*
	14		*ye-ked*	*tk-k*
REM 1333	6		*ye-ked*	
	13		*ked*	
	14		*ked*	*kbxelo* (< *kb-bxe-l-o*)
	16–17	(20)	*ked*	*arohe-bx; tk-bxe-l-o*
	18		*ye-ked*	
	20		*ked*	
	24		*kede-bx*	
REM 0094	11		*kede-bxe*	
	20–21		*kede-bx*	*kb-b-te*

Table 2. Forms of the verbs "kill" and "seize" (*vel. sim*) in REM 1044, 0092, 1003, 1333, and 0094.

The verbal forms listed above show a great diversity of suffixes. The plural verbal marker *-bx(e)* in REM 1333, variant *-b* in REM 1044/149–150 and 0094, and the pluractional suffix *-k* in REM 1044/5 and 1003, which were studied both in § 3.3.6, are irrelevant in the quest for personal markers. The suffixes *-td* (only in REM 1044), *-to* in REM 1044 and 0092, *-te* in REM 0094 are probably tense or aspect markers, which are in final position in all the other NES languages.[100] The morpheme *-i* in REM 1003 is obviously optional, as it can be present or absent in identical sequences such as *abr-se-l: ye-ked-i* "I killed each man" in l. 4 vs. *abr-se-l ye-ked* in l. 11.[101] The vocalic sign *-e* appended to the stem in *(e)-kede-to* (REM 1044 and 0092) is probably an epenthetic vowel inserted before the suffix *-to*. In the other verbal forms ending with this suffix that occur in the same texts, the vowel *-e* is generally absent, but no obvious rule, as for now, can predict its appearance. Finally, the forms ending with *-l-o* in REM 1333 are very probably periphrastic, as they include participles followed by the article *-l* and the copula *-o*. The multiplicity of tense or aspect markers that occur in these narrative texts is by no means unexpected or dubious, but is a further aspect of the *varietas* that is so peculiar to the Meroitic texts, when compared with their formulaic Egyptian counterparts.[102] A similar variety in narrative tenses can be found in many languages. In French, for example, historical records can of course use simple past and imperfect, but present is possible (*présent de narration*) and even future, in this case referring to past events (*futur historique*).

Coming back to **Table 2**, the only marker that can actually refer to the person is the prefix *(y)e-*, since it has no alternative, unlike the diverse suffixes that are listed above. As explained in § 2, the form *ye-* is just a later spelling of *e-*. Both were similarly pronounced /e/. In early inscriptions such as Taneyidamani's stela (REM 1044), the prefix is spelled *e-* everywhere. In classical Meroitic texts such as Akinidad's stela (REM 1003), *e-* (in *erk*) and *ye-* (in *yerki*) are alternately used for the same verb. Finally, in the late stela of viceroy Abratoye (REM 1333), the only spelling is *ye-*. One may wonder why this personal marker was not identified earlier. Actually, there were two difficulties. First, the prefix is missing in several clauses in REM 1003 and is completely absent in REM 0092 and 0094; second, a prefix *ye-* is attested in the final benedictions of the funerary texts, in a context where only the 2nd person plural is expected.

4.3. The Distribution of the Prefix *(y)e-* and Homonymy

The first difficulty can be easily resolved. Once again, this issue is connected with the chronology of the inscriptions. In the early text REM 1044, the prefix is present everywhere, before *ked* "kill" as well as before the verbs meaning "take" in the following clauses, except for *tk-to* in l. 151. In the classical Meroitic stela REM 1003, it is always present in the first clause ("kill") and can be omitted in the second clause ("take"), especially when the verb *tkk* is used. In the late inscription REM 1333, *(y)e-* is present before *ked* in the first instance of this verb, that is, at the beginning of the narrative part of the funerary stela. It is omitted in the subsequent occurrences of *ked* until l. 18, at which point it appears again. Furthermore, it is never present before the verbal forms of the second clause ("take" *vel sim.*). Curiously, the prefix *(y)e-* is lacking in REM 0092, which is contemporaneous with REM 1003, as they both mention Prince Akinidad. It is also absent from the occurrences of "kill" and "take" in the very late inscription of kinglet Kharamadoye (REM 0094).

How can we account for these variations in the distribution of the prefix *(y)e-* in the royal and princely inscriptions? In the early stela REM 1044, the prefix is systematically present on all the verbal forms. In REM 1003, a century and a half later, the prefix is used with the first verbal form ("kill") but is omitted in the following clause ("take") for reasons of economy, since the subject is the same as in the previous clause. In the late stela REM 1333, the first occurrence of the verb *ked* includes the prefix *ye-*, but the next three occurrences of the same verb are again subject to ellipsis, as are all the verbs of the second clauses ("take" *vel sim.*). In l. 18, the personal prefix is resumed, as a reminder for the two last occurrences of *ked,* where it is omitted again. In the very late inscription of the post-Meroitic kinglet Kharamadoye, the prefix is totally missing in the forms meaning "kill" or "take." However, a previous sequence in l. 8, *yetolxe,* could be a verbal form with prefix *ye-*.[103] Finally, the inscription REM 0092, though written at the same time as REM 1003, shows no prefix in the verbal forms for "kill" and "take." However, in a previous passage in l. 5, the verb is illegible because the stone is damaged in this place. This lacuna possibly contained the prefix *e-,* whose lower stroke seems partly visible on some photographs taken prior to the relocation of the temple of Dakka when the Aswan dam was built.

It seems that, in the course of time, the personal marker *(y)e-* shifted from compulsory verbal affix to quasi-independent subject pronoun. On the one hand, it could be present or absent if implicit, just like personal pronouns in English *he came and saw*. On the other hand, it was never separated from the verb by an intermediary element such as an object noun group or an adverbial phrase. Its close connection with the following verbal form is also showed by the total absence of a word-divider (:) between them in all the texts. In addition, ellipsis was likely more frequent in everyday speech than in the literary inscription. This could explain the difference in the use of the prefix between the contemporaneous texts REM 0092 and 1003: REM 0092 is a simple graffito carelessly engraved in the temple of Dakka during the visit of prince Akinidad, whereas REM 1003 was an official stela erected at the entrance of the temple of Amun in Hamadab.

The second difficulty is that a homonymous prefix *ye-* is attested in verbal compounds of the funerary benedictions, which are clearly in the 2nd person plural since these passages are prayers to Isis and Osiris. This rare alternative prefix can replace the element *p(V)s(V)-* that is generally found at the beginning of the complex verbal forms of the benedictions A and B.[104] It is altogether the most frequent in the rare benediction D.[105] The suffixes of the verbal compounds of the benedictions are now relatively well understood (see §⁄5.1), though their prefixes still remain puzzling. Both *ye-* and *p(V)s(V)-* can best be interpreted as causative markers, as they always appear before the verbal stems meaning "drink" (*he* in benediction A) and "eat" (*xr* in benediction B), but are optional before the verb "offer, present" (*hol* in benediction C). The deities invoked in the funerary texts would be invited to "make" the deceased "drink" and "eat," but they could either "present them with a good meal" or "have them presented with a good meal." Prefixes are extremely rare in NES languages and only the Taman group has verbal prefixes, used exclusively for marking the person (a point to which we return below).

The most plausible solution would be to regard *ye-* and *p(V)s(V)-* as causative verbs, such as "make" or "have" in English. In the case of *p(V)s(V)-*, a possible cognate could be Old Nubian ⲡⲉⲥ- "tell, speak, say." The gods of the underworld could in this case could be invited, literally, to "tell" that the deceased eat and drink, that is, to make them eat and drink. As for the alternative verb *ye-* in these passages, it could be linked with Old Nubian ⲉⲓ- and Nobiin *íí-* "say," especially because *ye-* has a variant *yi-* which is three times more frequent in funerary texts.[106] This solution may be semantically acceptable, but it faces a major obstacle: Meroitic, like all the NES languages, is a head-final language, in which the verb is placed at the end of sentences and the auxiliary is expected to occur after the verb. In addition, the absence of TAM markers after *p(V)s(V)-*, and *ye-/yi-* points to a serial verb construction, where only the last verb is inflected for TAM. However, this is cross-linguistically attested only for consecutive verbs that share a common subject.[107] For all these reasons, the verbal compound of the funerary benedictions requires further study. Nevertheless, the element *ye-* in these benedictions has nothing to do with the prefix *ye-* we found in the royal texts. It is just a further instance of the many homonymous morphemes that are attested in Meroitic.

Finally, another element *ye-* is attested in several kinship noun phrases, also in funerary inscriptions. The "filiation" part of these texts specifies the mother and father of the deceased, who is said to be "the person born of X" and "the person begotten by Y." In the major part of the inscriptions, these two compounds are *te-dxe-l* (or *t-dxe-l*) and *t-erike-l.* They include a prefixed element *t(e)-*, the participles *dxe* "born" and *erike* "begotten," and the final article, which has a nominalizing role. Several texts include a variant with a first element *y(e)-*, namely *ye-dxe-l* and *y-erike-l.* The forms including *y(e)-* and *t(e)-* can even be found together in the same inscription, giving a further example of the aforementioned *varietas* sought by Meroitic scribes. Another kinship term, *yetmde* "younger in the maternal line, i.e., nephew/niece," may provide the key to the element *ye-* in filiation clauses. It includes the word *mde* which refers to the mother's family in this matrilineal society. The first element is *yet-* (pronounced /eta/ or /eda/), but has many variants: *yete, yed, yen* (with assimilation before *mde*). The elements *te-* and *ye-* in filiation are probably two eroded forms of *yet-*, which can be compared with Proto-Nubian **id,* Proto-Taman **at* "person," and Nara *eítá* "body."[108] "The person born" and "the person begotten" are therefore accurate translations of *ye-dxe* and *y-erike.* The element *ye-* in these contexts is therefore originally a noun and has nothing to do with the homonymous prefix found in royal inscriptions.

4.4. Comparative Evidence from NES Languages

In light of the above, it seems certain, first, that the verbs in the narratives of the royal inscriptions are in the first person singular and, second, that the prefix *(y)e-* is the personal subject marker of the verbs "kill" and "take." Consequently, *ye-ked* (archaic *e-ked*), can be translated "I killed" or "I have killed" and *yerki* (archaic *erk*) as "I took," "I have taken," or the like. Given the meaning of these passages, the basic tense/aspect using simple stems like *ked, tkk,* and so on, must be a perfective. Alternative tenses with suffixes also are attested, as shown in **Table 2**, but for now, it is impossible to explain them. The first person singular marker *(y)e-* is probably the Meroitic reflex of the Proto-NES pronoun **a(-i),*[109] reconstructed from Proto-Nubian **a-i,*[110] Nara **a(-ga),*[111] and Proto-Nyima **a-i.* The stem of this pronoun is **a,* to which a suffix **-i* has been appended. This ending was probably a deictic particle and can be found at the end of persons' and gods' names in Meroitic and in Old Nubian.[112] The Meroitic form seems to have undergone crasis[113] /a/ + /i/ > /e/, which is also found for this pronoun in several Ajang dialects.[114]

If the form of the Meroitic marker matches its cognates in other NES languages, its syntactic use shows a substantial difference to them. In all these languages, the subject pronoun is located at the beginning of the sentence and the verb at the end (SOV word order) as in these examples from Nobiin and Ama.[115]

(45) **Nobiin**

ày	*tùuɲì-n*	*mèdrèsá-l*	*júù-r*
1SG	boys-GEN	school-LOC	go-1SG

"I go to the boys' school."

(46) **Ama**

à	*ɲúfà-ŋ*	*ēlò-ɔ̀*	*têg*
1SG	father.2SG.GEN-DAT	milk-ACC	give.IPFV

"I give (some) milk to your father."

The only NES-languages which have personal prefixes appended to the verb are the Taman languages, that is, Tama and Mararit. However, these suffixes, namely *nV-* for the 1st person, *V-* for the 2nd person, and Ø- (zero suffix) for the 3rd person,[116] are distinct from the subject pronouns, which are optional as shown in the following examples.[117] In the second sentence, the subject pronoun is here for emphasis and could be translated "as for me."

(47) **Tama**
dɔ́t n-ànɨ́
big 1SG-be
"I am big."

(48) *wâ tàmɔ́t n-ànɨ́*
1SG Tama 1SG-be
"I am a Tama."

This structure seems an innovation of the Taman group within the NES languages. Generally speaking, the personal affixes appended to the verb in Nara, Nubian, and Taman strongly differ from each other and cannot be reconstructed in Proto-NES. It seems that the original person marking combined independent pronouns (which are clearly related in the daughter languages) and verbal plural suffixes, which have been studied above. This system still operates in the Nyima languages. The Meroitic system — at least in the passages of the royal inscriptions under examination — seems close to the Proto-NES and Nyima system, but has innovated by displacing the subject pronoun before the verb. This innovation created a specific OSV word order for sentences including a subject pronoun, whereas the original SOV order was preserved in sentences with nominal subject.

4.5. Another Person Marker in Meroitic Royal Texts?

Instead of *(y)e-*, an alternative prefix *w-* appears before the verbal forms of *er-k* "take, capture," *kb* "seize, and *bqo* "take control" within the royal texts REM 1044, 1003, and 0094. It never occurs with *ked* "kill," as can be seen in the examples below.[118]

(49) **Meroitic**
heHle qoleb : ahtero-l am ***w****-k[b]-bx-te*
? 3PL ? ? PM-seize-VNM-TAM
"? seized ? them ???" (REM 1044/68–70)

(50) *qorte* *dxe-leb :* *wide-bese*
palace(?).GEN child-DET-PL brother-3PL.GEN
aroqitm *tdxsene* ***w**-er-k*
Aruqitama Tadakhesene(?) PM-take-PLC
"? captured the children of the palace (and) their brothers
Aruqitama (and) Tadakhesene(?)"

(51) *kdi-se-l-w :* *abr-se-l-w :*
woman-each-DET-ACC man-each-DET-ACC
yemoqe : *eqebese-wit :* ***w**-kb-te*
belongings(?) 3PL.GEN-DET(?) PM-seize-TAM
"? seized each man, each woman (and) their belongings(?)"
(REM 1003/23–24)

(52) *kdi-se-l-w :* *abr-se-l-w :*
woman-each-DET-ACC man-each-DET-ACC
emoqe : *eqebese-wit :* ***w**-kb-te*
belongings(?) 3PL.GEN-DET(?) PM-seize-TAM
"? seized each man, each woman (and) their belongings(?)"
(REM 1003/31–35)

(53) *wedi* *dxe* *mte-kdi* *Aqtoye : -se* *2*
? child young-woman Aqatoye-GEN 2
***w**-bqo-b-te*
PM-take.control-VNM-TAM
"? took control of ??? the two young daughters of Aqatoye"
(REM 0094/24)

There is no doubt that the prefixed element *w-*, which is paradigmatically parallel to the morpheme *(y)e-*, is also a person subject marker. We should expect it to mark a different person, which can only be the 1st plural or the 3rd singular or plural, since there is no interlocutor in these sections of the royal inscriptions. Unfortunately, the context of these passages with *w-* does not provide much information, chiefly because of our scanty knowledge of Meroitic, but also because of the poor preservation of some parts of the stelae REM 1044 and 1003. However, it seems that these passages are the continuity of the sentences where the subject is in the first person, either explicitly or implicitly. The passage below precedes (50) in Taneyidamani's stela (REM 1044/141–155). The lines that follow are unfortunately badly eroded.

> (54) *Ahotone qorte : drteyose-l :**e**-kede-to :*
> "I killed Akhutune, the ??? of the palace(?).
> *Nhror wide-l :**e**-kede-to :*
> I killed (his) brother Nakharura.
> *kdi : ste-bese : dnetro :*
> I ??? their mother [lit. 'woman-tutor'].
> *sxseli : holno-leb : asxdose : tedd : qoleb : axro tewideb-wit :**e**-ked-b-to :*
> I killed ??? them, namely the ???, the ???.
> *krtedse : xrpxe-se-mlo-l : tk-to :*
> I seized the good ??? governor.
> *qorte : dxe-leb : wide-bese : Aroqitm : Tdxsene :**w**-erk :*
> ? captured the children of the palace(?) (and) their brothers Aruqitama and Tadakhesene(?)." (= ex. 51)

Three of these sentences include the subject pronoun marker *e-* "I" in the verbal compounds *e-kede-to* (twice) and *e-ked-b-to*. In two other sentences, the prefixed pronoun is absent, but implicit, in *dnetro*(?) and *tk-to*. It is difficult to account for the subject shift in the last sentence (50), where the prefixed pronoun *w-* replaces *e-*. No solution is fully satisfactory, but the most acceptable is to assume that the antecedent of the prefixed pronoun is one of the nouns of the same sentence that would be placed as its topic. These topicalized constructions are well documented in Meroitic.[119] They can also be found, under Meroitic influence, in the Egyptian texts of the late Napatan royal inscriptions, as in this example from king Nastasen's stela (ll. 12–13, after *FHN* II: p. 478):

> (55) **Egyptian**
> *jr=w šn jr=j rmt-ꜥꜣ, ḥ(m)-ntr Jmn dr=w*
> "They made obeisance to me, (to wit) all the notables and priests of Amun
> *jry=w smꜣ jr=j, rꜣ nb*
> They blessed me, (to wit) every mouth."

If so, the tentative translation of (50) suggested above must be thoroughly corrected. A singular object is expected, because there is no plural object marker at the end of the verbal compound. Maybe the translation should be "(as for) the children of the palace (?) (and) their brother Aruqitama, they captured Tadakhesene." If this solution is syntactically acceptable, it is less so morphologically. A plural marker would be expected, like in *qe-be-se* "of them" (§3.2 above). In addition, an element *w-* is attested in the late text REM 0094 as a variant of the singular 3rd person pronoun *qo/qe* "he/she, this" (cf. §3.1). Instead of *qe-se, qo-se* "his/her" (lit. "of him/her"), a form *w-se,* with variants *we-se,* and even *w-si,* in the same text, is attested: *semle: w-si* "his wife," *ste: wese* "his mother" (line 26). Finally, no cognate can be found in other NES-languages, all of which have for "they" at least traces of a plural element **-gV.* In conclusion, the prefixed element *w-* in verbal compounds remains unexplained and needs further examination.

5. The Second Person Markers

Many Meroitic texts include prayers to the gods. They are chiefly present, of course, in the funerary inscriptions, which begin with an invocation to the deities of the underworld and finish with several "benedictions," in which a fictive enunciator beseeches them to provide the deceased with water, bread, and a good meal in the afterlife. Similarly, in the temples and on a few stelae, the depictions of the kings and their family in front of the gods are accompanied by captions, most of them in Meroitic hieroglyphic script. They also include prayers, uttered by a fictive enunciator again, that invite the deities to shower their gifts (life, strength, health, etc.) upon the ruler.

In all these inscriptions, the requests to the gods use verbal moods that fit with wishes, namely imperative or optative. The forms are in the singular in the temples because there is a specific prayer for each deity. They are in the plural in funerary inscriptions because they are addressed to Isis and Osiris together. Unlike in Egyptian and Napatan texts, the gods are never answering. Such sentences as "I gave you all life and all power," which are so common in Napatan texts and could give us details about the first and second person pronouns, are unfortunately missing from the Meroitic religious texts. However, a small stela found in 1999 has miraculously provided the genitive of the 2nd person pronouns singular and plural. Finally, recent researches on the Meroitic names of person have shown that they sometimes comprised short sentences, which in two cases include a second person singular pronoun.

5.1. Second Person Verbal Suffixes in Optatives and Imperatives

The final prayers of the funerary texts, which Griffith termed "benedictions," amount to thirteen different types, classified with uppercase letters from A to L, plus a formula "X" added by Hofmann.[120] The general scheme for benedictions A to D, by far the most frequent, is presented in (56).[121]

(56) Formula A

ato *mhe* *pVsV-/yi-* *he* *-x(e)/bx(e)*
water plentiful CAUS drink VNM.SG/PL
-k(e)te
OPT.2PL
"May you PL make her/him/them drink plentiful water."

Formula B

at *mhe* *pVsV-/yi-* *xr* *-x(e)/bx(e)* *-k(e)te*
bread plentiful CAUS eat VNM.SG/PL OPT.2PL
"May you PL make her/him/them eat plentiful bread."

Formula C

x(re) *mlo* *(pVsV-/yi-)* *hol/tx* *-x(e)/bx(e)*
meal good CAUS present VNM.SG/PL
-k(e)te
OPT.2PL
"May you PL present her/him/them (or have her/him/them presented) with a good meal."

Formula D

x(re) *lh-l* *(pVsV-/yi-)* *hol/tx* *-x(e)/bx(e)*
meal large-DET CAUS present VNM.SG/PL
-k(e)te
OPT.2PL
"May you PL present her/him/them (or have her/him/them presented) with a large meal."

The prefixed elements *pVsV-* or *yi-*, which obviously have a causative value but are not yet fully understood, have been studied above in §4.3. The element *-x(e)* in the singular, *-bx(e)* in the plural, is a verbal number marker that has been analysed in section §3.3. As the funerary benedictions are basically prayers to the gods, imperative or optative in the 2nd person plural are expected. The verbal TAM ending here is *-k-te* or *-ke-te* with a plural suffix *-k(e)*. The singular TAM ending is *-te*, as seen in examples (19), (29)–(31), each of which contains a prayer to a single god. Cross-linguistically, the singular imperative is generally a simple verbal stem, e.g., English *see!*, Latin *vide!*, and Middle Egyptian *m3!* This is also true for the living NES languages: Nobiin *nàl!*, Midob *kóod!*, etc.[122] For this reason, the verbal form with ending *-te*, which is used in the royal blessings and funerary benedictions, must be regarded as an optative rather than an imperative. However, an optional particle *-se*, which is added to the verbal compound in several funerary inscriptions,[123] has an Old Nubian parallel in the command marker -co or -cω.[124] Be it related or borrowed, this particle shows the semantic proximity of the Meroitic optative with the Old Nubian imperative.

The imperative proper, in all likelihood, is the verbal form devoid of TAM markers which is used instead of the optative in several funerary texts. As shown in the following examples, it occurs either in one or two of the three main benedictions A, B, and C (a further example of *varietas*), or in all of them. Example (57) is drawn from REM 0369, an offering table from Shablul engraved for a single deceased. Example (58) is cited from a stela found in the same cemetery, REM 0381, and engraved for two persons, hence the plural verbal marker at the end of verbal compounds.[125]

(57) **Meroitic**

Benediction A

a<to> *mhe* *pso-h :*

water abundant CAUS-drink.IMP.2

"Make her/him drink plentiful water."

Benediction B

at *mhe* *psi-xr* [:]

bread abundant CAUS-eat.IMP.2

"Make her/him eat plentiful bread."

Benediction C

x(re) *mlo-l* *hol :*

meal good-DET present.IMP.2

"Present her/him with a good meal."

(58) Benediction A

ato *<m>he* *pso-he-b :*

water abundant CAUS-drink.IMP.2-VNM

"Make her/him drink plentiful water."

Benediction B

at *mhe* *psi-xr-b :*

bread abundant CAUS-eat.IMP.2-VNM

"Make her/him eat plentiful bread."

In these imperative forms, there is virtually no plural marker. A final suffix *-k(e)* for the 2nd person plural is expected, but it is only attested in a very small number of funerary inscriptions.[126] However, it seems that in some epitaphs, the two deities Isis and Osiris, to whom these prayers were addressed, were syntactically regarded as a single god, as shown by the use of a single vocative suffix for both, located after the second noun.[127] Moreover, in the final invocations that resume the initial call to the deities, Osiris is sometimes omitted.[128] Finally, Isis (or one the goddesses assimilated to her in the Meroitic funerary cults, namely Nephthys, Nut, or Maat), is often figured in the private offering tables and the funerary chapels, whereas Osiris is never present, at least in the non-royal contexts with with which here we are dealing.[129] I surmise that the instances of the imperative are addressed to Isis. This would explain why the 2nd person singular, and not plural, is used.

Furthermore, a not uncommon variant of the verbal suffix *-te*, found only in the late funerary benedictions, is *-to.*[130] It is directly appended to the verbal stem and, unlike *-te*, is never preceded by the plural marker *-ke*. In REM 0368, an offering table from Shablul, there are four benedictions, A, B, C, D. The verb in benediction A has no suffix, so that it should be an imperative in the 2nd person singular. In the subsequent three benedictions, the verbs are in the optative with the final suffix *-to*. The four verbs, most likely, are all in the singular and convey prayers to Isis.

(59) Benediction A

ato *mhe* *pso-he*

water abundant CAUS-drink.IMP.2

"Make her/him drink plentiful water."

Benediction B

at *mxe :* *psi-xr-to*

bread abundant CAUS-eat.OPT.2SG

"May you make her/him eat plentiful bread."

Benediction C

x(re) *mlo-l :* *psi-tx-to*

meal good-DET CAUS-present-OPT.2SG

"May you have her/him presented with a good meal."

Benediction D

x(re) *lh-l :* *psi-hol-to*

meal large-DET CAUS-present-OPT.2SG

"May you have her/him presented with a large meal."

From the above, it appears that the markers of the Meroitic imperative and optative moods are as follows:

	2SG	**2PL**	**IMPP**
Imperative	-Ø	*-k(e)*	*(-se)*
Optative	*-Ø-te/-to*	*-k(e)-te*	*(-se)*

Table 4. Meroitic imperative and optative suffixes.

The use of the suffix *-k/-g* to express the plurality of actors in the imperative (and in other moods) is widespread in Nilo-Saharan languages and particularly frequent in the NES family. Although it may have the same origin as the verbal plural marker, it must not be confused with it. The exception here is Ama, where the same morpheme *-(ì)d̪ì* is used both verbal plural marker (§3.3.2) and marker of the plural imperative: *kílí* "hear!," PL*kíld̪ì* "hear ye!"[131] In Nara, the plural imperative is marked with a suffix *-aga*. This morpheme is attested in the two major dialects, namely in Higir *ay* "make!," PL*ay-aga* "make ye!"[132] and in Mogoreeb, *aw* "make!," PL*aw-aga* "make ye!"[133] In Mararit (Taman group), the plural imperative is marked with a morpheme *-k-*, which can be prefixed or suffixed according to the verb classes: *sîn* "eat!," PL*kí-síŋ-gì* "eat ye!" (prefixed); *kɛ̀dɛ̀k* "cut!," PL*kɛ̀d-k-ɛ̀k* "cut ye!" (suffixed).[134] In the Nubian group, the suffix *-*k/-g* is perhaps preserved in Midob in a palatalized form *-ic*: *kóod* "see!," PL*kóod-íc* "see ye!,"[135] but the difference with the plural verbal marker, as in Ama, is not clear. The other branches of Nubian seem to have innovated separately. In Andaandi, the 2PL imperative is marked with a suffix *-we*[136] and with a suffix *-an* in Old Nubian and Nobiin.[137] However, Old Nubian has a morpheme *-ke* "you," which Van Gerven Oei analyzes as a subject clitic.[138] It is not used for the "positive" imperative like in Meroitic, but is part of the jussive -ⲚⲔⲈ, vetitive -ⲦⲀⲚⲔⲈ(ⲤⲞ), and affirmative -ⲖⲔⲈ/-ⲤⲔⲈ. This morpheme is probably related to the Meroitic suffix *-k(e)* used in the plural imperative.

5.2. The Second Person Singular and Plural Pronouns

5.2.1. Interpretation of the Pronominal Forms in REM 1293

In 1999, the archaeological team of the Berlin Museum in Naga found a small stela (REM 1293) in the temple of Amun. It was nearly complete, but broken into three joining pieces. On the obverse, Queen Amanishakheto is depicted standing between god Apedemak and his wife, Amesemi. The Lion-god is seated on a throne whereas the goddess is standing behind the ruler. The two deities hold her elbows with their right hands in a gesture of legitimization.

On the reverse of the stela, an inscription in Meroitic cursive script is engraved on six lines. The first three lines include the following prayer.

(60) *apedemk :* *dqri-te-l-i :* *amni[sxeto :]*
Apedemak Daqari-LOC-DET-VOC Amanishakheto
qor : (< qore-l) *kdke-l :* *pwrit(e)* *(a)rese :*
ruler.DET candace-DET life 2SG.GEN
yel-x-te : *pwrite* *debse :* *el-x-te*
give-VNM-OPT.2SG life 2PL.GEN give-VNM-OPT.2SG
"O Apedemak (who is) in Daqari, to Amanishakheto, the ruler, the Candace, give the life from you SG, give the life from you PL!" (REM 1293)

The god is here invited to shower his gifts upon the ruling queen, and chiefly the most precious of them, *pwrite* "life, vital strength." Similar instances of this prayer for King Amanakhareqerama have previously been quoted in (29) and (30). The royal text REM 1293 is engraved with great care and a sense of aesthetics that is missing in so many private inscriptions. The different phrases are accurately separated by word dividers. Conspicuously, the phrases *pwritrese* and *pwrite debse* do not include a word divider after *pwrite.* Furthermore, in the first group, *pwrite* and its extension are agglomerated into a single unit. Due to the conventions of the Meroitic alphasyllabary (see §/2), the second element must have been *arese,* with an initial /a/ which was not explicitly written, because it occurred in internal position in this contracted phrase. The noun *pwrite* was pronounced /bawarit/ with the zero value of the grapheme *e.* So, the sequence *pwrite + arese* was pronounced /bawaritaresə/ and was accordingly spelled *pwritrese,* with default vowel /a/ after *t.* Additionally, the second term could not be **rese* because the phoneme /r/, in Meroitic as well as in all the NES languages, cannot occur in initial position.[139]

The close connection between *pwrite* and its successive extensions, *arese* and *debse* is best explained if the latter are determiners. They both include the genitival postposition "of," which also was part of the possessives *qe-se* "his/her" and *qe-be-se* "their" (§/3.2). Consequently, in the sentence from REM 1293 cited above, the sequences *are-se* and *deb-se* must be considered as possessive adjectives, that is, genitival forms of two personal pronouns, *are* and *deb.* As the context is a prayer to a deity, the only possibility is the second person: "O Apedemak, give your life to the queen," that is "give her the life (coming) from you."

5.2.2. Egyptian Parallels

This wording was already used in the Egyptian texts of the royal inscriptions engraved for the kings of the 25th Dynasty and their Napatan successors. Example (61) below is cited from the dedication engraved in the Temple of Mut, built by King Taharqo inside the cliff of Jebel Barkal (ca. 680 BCE). Example (62) is a text written on each side of the figure of goddess Mut in the same temple (after *FHN* I: p. 133). Example (63) is an excerpt from a stela of the Napatan king Anlamani (late 7th c. BCE) erected in the temple of Kawa (after *FHN* I: p. 322). In the three texts, the passages of interest to the question under study are in bold characters.

> (61) **Egyptian**
> *dd-mdw n Mwt, nb<.t> Tꜣ-Sty*
> "Words to be said by Mut, mistress of Nubia:
> *Jmn-Rꜥ nb ns.wt Tꜣ.wy ḥry-jb <m> Dw wꜥb*
> 'O Amun-Re, Lord of the thrones of the Two-Lands who is in the Pure Mountain
> *sꜣ=k mry=k Thrq ꜥnḫ d.t*
> (as for) your beloved son, Taharqo, may he live forever,
> *dj=k <n>=f* ***ꜥnḫ dd wꜣs nb ḫr=j***
> you have given to him **all life, stability and power from me,**
> ***snb nb ḫr=j****mj Rꜥ d.t*
> **all health from me**, like Re, for ever'." (Temple of Mut, inscription beside of the goddess standing behind Amun)

(62) *jr.n=f m mnw=f n mw-t=f Mwt*
"He made (this) as his monument for his mother Mut,
nb<.t> p.t ḥnw.t Tꜣ-Sty
Lady of Heaven, Mistress of Nubia
qd=f pr=s: sꜥꜣ=f ḥw.t-ntr=s m mꜣw m jnr ḥd nfr rwd
he built her house and enlarged her temple anew in fine, white sandstone,
dj=s n=f ***ꜥnh nb ḫr=s,***
so that she might give him **all life from her,**
***dd nb ḫr=s, wꜣs nb ḫr*[*=s*]**
all stability from her, and all power from [her]." (Temple of Mut, dedication to the goddess)

(63) *ḫꜥ Jmn-Rꜥ Gm-Jtn jw=f ꜥḥꜥ m-bꜣḥ=f*
"Amun-Re of Gematon (Kawa) appeared as he (the king) stood before him,
dj ntr pn ḥr=f r=f
and this god turned his face to him
jr=f ꜣ.t ꜥꜣ.t ꜥḥꜥ ḥr sdm ḏd.wt=f nb
and spent a long time standing and listening to all that he said
dj=f n=f ***ꜥnḫ dd wꜣs nb ḫr=f***
and gave him **all life, stability, and power from him (Amun),**
snb [***nb***] ***ḫr***[***=f***] ***ꜣw.t-jb nb ḫr=f***
[**all**] **health from him, and all joy from him.**" (Enthronement stela of Anlamani (Kawa VIII/ 27–28))

In all these passages, the Egyptian preposition *ḫr* is used: *ꜥnḫ nb ḫr=j* "all life from me," *ꜥnḫ nb ḫr=f* "all life from him." Its primary meaning is "near," but it can be also used with the agent of a passive verb in which it is usually translated with "by,"[140] a closer meaning to the sense of this proposition in examples (61)–(63). In these passages, the deity connected with the gift of life is the source of this gift, but not necessarily the one who provides it. In (62) the goddess gives to the ruler the life which is coming from her, and in (63) Amun is also the source and the giver of life. By contrast, in (61) Mut is asking her husband Amun to give Taharqo the life coming from her.[141]

In the Meroitic stela from Naga, the context bears similarities to the situation in (32). There are also three persons, namely the ruler, Amanishakheto, the lion-god Apedemak and his wife Amesemi, all of them figured on the obverse of the stela. The great difference between the Egyptian and the Meroitic texts is the position of the enunciator. In (32), Mut is the enunciator (1st person) and speaks to Amun (2nd person) about the king (3rd person). In REM 1293, the enunciator, as is common in the Meroitic prayers, is a fictive individual, who is never present in the text, so that there are no 1st person markers. He speaks to Apedemak and possibly to Amesemi (2nd person) about the queen (3rd person). The gift of life is presented to the ruler by Apedemak and the source of this life is expressed, first, by the phrase *are-se* and second by the phrase *deb-se.* The latter obviously includes the pronominal plural marker *-b,* cf. *qe-be-se* "their," lit. "of them, from them" (§/3.2)[142] In conclusion, the only solution is to regard *are-se* as a 2nd person singular possessive referring here to Apedemak, and *de-b-se* as a 2nd person plural possessive referring to both Apedemak and Amesemi.

5.2.3. Personal Pronouns in Proto-Nubian

The two possessive pronouns discussed above suggest a basic form *are* for "you SG" and *de-b* for "you PL" These forms differ considerably from the pronouns I reconstructed in proto-NES, namely **i* for "you SG" and **i-gi* for "you PL."[143] For Proto-Nubian, I suggested **i-r/*i-n* SG and **i-gi/*u-gi* PL. It is beyond the scope of this article to explain in detail on which bases these proto-forms were put forward. Suffice it to say that the pronouns attested in the Taman and Nyima groups, alongside with the most conservative dialects of Nara, are very similar to each other and provided the main basis for my reconstruction. By contrast, the personal pronouns in the Nubian family show considerable variations that are difficult to reconcile. The two proto-forms I worked out were mostly based on the genitives of these pronouns, which have a better consistency among Nubian languages and with the other branches of the NES family.

During the 14th Nilo-Saharan Linguistics Colloquium held in 2019 in Vienna, Angelika Jakobi, the leading expert on Nubian, delivered a paper entitled "The Nubian Subject Pronouns." She revisited the reconstruction of these morphemes in Proto-Nubian and suggested new proto-forms. For the 1st person singular and the 3rd person singular and plural, her reconstructions are not so different from mine. However, there are significant discrepancies for the 1st person plural and the 2nd person singular and plural. For the latter, she suggests *ed* "you SG" and **ud-i* "you PL." These proto-forms are very close to the Birgid forms *edi* and *udi,* but quite different from the Midob counterparts *íin* and *ùŋŋú.* Of course, it is tempting to believe that Jakobi's reconstruction is mainly based on Birgid. However, this language, in many respects, is the most conservative within the Nubian family, whereas Midob is one of the most innovative.[144]

In Old Nubian, we find ⲉⲓⲣ "you SG" and ⲟⲩⲣ "you PL," in Nobiin, *ìr* and *úr* respectively, and Mattokki–Andaandi *er* and *ir.* I had previously interpreted the final *-r* as an original article appended to personal pronouns in Proto-Nubian.[145] In Midob and in Tama, the article is actually *-r,* but it was *-l* in Meroitic and early Old Nubian, so that it must also have been *-l* in Proto-Nubian. In addition, the Midob reflexes of the Proto-Nubian liquids are often unpredictable,[146] whereas they are stable in Nile Nubian. For these reasons, I now think that at least in Proto-Nubian, the final *-r* was part of the stem of these personal pronouns.

On the other hand, Nubian languages have a propensity for intervocalic /r/ to shift to /d/. Many words for which the Proto-Nubian etymon included the sonorant **r* in intervocalic position, are written in Old Nubian with a delta, which later shifted back to /r/ in Nobiin, its modern descendant. As shown in **Table 5** below, Birgid and sometimes, Midob, can also have /d/ from Proto-Nubian **r.*

Gloss	**Proto-Nubian**	**Old Nubian**	**Nobiin**	**Birgid**
black	**ur(r)-i*	ⲟⲩⲇⲙ	*úrúm*	*úudè*
great	**ŋoor*	ⲅⲟⲇ "Lord"	*Nóor* "Lord"	*-gor* "old"
24 hours	**ugur*	ⲟⲁ̄ⲣ/ⲟ̄ⲁ̄ⲇⲉ "night"	*áwá,* PL *àwàrìi* "night"	*(nergi)*
six	**gorji*	ⲅⲟⲣⲟ̄ⲟ	*górjò*	*korʃi*
sorghum	**usi*	ⲙⲁⲇⲉ	*márée*	*(uze)*
sword[147]		ⲡⲁⲇⲁⲣ	*fáráɲ*	*(ʃíbídí)*
white	**arr-e*	ⲁ̄ⲇⲱ	KD *aro*[148]	*éelé* (M. *áddè*)[149]

Table 5. Alternation between intervocalic /r/ and /d/ in Nubian.

As this vacillation between /r/ and /d/ is shared by languages that belong to different branches of the Nubian family, it was in all likelihood present in Proto-Nubian. As a result, the proto-form **ed* for "you SG," which is suggested by Jakobi, is certainly possible. Likewise, it is possible that already in Proto-Nubian, a variant **er* was present.

In my previous reconstruction of Proto-Nubian, I assumed that the plural marker of the subject pronouns "we," "you PL," and "they" was **-gi* and consequently suggested **agi* for "we" and **igi* ~ **ugi* for "you PL." That assumption was based on parallels with Taman and Nyima, where this morpheme is easily reconstructable. However, I could not account for the consonant /d/ in the Birgid reflexes *adi* and *udi.*[150] If the Proto-Nubian pronoun of the second person singular is **ed,* the Birgid reflexes become perfectly regular and the Proto-Nubian plural marker is definitely **i.* This could be a development of Proto-NES **-gi,* which implies that **g* was already lost in Proto-Nubian, like in modern English *night* and *brought.* In conclusion, if Proto-Nubian "you SG" was indeed **ed,* a plural form **ud-i* is a consistent reconstruction. The initial vowel **u* instead of the expected **e* still has to be explained, but it is substantiated by the Old Nubian, Ajang,[151] and Birgid reflexes.

This alternation between /d/ and /r/ is obvious when comparing Meroitic and Nubian. Several Meroitic words related to Nubian have /d/ where Nubian has /r/. This is for instance the case for the words for "brother," in Meroitic *wide* and in Proto-Nubian *wer-i.*[152] In addition, the Meroitic phoneme /d/ has two different realizations: alveolar [d] in initial position and after another consonant, retroflex [ɖ] in intervocalic position.[153] The retroflex consonant was acoustically so close to [r] that Egyptians and Greeks transcribed this sound with the grapheme "r." That is why the capital of the kingdom, spelled *Medewi* in Meroitic, was written *Mrw.t* by the Egyptians and Μερόη by the Greeks.

Consequently, the two Meroitic pronouns *are* and *deb* for the second person singular and plural, are reliable cognates of the Proto-Nubian forms **ed* and **ud-i.* The singular *are* was pronounced /ar/ (§5.2.1) and strongly resembles its Dongolawi counterpart *er.* The plural form *deb* was pronounced /deba/ and must derive from an older form **adeb.* For prosodic reasons, the initial vowel was weakened and finally dropped.[154] Thus, the vacillation between /d/ and /r/, which was evidenced in the Nubian group, was also present in Meroitic, with /r/

in the singular and /d/ in the plural. Another possibility would be to that the original pronoun was **areb,* pronounced /areba/. This form would also have undergone the same apheresis, but, as /r/ can never be initial in Meroitic, it would have shifted to /d/, the closest stop to this vibrant. Finally, recall that /ba/ is the regular Meroitic reflex of Proto-SON **-gu,* which is known as plural marker for demonstratives in the eastern branch of the NES family.[155] In this respect, the formation of the plural form in Meroitic differs not only from Proto-Nubian, where a plural marker **i* was used, but also from Proto-NES, where this morpheme was **gi.*

5.2.4. The Second Person Singular Subject Pronoun in Personal Names

Most Meroitic personal names, and particularly the rulers', are complex compound words. This resulted in names being unique most of the time, and it may actually have been the purpose of this complexity and length. Among the royal names, only Arkamani was used twice, a sharp contrast to the seven Mentuhoteps and the eleven Ramesseses of the Egyptian history. These Kushite royal names seem to have been the birth-names of the rulers, to which the name of a god, most frequently Amun, was possibly — but not systematically — added at the time of their ascension to the throne. In some of them, "Amun" is fully integrated into the syntax of the compound, so that it may originally have been present, be it an actual birth-name or a completely new name given to the ruler. For instance, Amannote-erike means "the one whom Amon of Thebes has begotten" and it is obvious that in this case, the god name was not added at a later stage. Many Kushite royal names are theophoric and probably fall within the Egyptian naming tradition. For example, "Natakamani" probably means "Amun is strong" and is the Meroitic counterpart of Egyptian Nakht-Amun or Amun-Nakht.

However, several royal names seem to follow a local tradition of naming an individual from physical features or temperament and can therefore be considered genuine birth-names. A stunning example of this tradition among private individuals is the name of the mother of a deceased woman from Sedeinga. She was called *Xmlowiteke,* which means "she who likes a good meal."[156] It can be either the birth-name of a greedy baby or a nickname given later during her lifetime. In the royal sphere, a name like Aspelta falls in the same tradition. The name of this Napatan king, written in Meroitic, was recently identified by the author among the graffiti of Great Enclosure in Musawwarat es-Sufra. It was written *Isplto.*[157] If the first segment *Is-* is the Meroitic cognate of Old Nubian ⲉⲓⲥ- "other,"[158] it could mean "another is given" and refer, for example, to the birth of a second son, a possible heir to the throne. This name would be appropriate for a ruler like Aspelta, who succeeded his brother Anlamani at a very young age.

This naming tradition, in spite of the increasing influence of Islam, still exists in some parts of Sudan. In her study of the personal names among the Midob, a Nubian-speaking population of Northern Darfur, Abeer Bashir gives several examples of personal names whose meaning is connected with physical or social particularities, or with events that happened at the time these individuals were born:[159]

> (66) **Midob**
> *Óndìtè* ← *óndì* "camel" + *tè* "own" = "rich, lit. owner of a large herd of camels"
> *Úccí* ← *údí* "black" + suffix *-(i)cc* = "person of black skin"
> *Ábágàlò* ← *ábá* "grandmother" + *gálò* "lost" = "who has lost his/her grandmother"

Interestingly, two royal names belonging to this category of "contextual" names include a first element *are* which is obviously the same as the 2nd person pronoun identified above. They are the names of Queen Amanirenas (*Amnirense*) and king Amanakhareqerema (*Amnxreqerem*).[160] The god names *Mni* "Amun" and *Amnxe* "Amanakh" were added to their original names when they received the royal crown of Kush.[161] Their former names were *Arense* and *Areqerem* respectively. The vowel /a/ is never written in internal position (here after *Amni-* or *Amnax-*). However, it must have been present at the beginning of *Arense* and *Areqerem,* because, as addressed above in *§*/5.2.1 when analysing the compound *pwritrese* "the life from you," /r/ can never be initial in Meroitic and its related languages.

The first element, *are* "you " is followed by the sequences "-nase" (written *nse*) in the first name and "-qerema" (written *qerem*) in the second. They display striking resemblances with the Nubian adjectives "tall" and "black." In Old Nubian, these are ⲅⲁⲥⲥ- and ⲟⲩⲁⲙ- respectively, in Nobiin *nàssí* and *úrúm,* and in Andaandi *nosso*

) in the first name and "-qerema" (written *qerem*) in the second. They display striking resemblances with the Nubian adjectives "tall" and "black." In Old Nubian, these are ⲛⲁⲥⲥ- and ⲟⲩⲇⲙ- respectively, in Nobiin *nàssí* and *úrúm*, and in Andaandi *nosso* and *urumme*. In addition, the correspondence in initial position between Meroitic *qe/qo* /kʷu/ and Nubian /u/ is well attested, for instance between Meroitic *qore* "king" and Old Nubian ⲟⲩⲣⲟⲩ. The birth-name of the queen, namely *(A)rense* "Are-nase" would therefore mean "you are tall" and the birth-name of the king, namely *(A)reqerem* "Are-qerema" "you are black." The elision of the copula (*-o* was expected in final position) is noteworthy, but this morpheme has so far been attested only with 3rd person constructions.[162] The names were possibly given to them soon after they were born and described the physical appearance they had at this young age. When they ascended to the throne, these names were not considered incompatible with royal status: tall stature and black skin are, for example, features that were commonly associated with Osiris, the mythical first king of Egypt. The names of Amun or his hypostasis Amanakh were just added to their birth-names, according to the custom mentioned above.

5.3. The Prefixed Second Person Singular Marker in the Verbal Complex

We have previously seen that there were in Meroitic two types of person markers encoding the subject of the verb. First, independent pronouns such as *qo* "he, she" or *are* "you SG," attested so far only in non-verbal clauses, and second, prefixed elements which are appended to the verbal compound, such as *ye-* "I" and *w-* "he/she(?)," in verbal clauses. For the 2nd person singular, a morpheme *d-*, which has remained unexplained for twenty years, is very likely the prefixed person marker that matches the independent pronoun are "you SG."

In the 2000 issue of the *Meroitic Newsletter*, I published an article to show that a small corpus of Meroitic inscriptions on papyrus, leather strips, and ostraca, which were hitherto regarded as private letters, were actually protection spells.[163] They were purchased by pilgrims from the temples, especially the temple of Amun in Qasr Ibrim, where the major part of these texts were found by the British team of the Egypt Exploration Society. I termed them "Amuletic Oracular Decrees," after the name of the same type of texts attested in Egypt in the early first millennium BCE. Because of the rich vocabulary they include, describing all kind of misfortunes from which their owner will be protected, the translation of these inscriptions is still in an early stage. However, the scheme of the introductive parts of the texts is clear. They are divided in two groups according the prefixes of the verbal forms, *y(i)-* or *d-*.

(66) **Meroitic**
Prefixy(i)- (REM 0345, 1096, 1152(?), 1317/1168 (?), 1319, 1321, 1325, 1326)
Formula A
name-*i* *wte-li* *pke-li* *y-irohe-se-l-o-wi*
PN-VOC life-DET N-DET PM-VC-DET-COP-EMP
Formula B
God names and epithets
Formula C
mlowi *y-ni* *bnebeseni*
health PM-VC ?

(67) **Prefixd-** (REM 0361, 1174(?), 1236, 1322, 1323, 1324)
Formula A
noun-*l* *wte-li* *pke-li* *d-irohe-se-l-o-wi*
N-DET life-DET N-DET PM-VC-DET-COP-EMP
Formula B
God names and epithets
Formula C
mlowi *d-n-se-l-o* *bnebeseni*
health PM-VC-DET-COP ?

The decrees always begin with the mention of the beneficiaries in the vocative. They can be called either by their name or by their title. The verbal compound in formula A (*yirohe-se-l-o-wi/d-irohe-se-l-o-wi*) is partly obscure, but it is not an optative or an imperative (§/5.1). It is a periphrastic form — probably with an aspectual or modal value — since it includes the determiner *-l* used as nominalizer, followed by the copula. Accordingly, an explicit personal marker is expected, more precisely a 2SG, because of the vocative. Many texts are so damaged that it is impossible to know whether the initial vocative phrase included a name or a title, but each time it is preserved, the formulae with initial *d-* occur after the titles and those with initial *y(i)-* after the proper names. This initial *d-* is very likely the expected 2nd person subject prefix, a short version of the independent pronoun *are/*ade* "you SG" or the singular of *de-b* "you PL," without the plural suffix *-b.*

The verb used in formula A is *arohe,* which, in these oracular decrees, probably means "take under someone's protection."[164] It can also signify "take control," hence "take prisoner" in military contexts (see (20)). From the two nouns groups present in formula A, only *wte-li* "life(time)" is known. A very tentative translation of formula A with prefix *d-* would be "Oh you, the XXX, you shall (?) be protected for your lifetime and your ???." The other prefix *y(i)-* remains an enigma. It is not certain that it can be also regarded as a personal marker. Since *yi-* is a late spelling for initial /i/, it may be present in the form of the sign *i* in the verbal compound *d-i-(a)rohe-se-l-o-wi.* In that case, *yiroheselowi* would be a variant of *d-irohe-se-l-o-wi* unmarked for person.

6. Conclusion

In conclusion, a general table of the personal markers that have been identified or merely hypothesised in this article is given below. The reader must keep in mind that some of those results are still tentative. However, they illustrate the significant advances that the linguistic comparison has recently made possible in the decipherment of the Meroitic texts.

	1SG	2SG	3SG	1PL	2PL	3PL
Independent Subject Pronoun	?	*are* (< **ade*)	*qo*	?	*deb*	*qoleb*
Prefixed Person Marker	*(y)e-*	*d-*	*w-(?)*	?	?	?
Possessive Pronoun	?	*arese*	*(a)qese*	?	*debse*	*(a)qebese*
Imperative Person Marker	–	*-Ø*	–	–	*-k(e)*	–
Optative Person Marker	?	*-Ø-te*	?	?	*-k(e)-te*	?

Table 6. Meroitic Person Markers

	SG	PL
Subject	*-Ø*	*-b*
Object	*-x(e)*	*-bx(e)*

Table 7. Meroitic Verbal Number Markers

7. Abbreviations

- [...]: signs missing
- [*x*]: signs reconstructed
- *:* (colon): Meroitic word divider
- 1, 2, 3: 1st, 2nd, 3rd person marker
- ACC: accusative
- ADJ: adjective
- ASP: aspect marker
- APP: applicative voice
- COP: copula
- CONT: continuous (tense)

› DAT: dative
› DEC: declarative
› DET: determiner
› DISC: discursive (direct discourse marker)
› DU: dual
› EMP: so-called "emphatic particle" after the copula in Meroitic (-*wi*)
› CAUS: causative
› *FHN*: Eide et al., eds., *Fontes Historiae Nubiorum*
› FIN: final element
› FRQ: frequentative
› FUT: future tense
› GEN: genitive (genitival postposition)
› IMP: imperative
› IMPP: imperative particle (-*se*)
› IPA: International Phonetic Alphabet
› IPFV: imperfective
› LOC: locative
› N: noun
› O: object
› OBJ: objective (= accusative/dative) marker
› OPT: optative
› PL: plural
› PLC: pluractional
› PRT1: preterite 1
› PM: personal marker
› PN: person name
› PURP: purposive
› REM: *Répertoire d'épigraphie méroïtique*
› S: subject
› SG: singular
› TAM: tense, aspect, and mood markers
› VER: veridical
› VNM: verbal number marker
› VOC: vocative suffix
› VC: verbal compound

8. Bibliography

Armbruster, Charles. H. bib/*Dongolese Nubian: A Grammar.* Cambridge: Cambridge University Press, 1960.

Bashir, Abeer. bib/"Address and Reference Terms in Midob (Darfur Nubian)." *Dotawo: A Journal of Nubian Studies* 2 (2015): pp. 133–153. DOI: www/ 10.5070/D62110004.

Bossong, Georg. bib/"Differential Object Marking in Romance and Beyond." In *New Analyses in Romance Linguistics: Selected Papers from the XVIII Linguistic Symposium on Romance Languages, Urbana-Champaign, April 7–9, 1988,* edited by D. Wanner and D. A. Kibbee. Amsterdam: John Benjamins, 1991: pp. 143–170.

Browne, Gerald M. bib/*Old Nubian Dictionary.* Leuven: Peeters, 1996.

Carrier, Claude. bib/"La stèle méroïtique d'Abratoye (Caire, J.E. n° 90008)." *Meroitic Newsletter* 28 (2001): pp. 21–53.

Comrie, Bernard. bib/*Language Universals and Linguistic Typology.* Chicago: University of Chicago Press, 1981.

Cotte, Pierre. *Langage et linéarité.* Villeneuve d'Ascq: Presses universitaires du Septentrion, 1999.

Creissels, Denis. bib/*Syntaxe générale, une introduction typologique, vol. 1: Catégories et constructions.* Paris: Lavoisier, 2006.

Creissels, Denis. bib/*Syntaxe générale, une introduction typologique, vol. 2: La phrase.* Paris: Lavoisier, 2006.

Dimmendaal, Gerrit J. bib/"Pluractionality and the Distribution of Number Marking across Categories." In *Number: Constructions and Semantics. Case Studies From Africa, Amazonia, India & Oceania,* edited by Anne Storch and Gerrit J. Dimmendaal. Amsterdam: John Benjamins, 2014: pp. 57–76.

Dimmendaal, Gerrit J. bib/"Tama." In *Coding Participant Marking: Construction Types in Twelve African Languages,* edited by Gerrit J. Dimmendaal. Amsterdam: John

Benjamins, 2009: pp. 305–333.

Eide, Tormod, Tomas Hägg, Richard Holton Pierce & László Török, eds. bib/*Fontes Historiae Nubiorum: Textual Sources for the History of the Middle Nile Between the 8th Century BC and the 6th AD, vol. I: From the Eighth to the Mid-Fifth Century BC.* Bergen: University of Bergen, Department of Classics, 1994.

Eide, Tormod, Tomas Hägg, Richard Holton Pierce & László Török, eds. bib/*Fontes Historiae Nubiorum: Textual Sources for the History of the Middle Nile Between the 8th Century BC and the 6th AD, vol. II: From the Eighth to the Mid-Fifth Century BC.* Bergen: University of Bergen, Department of Classics, 1996.

Eide, Tormod, Tomas Hägg, Richard Holton Pierce & László Török, eds. bib/*Fontes Historiae Nubiorum: Textual Sources for the History of the Middle Nile Between the 8th Century BC and the 6th AD, vol. III: From the First to the Sixth Century AD.* Bergen: University of Bergen, Department of Classics, 1998.

El-Guzuuli, El-Shafie. bib/"The Uses and Orthography of the Verb ‘Say’ in Andaandi (Nile Nubian)." *Dotawo: A Journal of Nubian Studies* 2 (2015): pp. 91–107. DOI: www/10.5070/D62110010.

El-Nazir, Mustafa. *Major Word Categories in Mararit.* MA Thesis, University of Cologne, 2016.

Elsadig, Omda. *Major Word Categories in Nara.* MA Thesis, University of Cologne, 2016.

Ferrandino, Gilda. bib/*Studio dei testi reali meroitici (III a.C.-IV d.C.). Approccio interdisciplinare per la comprensione dell'evoluzione di una cultura dell'Africa Subsahariana.* PhD Thesis, L'Orientale University, Naples, 2016.

Gardiner, Alan H. bib/*Egyptian Grammar: Being an Introduction to the Study of Hieroglyphs.* 3rd edition. Cambridge: Cambridge Universite Press, 1957.

Gerven Oei, Vincent W.J. van. *A Reference Grammar of Old Nubian.* Leuven: Peeters, forthcoming.

Gerven Oei, Vincent W.J. van & El-Shafie El-Guzuuli. bib/*The Miracle of Saint Mina.* Tirana: Uitgeverij, 2013.

Griffith, Francis Ll. *Karanòg: The Meroitic Inscriptions of Shablûl and Karanog.* Eckley B. Coxe Jr. Expedition to Nubia 6. Philadelphia: University of Pennsylvania, 1911.

Griffith, Francis Ll. "Meroitic Studies IV: The Great Stela of Prince Akinizaz (Continued)." *Journal of Egyptian Archaeology* 4, nos. 2–3 (1917): pp. 159–173.

Haspelmath, Martin. "The Serial Verb Construction: Comparative Concept and Cross-linguistic Generalizations." *Language and Linguistics* 17, no. 3 (2016): pp. 291–319. DOI: 10.1177/2397002215626895.

Hintze, Fritz. *Beiträge zur meroitischen Grammatik.* Meroitica 3. Berlin: Akademie Verlag, 1979.

Hintze, Fritz. "Some Problems of Meroitic Philology." In *Sudan im Altertum: 1. Internationale Tagung für meroitistische Forschungen in Berlin 1971,* edited by Fritz Hintze. Meroitica 1 (1973): pp. 321–336.

Hofmann, Inge. *Material für eine meroitische Grammatik.* Veröffentlichungen der Institute für Afrikanistik und Ägyptologie der Universität Wien 16. Vienna: Afro-Pub, 1981.

Jacquesson, François. *Les personnes. Morphosyntaxe et sémantique.* Paris: CNRS Éditions, 2008.

Jakobi, Angelika. *Kordofan Nubian: A Synchronic and Diachronic Study.* Unpublished manuscript, 2001.

Jakobi Angelika. "The Nubian Subject Pronouns." Paper presented to the 14th Nilo-Saharan Linguistics Colloquium, Vienna (hand-out), 2019.

Jakobi, Angelika. "Verbal Number and Transitivity in Karko (Kordofan Nubian)." *Sprachtypologie und Universalienforschung* 70 (2017): pp. 117–142. DOI: 10.1515/stuf-2017-0007.

Jakobi, Angelika, Ali Ibrahim & Gumma Ibrahim Gulfan, "Verbal Number and Grammatical Relations in Tagle." In *Proceedings of the 2nd Nuba Mountain Languages Conference, Paris 2014,* edited by Nicolas Quint and Stefano Manfredi. Forthcoming.

Khalil, Mohamed K. "The Verbal Plural Marker in Nobiin." *Dotawo: A Journal of Nubian Studies* 2 (2015): pp. 59–71.

Kitchen, Kenneth A. *Ramesside Inscriptions Translated and Annotated: Notes and Comments, II.* Oxford: Wiley-Blackwell, 1999.

Kuckertz, J. "Amanakhareqerema: A Meroitic King of the 1st Century AD." *Der antike Sudan, Mitteilungen der Sudanarchäologischen Gesellschaft zu Berlin e.V* 29 (2018): pp. 119–144.

Loprieno, Antonio. "The 'King's Novel'." In *Ancient Egyptian Literature: History and Forms,* edited by Antonio Loprieno. Leiden: Brill, 1996: pp. 277–295.

Lukas, Johannes. "Die Sprache der Sungor in Wadai (aus Nachtigal's Nachlaß)." *Mitteilungen der Ausland-Hochschule an der Universität Berlin, dritte Abteilung. Afrikanische Studien* 41 (1938): pp. 171–246.

Millet, Nicholas B. "The Kharamadoye Inscription." *Meroitic Newsletter* 13 (1973): pp. 31–49.

Millet, Nicholas B. "The Kharamandoye Inscription (MI 94) Revisited." *Meroitic Newsletter* 30 (2003): pp. 57–72.

Norton, Russell. "Number in Ama Verbs." *Occasional Papers in the Study of Sudanese Languages* 10 (2012): pp. 75–93.

Peust, Carsten. *Das Napatanische. Ein Ägyptischer Dialekt aus dem Nubien des späten ersten vorchristlichen Jahrtausends. Texte, Glossar, Grammatik.* Göttingen: Peust & Gutschmid, 1999.

Reinisch, Leo. *Die Barea-Sprache.* Vienna: Wilhelm Braumüller, 1874.

Rilly, Claude. "Deux exemples de décrets amulétiques oraculaires en méroïtique: les ostraca REM 1317/1168 et REM 1319 de Shokan." *Meroitic Newsletter* 27 (2000): pp. 99–118.

Rilly, Claude. "Graffiti for Gods and Kings: The Meroitic Secondary Inscriptions of Musawwarat Es-Sufra: A Preliminary Study." *Der Antike Sudan* 31 (forthcoming).

Rilly, Claude. “Histoire du Soudan, des origines à la chute du sultanat Fung.” In *Histoire et Civilisations du Soudan. De la préhistoire à nos jours,* edited by Olivier Cabon. Paris: Soleb, 2017: pp. 25–445.

Rilly, Claude. bib/*La langue du royaume de Méroé: Un panorama de la plus ancienne culture écrite d’Afrique subsaharienne.* Paris: Champion, 2007.

Rilly, Claude. bib/*Le méroïtique et sa famille linguistique.* Leuven: Peeters, 2010.

Rilly, Claude. bib/“‘Les chouettes ont des oreilles’. L’inscription méroïtique hiéroglyphique d’el-Hobagi REM 1222.” In *La pioche et la plume. Autour du Soudan, du Liban et de la Jordanie. Hommages archéologiques à Patrice Lenoble,* edited by Vincent Rondot, Frédéric Alpi & François Villeneuve. Paris: Presses de l’université Paris-Sorbonne, 2011: pp. 481–499.

Rilly, Claude. *Répertoire d’épigraphie méroïtique. Analyse des inscriptions publiées. Tome IV. REM 0001 à REM 0073.* Habilitation Thesis, École Pratique des Hautes Études. Paris, 2018.

Rilly, Claude. “The Meroitic Inscriptions of Temple Naga 200.” In Josefine Kuckertz, *Naga: Temple 200 - Wall Decoration.* Berlin: Ugarit Verlag, forthcoming: pp. 283–328.

Rilly, Claude. bib/“The Wadi Howar Diaspora and Its Role in the Spread of East Sudanic Languages from the Fourth to the First Millenia BCE.” In *Reconstruction et classification généalogique: tendances actuelles,* edited by Konstantin Pozdniakov. Paris: Faits de Langue, 2016: pp. 151–163.

Rilly, Claude. bib/“Upon Hintze’s Shoulders: Today’s Challenges in the Translation of Meroitic.” *Der Antike Sudan* 28 (2017): pp. 25–33.

Rilly, Claude & Vincent Francigny. bib/“Excavations of the French Archaeological Mission in Sedeinga, Campaign 2011.” *Sudan & Nubia* 16 (2012): pp. 60–71.

Rilly, Claude & Vincent Francigny. bib/“Closer to the Ancestors: Excavations of the French Mission in Sedeinga 2013–2017.” *Sudan & Nubia* 22 (2018): pp. 65–74.

Schenkel, Wolfgang. bib/Meroitisches und Barya-Verb: Versuch einer Bestimmung der Tempusbildung der Meroitischen.” *Meroitic Newsletter* 11 (1972): pp. 1–16.

Schenkel, Wolfgang. bib/"Zur Struktur des Verbalkomplexes in den Schlußformel der meroitischen Totentexte." *Meroitic Newsletter* 12 (1973): pp. 2–22.

Spalinger, Anthony. "Königsnovelle and Performance." In *Times, Signs and Pyramids: Studies in Honour of Miroslav Verner on the Occasion of His Seventieth Birthday,* edited by Vivienne G. Callender et al. Prague: Faculty of Arts, Charles University of Prague, 2011: pp. 351–374.

Stevenson, Roland. bib/*Grammar of the Nyimang Language (Nuba Mountains).* Unpublished typescript, 1938.

Stevenson, Roland, Franz Rottland & Angelika Jakobi. bib/"The Verb in Nyimang and Dinik." *Afrikanistische Arbeitspapiere* 32 (1992): pp. 5–64.

Thompson, E. David. bib/"Nera." In *The Non-Semitic Languages of Ethiopia,* edited by M. Lionel Bender. East Lansing: African Studies Center, Michigan State University, 1976: pp. 484–494.

Vanhove, Martine. bib/*Le bedja.* Leuven: Peeters, 2017.

Weiss, Doris. bib/*Phonologie et morphosyntaxe du maba.* PhD Thesis, Université Lumière-Lyon 2, 2009.

Werner, Roland. bib/*Grammatik des Nobiin (Nilnubisch). Phonologie, Tonologie und Morphologie.* Hamburg: Helmut Buske, 1987.

Werner, Roland. bib/*Tìdn-áal: A Study of Midob (Darfur-Nubian).* Berlin: Dietrich Reimer, 1993.

Zibelius, Karola. bib/*Der Löwentempel von Naq'a in der Butana (Sudan). IV: Die Inschriften.* Wiesbaden: Ludwig Reichert, 1983.

Endnotes

1. I am grateful to Abbie Hantgan-Sonko for checking the English text. ↩

2. Griffith, *Karanòg.* ↩

3. Rilly, *Le méroïtique et sa famille linguistique.* ↩

4. Rilly, "The Wadi Howar Diaspora and Its Role in the Spread of East Sudanic Languages from the Fourth to the First Millenia BCE." ↩

5. For the definitions of the key terms in the Theory of Enunciative Operations, see www/https://feglossary.sil.org/page/definitions-key-terms-theory-enunciative-operations?language=en. ↩

6. Hintze, *Beiträge zur meroitischen Grammatik,* pp. 63–87. Nevertheless, he regards the 2nd person plural as an address to the visitors of the tomb. The interpretation of Inge Hofmann in her *Material für eine meroitische Grammatik,* p. 194, according to which the prayer is addressed to the gods of the afterlife, is much more convincing. See Rilly, *La langue du royaume de Méroé,* pp. 163–166, for a detailed review of the numerous hypotheses that were advanced since the decipherment of the scripts. ↩

7. This distinctive feature of the Meroitic writing-system was first evidenced in Hintze 1973. For an extensive study of the rules of Meroitic script, see Rilly, *La langue du royaume de Méroé,* pp. 277–314. ↩

8. Rilly, *La langue du royaume de Méroé,* pp. 359–407. ↩

9. See Rilly & Francigny, "Excavations of the French Archaeological Mission in Sedeinga, Campaign 2011," p. 67, no. 10. ↩

10. For further details, see Rilly, "Upon Hintze's Shoulders," pp. 28–29. ↩

11. Formerly known as "Hestermann's law," see Rilly, *La langue du royaume de Méroé,* pp. 415–420. ↩

12. In Arabic *ghâ'ib,* cf. Cotte, *Langage et linéarité,* p. 130. ↩

13. In addition to Latin, this feature can be found in Korean, Hindi, Panjabi, Marathi, Mongolian, etc. See Jacquesson, *Les personnes,* pp. 103–105. ↩

14. These similarities are due to common typological features and do not originate from a common genealogical origin. Turkish is, like Meroitic or Nubian, an agglutinative language, with no grammatical gender and an SOV word-order, cf. Rilly, *La langue du royaume de Méroé,* pp. 497–502. ↩

15. Creissels, *Syntaxe générale 1,* 2006: p. 91. ↩

16. In (2), Malutuna is traditionally transcribed “Maloton.” This viceroy of Lower Nubia (*peseto*), living at the end of the 3rd century CE, is famous for his beautiful *ba* statue kept in the Nubian Museum in Aswan. ↩

17. Griffith, *Karanòg*, p. 120. ↩

18. The function of this particle is not yet identified (Rilly, *Le méroïtique et sa famille linguistique*, pp. 386–387). ↩

19. Hintze, *Beiträge zur meroitischen Grammatik*, pp. 53–56. ↩

20. The frequent variants *qe/qo* here and in other words (for example *Aqedise/Aqodise* “Moon-god” in the texts from the Lion temple in Naga) is best explained by the labialized articulation /kʷ/ of the sign *q*: see Rilly, *La langue du royaume de Méroé*, pp. 374–379. ↩

21. See Rilly, *La langue du royaume de Méroé*, p. 547. The literal translation “this one, this is...,” which is used above, is somewhat unnatural in English. In spoken French, the topicalization of the subject is overwhelmingly frequent and sentences such as *celui-ci, c’est...* or even *ça, c’est...*, literally “this, this is” are very common. ↩ ↩

22. Rilly, *La langue du royaume de Méroé*, p. 98. ↩

23. Ancient Greek οὗτος ὁ ἀνήρ “this man,” literally “this the man.” ↩

24. Rilly, *La langue du royaume de Méroé*, p. 511. ↩

25. From the textual material so far available, the adjunction of the plural determiner *-leb* seems to be the only way to build the plural of nouns. For an alternative plural *qebe-*, see §/3.2. ↩

26. In (8), the titles *ssmrte* and *wtotrse* cannot yet be translated. The former is probably an early form of the title *ssimete* frequently attested in later texts and which is connected to the cult of the gods in several instances. The second one is a hapax legomenon. It is presumably a compound word (*wto-tr-se*) including possibly an indirect genitive with postposition *-se*. ↩

27. The final element *-bx* in (8), which could be considered as the object of the verb, is discussed in §/3.3. ↩

28. Hofmann, *Material für eine meroitische Grammatik,* pp. 334–338. ↩

29. In (9), the kinship term *yetmde* is applied to younger members of the same maternal line (Rilly, *La langue du royaume de Méroé,* pp. 526–527). It mostly designates "nephews" and "nieces," who are referring to a prestigious uncle in the descriptive part of their epitaph, but in rare cases such as this one, it can be applied to a younger brother. ↩

30. Rilly, *La langue du royaume de Méroé,* pp. 550–551. ↩

31. The initial *a* in *aqese* and in the variants of the 3rd plural possessive, *aqebese* and *aqobese* are unexplained. It is possible that this *a* is etymological and that, in this case, the forms *qese* and *qebese* result from apheresis (a widespread development in Meroitic, see Rilly, *La langue du royaume de Méroé,* pp. 290–291). In some instances, however, a non-etymological *a* is added at the beginning of a word for unknown reasons, for example *Ams-i* "oh (sun-god) Masha" in REM 0091C instead of expected *Ms-i.* ↩

32. Rilly, *Le méroïtique et sa famille linguistique,* p. 389. ↩

33. A third formula for "a good meal" is oftentimes added. A dozen of additional formulae are known, but they are less frequent. See Rilly, *La langue du royaume de Méroé,* pp. 163–183; Rilly, *Le méroïtique et sa famille linguistique,* pp. 68–74. ↩

34. See Comrie, *Language Universals and Linguistic Typology,* pp. 43–19 for an updated interpretation of this old classification of languages. ↩

35. Griffith, *Karanòg,* p. 14 and n. 1, pp. 25–26, 45. ↩

36. Hintze, *Beiträge zur meroitischen Grammatik,* pp. 65–66, 73–74. ↩

37. The form *-x* (= /xa/ or /ŋa/) and *-bx* (= /baxa/ or /baŋa/) are early. They later became *-xe* (= /x/ or /ŋ/) and *-bxe* (= /bax/ or /baŋ/). It is noted that the sign transliterated *e* can have a zero-vowel value (see §3 for the principles of the Meroitic script). ↩

38. The suffixes *-xe* and *-bxe* end with the consonant /x/, which assimilated to the subsequent suffix *-ke.* However, similar assimilation is rare with the plural suffix *-bxe.* In early texts, the suffixes were *-x* and *-bx,* with default vowel /a/. This final vowel explains why there was no assimilation with the following suffix. ↩

39. Rilly, *La langue du royaume de Méroé,* pp. 553–554. ↩

40. Jakobi, "Verbal Number and Transitivity in Karko," pp. 121–122 and n. 3. Nile Nubian (Nobiin and Mattokki/Andaandi) uses applicative suffixes that are nothing but a grammaticalized forms of the two verbs "to give," *deen* and *tir.* In other languages, they may result from the incorporation of adpositions in the verbal compound, as is the case in Amharic (Creissels, *Syntaxe générale 2,* p. 39). ↩

41. Adapted from Creissels, *Syntaxe générale 2,* pp. 74, 76. In (19c), the added gloss "3:1.s" means "subject 3rd person, Bantu nominal class 1." ↩

42. Carrier, "La stèle méroïtique d'Abratoye." ↩

43. Jacquesson, *Les personnes,* pp. 297–298. ↩

44. An in-depth analysis of this construction in Ama can be found in Norton, "Number in Ama Verbs." This author prefers to speak of "distributive" rather than "plural" (ibid., p. 78). His stance is supported by a series of five examples, which can be nonetheless analysed as a particular case of plural construction. In her study of verbal plural in Nubian, Jakobi states that "verbal number — realized by distinct singular and plural verb stems — can have both aspectual and morphosyntactic functions. On the one hand these stems may encode habitual, progressive, iterative, repetitive, distributive, or even single events, on the other hand these stems may encode the participants affected by these events" (Jakobi, "Verbal Number and Transitivity in Karko," p. 117). ↩

45. Werner, *Tìdn-áal,* p. 49. ↩

46. The suffix *-(i)j* is mentioned in Van Gerven Oei, *A Reference Grammar of Old Nubian,* §13.1 who calls it "pluractional" and in Werner 1989: 173–175, who speaks of "plural object extension" but not of plural subject marking. Recent and more explicit studies are Khalil, "The Verbal Plural Marker in Nobiin"; Jakobi, "Verbal Number and Transitivity in Karko"; and Jakobi et al., forthcoming. ↩

47. Examples from Khalil, "The Verbal Plural Marker in Nobiin," p. 65, ex. 9; p. 64, exx. 3, 4. ↩

48. Rilly, *Le méroïtique et sa famille linguistique,* p. 350. ↩

49. Ibid., p. 272. ↩

50. Khalil, "The Verbal Plural Marker in Nobiin," pp. 64–65. ↩

51. Van Gerven Oei, *A Reference Grammar of Old Nubian,* §13.1.3. ↩

52. In Kordofan Nubian language Karko, unlike in Nobiin, the verbal number marker refers to the direct object even in ditransitive construction (Jakobi, "Verbal Number and Transitivity in Karko," pp. 164–165). The example she gives ("Dry the pots for the woman"), compared with the Nobiin example (28) above, shows that at least in this language, the participant hierarchy is not connected with the degree of animacy of the two objects, direct and indirect. See, however, n. 59 below. ↩

53. Example from Norton, "Number in Ama Verbs," p. 86, ex. 35. ↩

54. Examples from Khalil, "The Verbal Plural Marker in Nobiin," p. 64, exx. 6, 7. ↩

55. cf. Rilly, *Le méroïtique et sa famille linguistique,* p. 90. ↩

56. Rilly, "The Meroitic Inscriptions of Temple Naga 200." ↩

57. Aritene and Makedeke/Makedoke, "the Great God," are two of Amun-Re's numerous hypostases. The name Aritene is obviously a nominal compound and is consequently followed by the article *-l,* though scribes frequently omitted it. This determiner is mandatory here because the name is a direct genitive (Rilly, *La langue du royaume de Méroé,* pp. 520–523). The meaning of Aritene is uncertain. It might be a Meroitic transcription *Ar-i-tene* of Egyptian *Harakhty* (Ḥr-ꜣḫt.y) "Horus of the Horizon," where the "horizon" is reinterpreted as the "west": cf. Meroitic *tene-ke-l* "west," Nobiin *tin-o,* Ama *ṭ̪êŋ* and words for "evening" or "night" in NES languages (Rilly, *Le méroïtique et sa famille linguistique,* p. 141). ↩

58. Example (8) above, which is two centuries earlier than (29)–(31), is apparently a counterexample. Admittedly, the contextual elements are much clearer and the meaning of the verb is better established in examples (29)-(31) than in (8). However, it may be that the marking of the direct/indirect object is governed by the degree of animacy/definiteness, as it is in Old Nubian (Van Gerven Oei, *A Reference Grammar of Old Nubian,* §13.1.3). According to Dimmendaal, "Tama," p. 324, this hierarchy is the following:

   1. Animacy: Human > animate > inanimate:

   2. Definiteness: Personal pronoun > proper name > definite NP > indefinite specific NP > non-specific NP.

   In (8), the beneficiary is a god designated by his proper name, Amun of Napata (*Amnp*). The logical direct object is the two men, also designated by their names. But they are referred to by a personal pronoun (*qoleb*) which is the grammatical object of the verb. The personal pronoun is higher in the definiteness hierarchy than the proper name, and this might explain why it is encoded in the verbal compound by the plural suffix. ↩

59. Data from Jakobi, "Verbal Number and Transitivity in Karko," p. 126, t. 6. Only three of these verbs have specific markers both in singular and plural ("hang up," "kindle," "wake up"). In Karko, most of the verbs operate according to a pattern "unmarked singular/marked plural." As in many languages where verbal number is present, the plural form can be a different verb (ibid., pp. 128–129). Several cases of replacive verbal forms for plural object marking are attested in Ama, see Norton, "Number in Ama Verbs," p. 77. ↩

60. Example from Weiss, *Phonologie et morphosyntaxe du maba,* p. 270, ex. 699. ↩

61. Examples from Werner, *Grammatik des Nobiin,* p. 173; Jakobi, "Verbal Number and Transitivity in Karko," p. 130, ex. 16. The original gloss PLR "verbal plural stem" has been replaced by VNM "verbal number marker" in accordance with the conventions of the present article. ↩

62. See also Khalil, "The Verbal Plural Marker in Nobiin," p. 37. ↩

63. Jakobi, "Verbal Number and Transitivity in Karko," pp. 130–132. ↩

64. Ibid., p. 128. ↩

65. See Jakobi, Ibrahim & Gulfan, "Verbal Number and Grammatical Relations in Tagle," §2, with further references, particularly Armbruster, *Dongolese Nubian: A Grammar,* §§2880f, 3031f. ↩

66. Jakobi, "Verbal Number and Transitivity in Karko," p. 122 with further references. ↩

67. The morphology of event plurality marking in Tama seems complex (Dimmendaal, "Tama," p. 316) and needs a specific study. In the closely related language Mararit, it seems reduplication, which is cross-linguistically a very common way to form verbal plurals, is used (El-Nazir, *Major Word Categories in Mararit,* p. 55). In Ama, the same suffix *-ī̯ḍì* (see exx. 21–22) is used for plurality of participants and plurality of events. ↩

68. Thompson, "Nera," p. 491. ↩

69. Several cases of "fossilized" suffix *-k* are attested in Meroitic, in which basic verb has disappeared whereas the form with *-k* has been preserved, but has lost its pluractional meaning. Examples are the verbs *erik-* "beget" and probably *tk-* "love" or "revere" in *Amni-tke-l* "beloved of Amun" (Rilly, *Le méroïtique et sa famille linguistique,* pp. 90–91). The former verb is still attested in Ajang (Kordofan Nubian) in both its forms: *ír-í* "give birth," pluractional *ír-k-í* "give birth to one child after the other" (Jakobi, *Kordofan Nubian,* p. 114). The second might be an assimilated form /takk/- of **tar-k-*, cf. Old Nubian ⲧⲁⲣⲟⲩ-, ⲧⲁⲣⲓ- "praise, bless," Tama *tár-* "love." ↩

70. In (36), "their" refers to the women and the men, who are quoted in the previous sentence. One may wonder whether the term *apote,* which is borrowed from Egyptian *wpwtj,* "envoy, ambassador," does not mean something like "tribal chief" in this particular context. ↩

71. Dimmendaal, "Tama," p. 130. ↩

72. Rilly, *Le méroïtique et sa famille linguistique,* p. 373. ↩

73. Ibid., pp. 303–304. ↩

74. Ibid., p. 329, n. 4. ↩

75. Ibid., p. 456, no. 72. ↩

76. Ibid., p. 523, no. 190 ↩

77. For this ruler, see *FHN* II, pp. 293–296. The name is known in Egyptian transcription only (first line of (38)), since the Meroitic script was invented only three centuries later. ↩

78. In the inscriptions of the temple of Apedemak in Naga, the verbal form *lbxte* "give them" is attested in REM 0003, where the beneficiary is the sole queen and in REM 0004, where it is the king alone. In her publication of these texts, Karola Zibelius (*Die Löwentempel van Naq'a in der Butana (Sudan). IV*, pp. 45–52) explains this plural form as an iterative. However, at this time (mid-1st c. CE), the verbal plural suffix *-bx* was already specialized to exclusively mark the object plurality. It never occurs in benedictions involving a single person, where only *lxte* is used at least since the 2nd c. BCE (REM 1044A, REM 1151). The plural marker in REM 0003 and 0004 refers to the three members of the royal family, who constitute an indissoluble trinity, even when the queen and the king are figured alone (cf. ex. 31 above). ↩

79. Example from Van Gerven Oei, *A Reference Grammar of Old Nubian*, §8.3.2.2. ↩

80. Van Gerven Oei & El-Guzuuli, *The Miracle of Saint Mina*, p. 99. He later refers to the same suffix as "pluractional" (Van Gerven Oei, *A Reference Grammar of Old Nubian*, §13.1.) ↩

81. See Rilly, *La langue du royaume de Méroé*, pp. 171–172 (formula C') and pp. 176–177 (formula J). ↩

82. The two suffixes are therefore used at the same period, but a dialectal difference is possible, since the Meroitic scribes had a marked taste for variety and commonly used dialectal variants in the same text (cf. Rilly, *La langue du royaume de Méroé*, p. 42). ↩

83. Rilly, *Le méroïtique et sa famille linguistique*, pp. 390–395. ↩

84. Dimmendaal, "Tama," pp. 323–328 after Bossong, "Differential Object Marking in Romance and Beyond." ↩

85. Rilly, *Le méroïtique et sa famille linguistique*, p. 394. ↩

86. See for instance the speech of Amun-Re in Anlamani's stela from Kawa (*FHN* I: pp. 217–218). ↩

87. See Loprieno, "The King's Novel" and Spalinger, "Königsnovelle and Performance." For an annotated edition of the poem of Kadesh, see Kitchen, *Ramesside Inscriptions Translated and Annotated: Notes and Comments, II.* ↩

88. Taharqo's stelae, Kawa IV: *ḥm=f* with a long speech of the king in the 1st person (*FHN* I: pp. 135–145), Kawa V: *ḥm=f,* with a long narrative told by the king in the second half of the text (*FHN* I: pp. 145–158), Kawa VI: *ḥm=f,* with a long speech told by the king in the second half of the text (*FHN* I: pp. 164–176), Kawa VII: *ḥm=f,* with a speech told by the king in the second half of the text (*FHN* I: pp. 176–181); Anlamani's stela, Kawa VIII: *ḥm=f,* but the raid against the Blemmyes uses the 3rd person plural ("soldiers") because the king stayed in Napata (*FHN* I: pp. 216–228); Aspelta's stelae from Jebel Barkal, Election stela: *ḥm=f* (*FHN* I: pp. 232–252), Banishment stela: *ḥm=f* (*FHN* I: pp. 252–258), Adoption stela (king hardly mentioned): *ḥm=f* (*FHN* I: pp. 259–268), stela for the mortuary cult of Prince Khaliut: *ḥm=f* (*FHN* I: pp. 268–279). ↩

89. Cf. *FHN* II: p. 487 (l. 46), p. 488 (l. 50), p. 489 (l. 52), p. 490 (l. 54, 56), p. 491 (l. 60), p. 492 (l. 64). ↩

90. *FHN* II: p. 475 (l. 4). This infringement of the Egyptian tradition puzzled the editor of the text, who appropriately translated "he says," but erroneously corrected in n. 151: "For 'I say'." ↩

91. Reading and translation by the author. See *FHN* II: p. 490 and Peust, *Das Napatanische,* pp. 42, 60, 64. ↩

92. See *FHN* II: pp. 522–532. The stelae, which are in very bad state of preservation, are dated to the late 4th or the early 3rd c. ↩

93. *FHN* III: pp. 1147–1153; Rilly, "Histoire du Soudan, des origines à la chute du sultanat Fung," pp. 385–388. ↩

94. Cf. Rilly, *Le méroïtique et sa famille linguistique,* pp. 74–80. ↩

95. The word appears in REM 1003/14 and in graffito MS 57 from Musawwarat. Its translation is inferred from the context of these two occurrences and from the comparison with Andaandi *daa* "residence" and Nara *dà* "village." See Rilly, "Graffiti for Gods and Kings." ↩

96. Griffith, "Meroitic Studies IV," p. 167. Note that Griffith mistook the noun phrase *ar-se-li* "all the boys" for the verbal form he translated "enslaving," which verb was actually *tkk.* ↩

97. Hofmann, *Material für eine meroitische Grammatik,* pp. 294–297. For a critical review of her translation of *ked,* see Rilly, *Le méroïtique et sa famille linguistique,* pp. 76–78. ↩

98. Millet, "The Kharamadoye Inscription," p. 38. ↩

99. Millet, "The Kharamandoye Inscription (MI 94) Revisited," p. 67. ↩

100. Wolfgang Schenkel, in his analysis of the verbal affixes in the Meroitic royal text ("Meroitisches und Barya-Verb"), assumes that *-td* is a durative suffix, which he compares with the durative ending *-ter/-der* in Nara. Note that this suffix is attested only in Reinisch's description of the language, which used second-hand material and is not entirely reliable (Reinisch, *Die Barea-Sprache,* p. 57). Schenkel suggests that the suffix *-to* includes an aorist marker *-t* followed by a 1st person singular *-o,* with similar comparisons with Nara. For a critical review of his hypotheses, see Hofmann, *Material für eine meroitische Grammatik,* pp. 214–216. Note that the suffix *-te* in REM 0094 (also frequent with other verbs in REM 1003) is not identical with the 2nd person plural suffix of the optative, which is also written *-te* (see §5.2 below). ↩

101. This morpheme may be the same as the particle *-wi* that is added *ad libitum* to the singular copula *-o* (cf. Rilly, *Le méroïtique et sa famille linguistique,* p. 186). The consonant *w-* could be either an epenthetic glide inserted between *o* (pronounced /u/) and *i,* or a dummy sign used to write the hiatus /u/ + /i/ according to the rules of the alphasyllabic Meroitic writing system (Rilly, *La langue du royaume de Méroé,* pp. 294–295). ↩

102. This is particularly true for the funerary texts. See Rilly, *La langue du royaume de Méroé,* pp. 202, 565. ↩

103. Millet, "The Kharamandoye Inscription (MI 94) Revisited," pp. 62, 70, considered this sequence a noun group *yeto-l-xe* "on (?) the river." The variant *yeto* for *ato* "water" is, however, attested only in REM 0307. ↩

104. See Rilly, *La langue du royaume de Méroé,* pp. 559–567. It accounts for 2% of the verbal forms used in the benedictions funerary texts according to Schenkel, "Zur Struktur des Verbalkomplexes in den Schlußformel der meroitischen Totentexte," p. 8. ↩

105. Rilly, *La langue du royaume de Méroé,* pp. 172–174. Only twenty occurrences are known so far. ↩

106. The frequency of *yi-* is 6,2% according to Schenkel, "Zur Struktur des Verbalkomplexes in den Schlußformel der meroitischen Totentexte," p. 8. For Nobiin *ií-*, more commonly used with a causative suffix in the compound *ií-gìr,* see Werner, *Grammatik des Nobiin,* p. 356. Note that "say" is frequently used as a light verb (but not as a causative auxiliary) in the languages of Sudan, regardless of the linguistic family. For Andaandi, see El-Guzuuli, "The Uses and Orthography of the Verb 'Say' in Andaandi"; for Ama, see Stevenson *Grammar of the Nyimang Language,* p. 147 (my copy of the manuscript, an annotated version transmitted by Roger Blench, has the light verb *she* on pp. 146–146a and 147. Page 146a is handwritten and the page numbers on p. 147 and 148 have been corrected manually) and Rilly, *Le méroïtique et sa famille linguistique,* p. 210; for Beja, see Vanhove, *Le bedja,* pp. 146–147. ↩

107. See Haspelmath, "The Serial Verb Construction," esp. pp. 409–411 (with possible exception in ex. 31, where two different subjects are found). ↩

108. Rilly, *Le méroïtique et sa famille linguistique,* p. 496, no. 141. ↩

109. Cf. Rilly, *Le méroïtique et sa famille linguistique,* pp. 467–468, no. 92. The Proto-Taman is curiously **wa,* which can result from **o* through vowel-breaking. The Proto-NES genitive of the 1SG pronoun seems to have been **on* and might have triggered an analogical shift for the nominative in Proto-Taman. ↩

110. Reconstructed **ay* in Proto-Nubian according to Jakobi, "The Nubian Subject Pronouns," tab. 2. The glide *y*, IPA [j], has no phonological status in Proto-Nubian according to my own research (Rilly, *Le méroïtique et sa famille linguistique*, p. 269). For this reason, I am inclined to reconstruct this word as vowels in hiatus. ↩

111. In the Nara group, the ancient accusative form (with regular **-ga* ending) of this pronoun has replaced the nominative when the distinction between both cases was lost: see Rilly, *Le méroïtique et sa famille linguistique*, p. 391 and n. 471. There is no way to know if the original nominative form was also **a-i*. ↩

112. In Meroitic, this particle is spelled *-i* in names of gods, for example *Amn-i* "Amun" or *Atr-i* "Hathor" and *-ye* in the names of people, for example *Abrato-ye*, name of a famous viceroy of Nubia. In Old Nubian, for example, Jesus is written ïⲏⲥⲟⲩⲥ-ⲓ. This particle may be connected to the Meroitic vocative ending *-i*: *Wos-i* "oh Isis!" ↩

113. Fusion of two consecutive vowels into one. ↩

114. For instance Karko *ê* "I" (Jakobi, *Kordofan Nubian*, p. 42) from Proto-Nubian **a-i*. ↩

115. Example (45) is based on Werner, *Grammatik des Nobiin*, p. 291. ↩

116. These prefixes (where *V* stands for a variable vowel) are the same for the singular and plural persons. ↩

117. The data are cited from the unpublished Tama grammar of Pierre Palayer. ↩

118. In (49), the reading of the first signs was made possible thanks to excellent photos and interpretation by Gilda Ferrandino in her doctoral thesis, *Studio dei testi reali meroitici,* p. 65 and pl. 29.1. For the archaic sign conventionally transcribed *H,* see Rilly, *La langue du royaume de Méroé,* p. 353. In all likelihood, the form *kbxte* comes from *kb-bx-te* after haplography, as the object seems to be a plural and, accordingly, should be marked in the verb by the suffix *bx.*

   In (50), the word *tdxsene* includes the noun phrase *t-dx-* meaning "child (of a mother)" but the following sequence *-se-ne* is obscure. It ultimately might be a proper name, Tadakhesene, with an ending *-ne* that is common in the Meroitic personal names.

   Examples (51) and (52) differ only in the spellings of *(y)emoqe* "belongings (?)"and *(e)qebese* "their'.

   In (53), a direct genitive *Aqtoye mtekdi 2* "the two daughters of Aqatoye" should be expected for unalienable possession (cf. Rilly, *La langue du royaume de Méroé,* pp. 525–527). However, the inscription REM 0094, engraved for the Blemmyan kinglet Khamaradoye after the fall of Meroe, is very late (c. 420 CE) and includes some strange features that could have resulted from language contact with Old Nubian and Blemmyan (Old Beja dialect), in which no distinction was made between alienable and unalienable possession (for Beja, see Vanhove, *Le bedja,* p. 40). ↩

119. Rilly, *La langue du royaume de Méroé,* pp. 547–548. ↩

120. Griffith, *Karanòg,* pp. 42–53; Hofmann, *Material für eine meroitische Grammatik,* pp. 198–200; synthesis in Rilly, *La langue du royaume de Méroé,* pp. 163–183 and Rilly, *Le méroïtique et sa famille linguistique,* pp. 68–74. A further type of benediction was used in a stela recently found in Sedeinga, Exc. No II S 055, cf. Rilly & Francigny, "Excavations of the French Archaeological Mission in Sedeinga, Campaign 2011," pp. 70–71. It remains unattested elsewhere. ↩

121. For benedictions A and B, see also (11)–(14) above. ↩

122. In the Nubian group, for Nobiin: Werner, *Grammatik des Nobiin,* p. 145; for Andaandi: Armbruster, *Dongolese Nubian,* pp. 194–195; for Midob: Werner, *Tìdn-áal,* pp. 58–59. In the Nara group, for Higir: Thompson, "Nera," p. 467; for Mogoreeb: Elsadig, *Major Word Categories in Nara,* p. 66. For Tama: Palayer's unpublished grammar, §4.3; for Sungor: Lukas, "Die Sprache der Sungor in Wadai," pp. 192, 198–199; for Mararit: El-Nazir, *Major Word Categories in Mararit,* pp. 57–58. For Ama: Stevenson, *Grammar of the Nyimang Language,* pp. 106, 110 and Stevenson, Rottland & Jakobi, "The Verb in Nyimang and Dinik," p. 30; for Afitti: ibid., p. 33. In all these languages, the singular imperative is generally the simple stem of the verb. However, a suffix *-i* is found for some verbs in Nubian, Taman, and Nyima. Suppletive forms for basic verbs are attested in Nara, Taman, and Nyima. ↩

123. The particle *-se* may have an emphatic role, such as *donc* in French *dis-moi donc!* or the use of the auxiliary *do* in the English counterpart *do tell me!.* The resulting verbal compound is *pVsV-k(e)-te-se,* often reduced to *pVsV-k(e)-se* with regressive assimilation (see (40) above); cf. Hintze, *Beiträge zur meroitischen Grammatik,* p. 75 and Rilly, *La langue du royaume de Méroé,* p. 563. ↩

124. Van Gerven Oei, *A Reference Grammar of Old Nubian,* §4.2. ↩

125. The verbal plural marker *-bxe* here appears as *-b,* without the objective case marker. See (43) and its comment above. ↩

126. One clear example is REM 0380, an offering table from Shablul, where benediction B is written with final verb compound *pisixrke.* The form is complete, since it ends with a word divider, it is located in the middle of a line and followed by benediction C. Note that, in this inscription, benedictions A and C have regular optative forms in *-kete.* There may be more instances of 2PL imperative in the benedictions. In particular, it cannot be ruled out that all or part of the verbal compounds ending with *-ke-se* are not assimilated optative forms deriving from *-ke-te-se,* but imperative with plural suffix *-ke* followed by the emphatic particle *-se* (see n. 124). ↩

127. Rilly, *La langue du royaume de Méroé,* p. 297. Another solution for the lack of plural marker *-ke* is again the principle of economy, which seems to play an important role in Meroitic, as in Tama (see n. 72). ↩

128. Ibid., p. 93. ↩

129. In the Meroitic private funerary iconography, the male counterpart to Isis is Anubis, or more rarely Thoth. The local names of these Egyptian gods are unknown. ↩

130. Cf. Griffith, *Karanòg,* p. 48. The alternation *-te/-to* is apparently a phonetic, not morphological, feature. It also occurs in person names. Queen Amanishakheto's name, for instance, is generally written *(A)mnisxeto,* but is spelled *(A)mnisxete* in REM 0706, 1055, 1293, and 1346. ↩

131. Recall that the dental stop ḓ is a development of Proto-NES **g* which is specific to the Nyima group. ↩

132. Thompson, "Nera," p. 487. ↩

133. Elsadig, *Major Word Categories in Nara,* p. 66. ↩

134. El-Nazir, *Major Word Categories in Mararit,* pp. 57–58 (version updated for tones, 2019). ↩

135. Werner, *Tìdn-áal,* pp. 145–146. ↩

136. Armbruster, *Dongolese Nubian,* pp. 194–195. ↩

137. Van Gerven Oei, *A Reference Grammar of Old Nubian,* §10.1.5, Werner, *Grammatik de Nobiin,* pp. 145–146. ↩

138. Van Gerven Oei, *A Reference Grammar of Old Nubian,* §10.1.6. ↩

139. Rilly, *Le méroïtique et sa famille linguistique,* p. 230. ↩

140. Gardiner, *Egyptian Grammar,* pp. 42, 121. ↩

141. The complex distribution of roles in the last sentence, which includes the three grammatical persons together, is rare in this genre of Egyptian texts. Some mistakes in the use of the Egyptian personal suffixes are attested in late Napatan stelae written in poor Egyptian by local scribes. By contrast, the texts engraved in the temple of Mut were prepared by Egyptian scribes working for Taharqo during the heyday of the Kushite power. Consequently, the use of personal suffixes in (32) must be considered correct and deliberate. ↩

142. The Meroitic postposition *-se* can be appended to the name of the giver in inscriptions found on funerary offerings. In this case, *-se* is best translated as "from"; see Rilly, "Les chouettes ont des oreilles," pp. 489–491. ↩

143. Rilly, *Le méroïtique et sa famille linguistique,* p. 519, no. 184 and p. 528, no. 200. ↩

144. For conservative aspects in Birgid, see Rilly, *Le méroïtique et sa famille linguistique,* pp. 367–368. ↩

145. Ibid., p. 383. ↩

146. Ibid., p. 254. ↩

147. The Old Nubian and Nobiin forms are reflexes of Proto-NES **mbar-e* "spear." The Birgid word is borrowed from Old Dongolawi **sibit,* ultimately from Egyptian *šf.t* "knife," probably through a still unattested Meroitic word. ↩

148. "White" is in Old Nubian ⲥⲟⲩⲗⲟⲩ, Nobiin *nùlù.* The adjective ⲁ̄ⲇⲱ is an Old Dongolawi word used in an Old Nubian letter. The modern form which is given here, *aro,* is Mattokki–Andaandi. ↩

149. The reflex /l/ in Birgid is unexpected. It could actually be a flap [ɾ], which is acoustically very close to [l] but is cross-linguistically a frequent allophone of /d/ in intervocalic position, particularly in American English. However, it was transcribed as *l* by both McMichael and Thelwall (cf. Rilly, *Le méroïtique et sa famille linguistique,* p. 425). Accordingly, the Midob form, which has an undisputable *d,* has been added here. ↩

150. Rilly, *Le méroïtique et sa famille linguistique,* pp. 250–251 and n. 7. ↩

151. Jakobi, "Verbal Number and Transitivity in Karko," t. 5. ↩

152. Ibid., pp. 367–368. ↩

153. Rilly, *Le méroïtique et sa famille linguistique,* p. 18. ↩

154. Rilly, *La langue du royaume de Méroé,* pp. 29–30, 289–291. ↩

155. Rilly, *Le méroïtique et sa famille linguistique,* p. 389. The eastern branch comprises Meroitic, Nubian, and Nara (§/1). ↩

156. This name occurs in the inscribed lintel II T 302 d2, found in 2017: see Rilly & Francigny, "Closer to the Ancestors," p. 70. ↩

157. Rilly, "Graffiti for Gods and Kings."" ↩

158. Nobiin *íccí,* Andaandi *ecce-l.* The verb *pl(e)-* "give, offer" is attested in the funerary bendiction D (Rilly, *La langue du royaume de Méroé,* p. 173). ↩

159. Bashir, "Address and Reference Terms in Midob," pp. 136–137. ↩

160. Queen Amanirenas reigned around the end of the first c. BCE and the beginning of the first c. CE, Amanakhareqerema at the end of the first c. CE. For their reigns, see Rilly, "Histoire du Soudan, des origines à la chute du sultanat Fung," pp. 242–252, 286–291 and Kuckertz, "Amanakhareqerema." ↩

161. Amanakh, written *Amnx(e)* or *Mnx(e),* was obviously a hypostasis of Amun, but his identity remains a mystery. The name is not dubious; it appears in the names of king Amanakhabale and of many princes and queens. However, it is never independently attested and no Egyptian parallel is known so far. ↩

162. The absence of copula (final *-o* expected) or of any verb "to be" (stem *ne-*) is certainly puzzling, but as this is the first time a sentence with a probable second person subject pronoun is attested, one cannot expect to find the same syntactic features as in sentences where the subject is a 3rd person and not a pronoun. ↩

163. Rilly, "Deux exemples de décrets amulétiques oraculaires en méroïtique" and *La langue du royaume de Méroé,* pp. 216–226. ↩

164. The Old Nubian verb ⲁ̄ⲣⲟⲩ-ⲁⲅⲁⲣ "protect" is probably related to the Meroitic verb *arohe,* rather than borrowed, if the link suggested by Browne with ⲁ̄ⲣⲟⲩ "rain" is correct (Browne, *Old Nubian Dictionary,* p. 19). ↩

article/ Ama Verbs in Comparative Perspective

author/ Russell Norton

abstract/ *Ama verbs are comparable with Nubian and other related languages in their clause-final syntax, CVC root shape, and some affixes. However, there is also considerable innovation in adjoined relative clauses, a shift from number to aspect marking traced by T/K morphology, and other changes in the order and meaning of affixes. These developments show a unique trend of concretization of core clause constituents, and internal growth in the complexity of verbs in isolation from other languages. On the other hand, Ama's stable distributive pluractional represents a wider Eastern Sudanic category. The late loss of pronominal subject marking supports a hypothesis that the Ama language was used for inter-group communication with Kordofan Nubians.*

keywords/ Ama, Northern East Sudanic, comparative linguistics, Nilo-Saharan, Nyimang, Afitti

1. Preliminaries

Ama is a Northern East Sudanic language spoken in villages to the west and north-west of Dilling, near to where Kordofan Nuḇian languages are spoken in the north-western Nuba Mountains. "Ama" (*ámá* "people") is the self-designated name of the language community identified by the ISO639-3 code [nyi] and replaces the name "Nyimang" in older sources,[1] as "Ama" is the name used in local literature in the language created over the last three decades. Nyimang is an altered form of "Nyima," one of the mountains in the Ama homeland, which is now used as the name of the branch of Eastern Sudanic consisting of Ama [nyi] and Afitti [aft]. I will assume that Nyima is one of a group of four extant northern branches of the Eastern Sudanic family, the others being Nubian, the Nara language, and Taman.[2]

Ama examples unless otherwise stated are from the author's fieldwork verified with leading Ama writers who oversee literacy in the language. For vowels, I distinguish five –ATR brassy vowels *ɪɛaɔʊ* and five +ATR breathy vowels *ieəou,* as represented fluently by Ama writers using five vowel letters {aeiou} and a saltillo {ꞌ} in breathy words. For tone, Ama's nearest relative Afitti has been described as having two contrastive tone levels,[3] but Ama has three levels, which play a role in the verb system as well as the wider lexicon as shown in **Table 1**.

kɛ́r	"woman"	*ní*	"kill" FACT	*ɕɪ́ɛ̄*	"do" TR
kɛ̄r	"crane" (bird sp.)	*nī*	"kill" PROG 3	*ɕɪ̄ɛ̄*	"say"
kɛ̀r	"around"	*nì*	"kill" PROG 1/2	*ɕɪ̀ɛ̄*	"do" ITR

Table 1: Level tone contrasts in Ama

A brief overview of Ama morphosyntax can be gained by locating it in the typology of Heine and Voßen,[4] which assesses African languages on the presence of nominal classification, nominal case, and verbal derivation. In Ama, the role of nominal classification is limited due to a remarkable lack of nominal number affixes, although there is some differentiated grammatical behavior of rational nominals.[5] However, case is extensive in Ama,[6] as is typical of Nilo-Saharan verb-final languages,[7] and likewise verbal derivation is extensive.

	Feature	Presence	Categories
1.	Nominal classification	limited	rational
2.	Nominal case	extensive	accusative, dative, genitive, ablative, locatives
3.	Verbal derivation	extensive	causative, applicative, reciprocal, directional

Table 2. Ama morphosyntax

In the remaining sections, we will examine Ama's verb syntax (§/2), verb stems (§/3) and verb affixes (§/4) from a comparative perspective, followed by a conclusion (§/5).

2. The Syntax of Ama Verbs

Ama verbs follow a syntax that is partly familiar from other Nilo-Saharan languages. It has SOV word order, although as we shall see, Ama is not strictly verb-final. It also has coverbs that occur with an inflecting light verb. As in Tama,[8] most Ama verbs take their own inflections but coverbs are also seen quite frequently. Many Ama coverbs fit Stevenson's characterization that the coverb occurs before the light verb stem *ɓɪɛ* "do/say" and is either an ideophone (with marked phonology such as reduplication or non-mid tone) or a word marked by the suffix *-ɛ̄n* (typically a borrowed verb).[9] The form of the Ama coverb suffix *-ɛ̄n* matches the Fur coverb suffix *-ɛn ~ -ɛŋ*.[10] The transitivity of the predicate is distinguished in Ama by the tone on the light verb *ɓìɛ̄/ɓíɛ̄*.

Intransitive coverbs		**Transitive coverbs**	
nɔ̄nɔ̄ɲ ɓìɛ̄	"hop"	*díɟí ɓíɛ̄*	"work"
ɟìɟìg ɓìɛ̄	"speak angrily"	*ɟɛ̀rɟɛ̀r ɓíɛ̄*	"scatter"
àr̪ìmɛ̀ ɓìɛ̄	"be angry"	*t̪úūl ɓíɛ̄*	"destroy"
ɔ̄lg-ɛ̄n ɓìɛ̄	"cry"	*dígl-ɛ̄n ɓíɛ̄*	"gather" (KN *ɖigil*)[11]
tɔ̄gl-ɛ̄n ɓìɛ̄	"tie oneself"	*fɔ̄ɹ-ɛ̄n ɓíɛ̄*	"make suffer"
sɛ̀g-ɛ̄n ɓìɛ̄	"complain"	*tīm-ɛ̄n ɓíɛ̄*	"finish"
		kɔ̄w-ɛ̄n ɓíɛ̄	"iron" (SA *kowa*)
		rɛ̄kb-ɛ̄n ɓíɛ̄	"ride" (SA *rikib*)
		mīskīl-ɛ̄n ɓíɛ̄	"give someone a missed call" (SA *miskil*)

Table 3. Ama coverbs

While Ama's verb-final word order and use of coverbs are reminiscent of other Nilo-Saharan languages, relative clauses in Ama are of a globally rare type. Ama uses adjoined relative clauses at the end of the main clause, and these modify the last noun of the main clause.[12]

(1) **Ama**

àì	*bā*	*ìr-ò*	*tὲlɛ̄*		*(ìn)*	*kwārāŋ-àʊ̀*
1SG	DECL.VER	elephant-ACC	see	[	3SG	field-LOC

túŋ
sleep:PROG]

"I definitely saw the elephant who was sleeping in a field."

(2)

āбīdī-ʊ̄ŋ	*kwɛ̄ɪ̄*	*d̪ɛ̄*	*īrīd̪ā*	*wʊ̄ɔ̄*
God-GEN	man	EV	message	keep:PROG

kɛ̄r-àʊ̀		*yʊ̄sʊ̄f-īl*	*tīŋ-ɛ́í*
girl (*kɛ̄rà*)-LOC	[	Joseph-LOC	choose-MED]

"An angel from God had a message for a girl who was engaged to Joseph."

The adjoined relative clause strategy means that verbs tend not to occur in noun phrases in Ama, although for completeness we should observe that they are not entirely excluded. Since it is impossible to modify the subject of a transitive clause by an adjoined relative clause, as it is separated by another object or oblique noun, speakers consulted confirmed that it is grammatically acceptable to modify a subject noun by a progressive verb within the noun phrase as in (3), although they felt this is not used much, and I have not found examples in texts. However, verb participles marked by the suffix *-ɔ̀* (or *-ò* by vowel harmony) also occur in noun phrases, including in texts as in (4) and (5).

(3) Unmarked relative clause in subject noun phrase (elicited)

ìr	*nɔ̄*		*mūɓ-èg*	*bā*	*āŋ*
elephant	this	[	run-DIR:PROG]	DECL.VER	1SG.ACC

t̪ὲlɛ̄
see:FACT

"This running elephant definitely saw me."

(4) Participial subject relative clause
ə́níŋè wád̪à kìr-d̪-ò wàá ɓìɽāgíd̪í
when [word cut-PCT-PTCP] people rule
wāg-áʊ́
keep-PST.PROG
"When the judges (lit. 'cut-word people') were ruling,"

(5) Participial object relative clause
mōrd̪à kōɟɔ̄-ɔ̀ d̪ɛ̄ ŋáŋà túɽāk
horse [saddle-PTCP] EV attention warn:PROG
"The saddled horse is warning, look out."

Nevertheless, the adjoined relative clause strategy is an innovative feature of Ama that tends to place information about participants outside the noun phrase where they are mentioned. A similar distribution applies to the expression of number. Within the noun phrase, there are no number affixes, although there is a plural specifier *ŋī* or *gī* that can be used with rational nouns as seen in (6). Speakers consulted assess this specifier the same way as unmarked relative clauses within the noun phrase: acceptable, but not used much. However, Ama also has a post-verbal quantifier *gàì* that can be used when there is a plural participant in the clause, as shown in (7).[13]

(6) Plural noun phrase specifier (elicited)
ābā dìà ŋī
father big PL
"grandfathers"

(7) Post-verbal plural quantifier
wàá dū fāɽāŋ fīl gàì
people TOP drum dance:PROG PL
"The people were all dancing to a drum."

We will return to this tendency to express relative clauses and number late in the clause after considering other evidence from verb stems.

3. Ama Verb Stems

Stevenson discovered the existence of two stems of each Ama verb.[14] The forms of the two stems are not fully predictable from each other in general, and their usage depends on aspect.

3.1. The Factative–Progressive Distinction

The aspectual functions of the two stems were described by Stevenson as definite and indefinite aspect, and relabeled as perfective and imperfective by more recent authors. However, the usage of the former stem meets the definition of "factative,"[15] such that it has a past perfective reading when used for an active verb like "eat," but a present continuous reading when used for a stative verb like "know." The other stem has a present progressive reading, which is marginal for stative verbs (as indicated by "?") where the meaning contribution of progressive to an already continuous verb is highly marked.[16] The factative–progressive analysis is helpful when we consider the history of these stems below.

	active verb	**stative verb**
FACT	*t̪àl* "ate" (past perf.)	*t̪ō-máí* "know" (pres. cont.)
PROG	*tām* "is eating"	?*máí* "is knowing"

Table 4. Verb stems of active and stative verbs

3.2. Stem Formation and the Verb Root

Although factative aspect is broader in meaning and more heavily used in text, the progressive stem is generally more basic in form, often consisting only of the bare root. However, neither the factative stem nor the progressive stem is predictable from the other in general because: (i) factative stems belong to various theme vowel classes, and some belong to a class taking a formative prefix *t̪V-*; (ii) in some verbs the two stems have two different suppletive roots; and (iii) the progressive stems of some verbs require certain obligatory incorporated affixes. When the root is extracted from any additional formatives, CVC is the most frequent verb root shape.

FACT	**PROG**	**Gloss**	**morphology other than FACT theme vowel**
sāŋ-ɔ̄	*sāŋ*	search	
kīr-ɛ̄	*kīr*	cut	
wāg-ā	*wɔ̄ɔ̄*	keep	suppletive roots
t̪ī-ə̀	*túŋ*	sleep	suppletive roots
t̪áw-ɔ̄	*gēd̪-ì*	cook	suppletive roots, final *-i* required after *d̪*
ɟɛ́g-ɛ̄	*ɟēg-īn*	leave s.th.	applicative *-(ī)n*
á-bīr̪-īŋ-ɔ̄	*á-bīr̪-īŋ*	invent	causative *á-* and inchoative *-īŋ*
t̪ī-ŋīl-ē	*ŋīl*	laugh	factative *t̪V-*
t̪ū-mūs-ò	*mús-èg*	run	factative *t̪V-* ~ directional *-èg*
t̪í-gɛ̄l-ɛ̄	*á-gɛ̄l*	wash	causative-factative *t̪V́-* ~ causative *á-*
ɓì-ɛ̄	*á-ɓī*	do (intr.)	causative *á-*

Table 5. Examples of verb stems

The CVC shape of verb roots is characteristic across Eastern Sudanic languages. In Gaahmg, for example, at least 90% of verb roots are CVC, whereas nouns are much more varied in shape.[17] CVC is also the predominant shape in the following comparative data for verbs across Northern branches of Eastern Sudanic.[18]

Gloss	Nubian	Nara	Taman	Nyima	Proto-NES
be	**-a(n)/*-a-gV*	*ne-/ge-* PL	**an-/*ag-*	**nV*	**(a)n/*(a)g* PL
burn	**urr*	*kál, war*	**wer	**wul* "boil"	**wul*, [**wel?*]
buy	**jaan*	*tol ~ dol*	–	**tar*	**tol*
come	**taar*	*til*	**or*, PF *kun	**t̪ar/*kud̪*	**tar*, [**kud?*]
cut	**mer*	*ked*	**kid*	– (Ama *kɪr*)	**kɛd*
dance	**baan*	*bàl, bàr*	–	**bal/fal*	**bal*
drink	**nii*	*l-, líí-*	**li*	– (Ama *li*)	**li*
eat	**kal*	*kal*	**ŋan*	**t̪al/*tam*	**kal/*kamb* PL
give	**tir* (2/3), **deen* (1)	*nin*	**ti(n)*	**t̪Vg*, **t̪ɔ́ŋ* (1)	**te(n)* [final C?], **den*
look	**guuɲ*	–	**gun*, PF **gud*	**t̪igol*	**guɲ* [final C?]
love, want	**doll, *oon*	*sol*	– (Tama *tar*)	– (Ama *war*)	**tor*
sit	**ti(i)g/*te(e)g*	*dengi, daŋŋi* "wait"	**juk*	**dɔɲ*	**daŋ*
take, carry	**aar*	–	**ar-i*	**-ur*	**ar*
take, gather	**dumm*	*nem*	– (Tama *tə-məɽ*)	– (Ama *dum-*)	**dəm*
take, raise	**eɲ*	*hind*	**eɲ*	– (Ama *ɲɔn* "carry")	**meɲ ~ *ɲeɲ*

Table 6. Verbs across Northern East Sudanic (NES)

3.3. T/K Morphology for Factative/Progressive

An alternation between *t̪-* and *k-* cuts into the characteristic CVC shape in one class of Ama verbs as a marker of aspect along with the theme vowel.

FACT	PROG	Gloss
t̪-ùg-è	*k-ūg*	build
t̪-īw-ò	*k-íw*	dig
t̪-ūɓ-ē	*k-úɓ-ín*	light (fire)

Table 7. T/K marking on Ama verbs

A longer list of examples of this alternation shown in **Table 8** was documented by Stevenson, Rottland & Jakobi, albeit with a different standard of transcription; they also detected the alternation in Afitti (*tosù/kosìl* "suckle"; *tòsù/kosìl* "light fire").[19]

FACT	PROG	Gloss
tugɛ̀	*kwò*	build
tàiɔ̀	*kaì*	chop
tìwò	*kìù*	dig
tìwò	*kèù*	fall (of rain)
twɛ̀	*kwài*	rear, bring up
twèr	*kweàg*	grow ITR
təwɛ̀	*kwɔ̀i*	grow TR
tuwɛlɛ̀	*kwɛlì*	guard
tugudò	*kwogidì*	mix up, tell lies
toromɔ̀	*kwòròm*	gnaw
toso	*kwoʃi*	suck (milk, of baby)
tɔʃig	*kwɔʃig*	suckle
tosùn	*kwosùn*	burn ITR
tuʃè	*kwuʃin*	light fire
tɛ̀nɛ̀	*kɛndìr*	climb
tɛnìg	*kɛndɛ̀g*	mount

Table 8. More verbs with T/K marking

T and K are well-known markers of singular and plural in Nilo-Saharan languages,[20] but in Ama and Afitti where there is no T/K morphology on the noun, essentially the same alternation (**t* becomes dental in the Nyima branch)[21] is found on the verb. It also cuts into the characteristic CVC verb root shape, implying that it is an innovation on the verb. I therefore propose that this class of verbs attests the Nyima cognate of the wider Nilo-Saharan T/K alternation. This entails a chain of events in which the T/K alternation first moved from the noun (singular/plural) to the verb (singulactional/pluractional), and then shifted in meaning from verbal number to verbal aspect (factative/progressive).

Both steps in this proposed chain are indeed plausible cross-linguistically. As to the first step, the possibility of nominal plural markers being extended to verbal pluractionals is familiar from Chadic languages, where the same formal strategies such as first-syllable reduplication or *a*-infixation may be found in plural nouns and pluractional verbs.[22] In the Nyima languages, the productive innovation at this step appears to have been the extension of singulative T to a verbal singulactional marker. This is seen in the fact that *t̪-* alternates with other consonants as well as *k* in Ama (*t̪ān-ɛ̄/wɛ̄n* "talk," *t̪ɛ̀l-ɛ̄/wɛ̄ɛ́n* "see," *t̪àl/tām* "eat"), or is prefixed in front of the root (*t̪ó-wár-ɔ̄/wār* "want," *t̪ī-ŋīl-ē/ŋīl* "laugh," *t̪ì-fīl-è/fīl* "dance," *t̪ū-mūs-ò/mús-èg* "run," *t̪ō-máí/máí* "know," *t̪-īlm-ò/ílím* "milk"). There is also external evidence from Nubian and Nara cited in **Table 6** above that **k* is the original initial consonant in **kal* "eat" replaced by *t̪-* in Ama and Afitti.

As to the second step, the prospect of verbal number shifting to verbal aspect is supported by semantic affinity between pluractional and progressive. Progressive aspect often entails that a process that is iterated ("is coughing," "is milking") over the interval concerned.[23] In Leggbo,[24] a Niger-Congo language, the progressive form can have a pluractional reading in some verbs, and conversely, verbs that fail to form the regular progressive *C#* → *CC-i* because they already end in *CCi* can use the pluractional suffix *-azi* instead to express progressive aspect. In Spanish,[25] a Romance language, there is a periphrastic paradigm between progressive (*estar* "be" + gerund), frequentative pluractional (*andar* "walk" + gerund), and incremental pluractional (*ir* "go" + gerund). The two Spanish pluractionals have been called "pseudo-progressives," but conversely one could think of progressive aspect as pseudo-pluractional. What is somewhat surprising in Ama is that progressive stems, being morphologically more basic (see **Table 5**), lack any devoted progressive affixes that would have formerly served as pluractional markers.[26] However, some progressive marking is found in irregular alternations that reveal former pluractional stems.

In *t̪àl/tām* "eat," the final *l/m* alternation is unique to this item in available word lists, although *l/n* occurs elsewhere (*kíl/kín* "hear," *t̪ɛ̀l-ɛ̄/wɛ̄ɛ́n* "see"). The final *l/m* alternation is nevertheless also found in Afitti (*t̪ə̀lə̀/tə̀m* "eat") and in Kordofan Nubian (**kol ~ kel/*kam* "eat").[27] Kordofan Nubian **kam* is used with a plural object, a pluractional function, so in the Nyima branch the proposed shift pluractional → progressive derives the progressive function of final m found in Ama, just as it does for the initial *k* in *t̪/k* alternations or the *t* in *t̪àl/tām* "eat." Furthermore, a final plosive in Old Nubian (ⲕⲁⲡ-[28]; Nobiin *kab-*) suggests that the unique *m* in "eat" arose by assimilation of the final nasal (realized as *n* in the other Ama verbs mentioned) to a following **b*, that was fully assimilated or incorporated in Old Nubian.

Seen in this light, the significance of moving T/K morphology onto verbs in the Nyima branch is that it renewed an existing system of irregular singulational/pluractional alternations. We then have a tangible account of where Ama's missing noun morphology went, because formerly nominal morphology is found on the verb instead.

3.4. Concretization of Core Clause Constituents

We can also now tie together this finding with the findings on verb syntax in §/ 2. Both T/K number marking and relative clause modification have moved out of the noun phrase, and in these comparable changes we can observe a trend towards concretization of noun phrases, with number and clausal information about the participant being expressed later in the clause.

The trend towards concretization also affects the verb itself. T/K and other irregular stem alternations did not maintain their pluractional meaning, as this evolved into a more concrete construal of the predicate over an interval of time as progressive aspect. Since concretization affected the verb as well as noun phrases, it affected the entire core SOV clause, with plurality as well as relative clauses largely deferred to after the verb.

A role for concreteness in grammar was previously proposed in the Pirahã language of Brazil by Everett.[29] Everett's approach remains highly controversial,[30] particularly, I believe, in its attempt to constrain grammar by culture directly in the form of a synchronic "Immediacy of Experience Constraint" on admissible sentence constructions and lexemes in Pirahã. My proposal here is deliberately less ambitious, appealing to concreteness as a diachronic trend in the Nyima branch, not as a constraint on the current synchronic grammar of Ama. Thus, Ama typically attests a separation between a concrete SOV clause and post-verbal modification, but this is not a strict division in the grammar, because it is not impossible to express number or relative clauses within the noun phrase, just infrequent. The concretization process in Ama must also have been specific enough not to have eliminated adjectives from the noun phrase. Ama has adjectives, as shown in examples (8)–(11), which occur as attributive modifiers of nouns in their unmarked form, whereas in predicates they are separated from the subject noun by a clause particle and occur as the complement of the inflecting copula verb *nɛ̄*. Ama adjectives include numerals and quantifiers, despite the limited role of number in the grammar.

> (8a) *kwɛ̄ɪ̄ tòɽū*
> man tall
> "tall man"

> (8b) *kwɛ̄ɪ̄ ā tòɽū nɛ̄*
> man DECL tall be
> "The man is tall."

> (9a) *kwɛ̄ɪ̄ gɔ̀ɽɛ̀*
> man old
> "old man"

> (9b) *kwɛ̄ɪ̄ ā gɔ̀ɽɛ̀ nɛ̄*
> man DECL tall be
> "The man is old."

> (10a) *ŋɔ̄ɽɪ̄ mūl*
> day five
> "five days"

> (10a) *ŋɔ̄ɽɪ̄ ā mūl nɛ̄-ɛ́d̪-ɪ̄*
> day DECL five be-DISTR-TH
> "The days are five." ("There are five days.")

> (11a) *wàá kàdúùŋ*
> people many
> "many people"

> (11b) *wàá ā kàdúùŋ nɛ̄-ɛ́d̪-ɪ̄*
> people DECL many be-DISTR-TH
> "The people are many." ("There are many people.")

4. Ama Verbal affixes

Research over the past century has also been gradually clarifying the complex morphological system of Ama verbs.[31] Factative and progressive aspect are distinguished in the affix system as well as in stems, and there is an evolving portfolio of pluractional affixes.

4.1. Affix Selection and Order

Some verbal affixes are selected depending on factative or progressive aspect in Ama, just as verb stems are. For example, different suffixes for past tense or for directional movement are selected in the different aspects:

	Stem	**PST**
FACT	*t̪àl*	*t̪àl-ɔ̀n*
PROG	*tām*	*tām-áʊ́*

Table 9a. Affix selection according to aspect: "eat"

	Stem	**DIR**
FACT	*dɪ̀ɟ-ɛ̄*	*dɪ̀ɟ-ɛ̄-g*
PROG	*dɪ̄ɟ-ɪ̄*	*dɪ̄ɟ-ɪ́r*

Table 9b. Affix selection according to aspect: "throw"

The same is true of passive and ventive suffixes, but in factative aspect the suffixes replace the theme vowel, so that the affixes are the sole exponent of aspect in many verbs:

	Stem	**PASS**
FACT	*ásīd̪āy-ɛ̄*	*ásīd̪āy-áí*
PROG	*ásīd̪āɪ̄*	*ásīd̪āy-àg*

Table 10a. Affix selection as sole exponent of aspect: "paint"

	Stem	VEN
FACT	*īr-ɛ̄*	*īr-īīg*
PROG	*īr*	*īr-íd̪ɛ̄ɛ̀g*

Table 10b. Affix selection as sole exponent of aspect: "send"

In passive and in past, affix order also varies according to aspect with respect to the dual suffix *-ɛ̄n*:

	Stem	DU PASS
FACT	*ásīd̪āy-ɛ̄*	*ásīd̪āy-áy-ɛ̄n*
PROG	*ásīd̪āī*	*ásīd̪āy-ɛ̄n-àg*

Table 11a. Affix order variation according to aspect: "paint"

	Stem	DU PST
FACT	*sāŋ-ɔ̄*	*sāŋ-ɛ̄n-ɔ̀n*
PROG	*sāŋ*	*sāŋ-áw-ɛ̄n*

Table 11b. Affix order variation according to aspect: "search"

The origin of this affix order variation is revealed by further evidence. Passive marking comes after dual in progressive aspect, whereas past marking comes after dual in factative aspect, but the common feature of both suffixes *-àg, -ɔ̀n* placed after the dual is that they both bear low tone. Two more suffixes with low tone, directional *-ɛ̀g* ~ *-g* (the second allomorph is toneless) and mediocausative -*àw* ~ *-ɔ̀* (the second allomorph is used word-finally) appear after the dual, but if another low-tone suffix is added after the dual, they appear before the dual instead. Hence, there is only one more affix slot in Ama after the penultimate dual suffix.

Gloss	throw	throw to DU	elicit DU
FACT	*dìɟ-ɛ̄-g*	*dìɟ-í-n-īg*	*kíl-ɛ̄n-ɔ̀*
	throw-TH-DIR	throw-VEN-DU-DIR	hear-DU-MEDCAUS
FACT IMP	*dìɟ-ɛ̀g-ɛ̄-ì*	*dìɟ-í-g-ɛ̄n-ì*	*kíl-àw-ɛ̄n-ì*
	throw-DIR-TH-IMP	throw-VEN-DIR-DU-IMP	hear-MEDCAUS-DU-IMP
FACT PST	*dìɟ-ɛ̀g-ɔ̄-ɔ̀n*	*dìɟ-í-g-ɛ̄n-ɔ̀n*	*kíl-àw-ɛ̄n-ɔ̀n*
	throw-DIR-TH-PST	throw-VEN-DIR-DU-PST	hear-MEDCAUS-DU-PST

Table 12. Inward displacement of suffixes by an imperative or past suffix

Both types of affix alternation in **Tables 11 and 12** involve low-tone suffixes in the final slot. Therefore, the development of all affix order alternations can be attributed to a single historical shift of all low-tone suffixes to the final slot. However, this shift is not realized in verbs containing two low-tone suffixes, because only one of them can go in the final slot. The only final-slot suffix that does not alternate is the imperative *-ì,* which leaves imperative as original to the final slot. Other suffixes originate from more internal slots to the left of the dual.

As for the origin of affix selection according to aspect, this presumably arose as an extension of the systematic stem selection that occurs for every verb in Nyima languages. This question remains complex, however, because each of the categories affected (past, passive, directional, ventive) will have its own history as to how alternating affixes were acquired in these conditions. One modest proposal is that the NES plural copula **ag* shown earlier in **Table 6** is the likely source of the progressive passive suffix *-àg* in Ama,[32] via the shift from pluractional to progressive (§3.3), and by a plausible assumption of a transition in passive marking strategy from use of a copula to morphological marking on the verb. This sourcing does not extend to the other passive suffix in factative aspect *-áí,* however, which does not resemble the singular copula **an*. Some similar proposals that other progressive suffixes have pluractional origins are made in the course of §4.2 below.

4.2. Pluractional Affixes

Ama has extensions that fall within the family of pluractionals that associate plurality with the verb in different ways, that has emerged as an area of study in language description in recent years.[33] These extensions are particularly comparable with Nubian and other related languages.

4.2.1. Distributive Pluractional

Ama has a distributive suffix *-íḏ* that marks incremental distribution of an event over time or over participants (*àì bā fōrā mōl ṯàl-íḏ-ɛ̀* "I ate until I had eaten five rabbits," *wùḏēŋ bā dōrɛ̄ŋ ṯɛ̀l-íḏ-ɛ̄* "The child saw each of the children").[34] Called "plural" in earlier works, it is remarkable that this category was largely unaffected by the shift of pluractional → progressive analyzed in §3.3 above,[35] indicating that we are dealing with two distinct pluractionals, a distributive pluractional and another former pluractional that is now progressive. Ama has a second distributive suffix *-r* used only on verbs with the theme vowel *-a* (*wāg-ā* "keep," distributive *wāg-íḏ-ā-r*).[36] Ama's immediate relative Afitti has a "verbal plural" suffix *-tər,*[37] which corresponds to Ama *-íḏ* and *-r* combined, reminiscent of their use in that order in Ama on verbs with the theme vowel *-a,* but regularized to all verbs in Afitti. The Ama suffix *-íḏ* also closely resembles a "plural action" suffix *-(ɨ)ṯ* in the nearby Eastern Sudanic language Temein,[38] and a "plurality of action" suffix *-íd* in Midob.[39] The distributive suffix *-ij* in Mattokki (Kunuz Nubian) is also similar.[40]

Distributive pluractionals are characterized by optionality with a plural participant (distributivity implies plurality but is distinct from it),[41] which distinguishes them from plural-object pluractionals found in many Nubian languages that mark, and are thus obligatory with, plural objects.[42] Distributives are also characterized by non-occurrence with dual participants (to be non-trivial, distribution requires at least three targets).[43] The Ama distributive has the first property of optionality in transitive (but not intransitive) verbs, and the second property of non-duality with respect to subjects (but not objects).[44] This second property is shared by the Afitti suffix *-t(ə)r* which likewise does not occur with dual subjects.[45] This is shown in Afitti field data below,[46] where the suffix -

t(ə)r contrasts in this respect with plural pronominal affixes 1PL*ko-*, 2PL*o-*, and 3PL*-i* which do occur with dual subjects.

1	Gloss	2	Gloss	3	Gloss
gə́-gaɲal	I milk	*é-gaɲal*	you SG milk	*kaɲál*	he/she milks
kó-gaɲal	we DU milk	*ó-gaɲál*	you DU milk	*gaɲál-i*	they DU milk
kó-gaɲa-tr̀	we PL milk	*ó-gaɲa-tr̀*	you PL milk	*gaɲá-tər-i*	they PL milk

Table 13. Afitti pluractional *-t(ə)r* not used with dual subjects

Beyond the Nyima branch, the Temein "plural action" suffix *-(ɨ)t̪* shares the first property of optionality as it "is by no means always added with plural objects."[47] It actually marks a distributive effect of the verb on the object (*ŋɔŋɔt-ɨt̪-ɛ dʉk* "I break the stick into pieces"), as also found with the Mattokki distributive suffix -*ij* (*dugu:g gull-ij-ossu* 'She threw the money here and there').[48] Information on non-occurrence with dual subjects is not reported in these languages, but it appears that this is because non-duality is a feature of incremental-distributive marking as found in Nyima, and not distributive-effect marking as found in Temein and Mattokki which can even occur with a singular object, as in the Temein example.

The confirmation of distributive markers across Nubian, Nyima, and Temein implies that a distributive pluractional was present in Eastern Sudanic from an early stage, with a form like **-id.* In Nubian the consonant is palatal,[49] and although palatals are a difficult area for establishing wider sound correspondences,[50] the palatal arises in the plausible conditioning environment of a high front vowel.

4.2.2. Second Historic Pluractional

Ama's second distributive suffix *-r* corresponds to the Nubian plural object marker **-er,*[51] and since this suffix is much less productive in Ama, it may well have been bleached of its original meaning. In the Kordofan Nubian language Uncu, the cognate extension *-er* has the same function as the irregular pluractional stem *(kol/)kom* "eat," as both occur with plural objects.[52] Similarly in Ama, some trills shown below occur in the same category as the irregular progressive stem *(t̪àl/)tām* "eat," providing evidence that the trill originally marked the second Nyima pluractional that is now progressive.

The Ama suffix *-ar* can be added to a progressive verb as a mirative that marks unexpected events (*swāy-ɔ́* "was cultivating" → *swāy-ɔ̄r-ɔ́* "was unexpectedly cultivating," where the vowel has harmonized to the following vowel). However, this suffix is also used to disambiguate progressive verb forms from otherwise indistinguishable factatives (*sāŋ-ɛ̄n/sāŋ-ɛ̄n, sāŋ-ār-ɛ̄n* "search DU"),[53] providing what looks like an alternate progressive stem to take the dual suffix. Similarly, the negative imperative construction in Ama requires a progressive stem with *-ar* after the negative particle *fá* as shown in **Table 14** below. Inflections occurring in this construction are a plural subject marker *à-* on the particle, and dual or distributive marking on the verb. Only the dual suffix can occur without *-ar*, where in my data the dual suffix adds to the longer stem with *-ar* unless the short stem is suppletive (*t̪ī-ə̀/túŋ* "sleep," t̪àl/*tām* "eat") and can take the dual suffix without ambiguity with factative aspect.

SG	DU	DISTR PL	Gloss
fá kīr-ār	*à-fá kīr-ār-ɛ̄n*	*à-fá kīr-íd̪-ār*	don't be cutting!
fá sāŋ-ār	*à-fá sāŋ-ār-ɛ̄n*	*à-fá sāŋ-íd̪-ār*	don't be searching!
fá túŋ-ār	*à-fá túŋ-ɛ̄n*	*à-fá túŋ-íd̪-ār*	don't be sleeping!
fá tām-ār	*à-fá tām-ɛ̄n*	*à-fá tām-íd̪-ār*	don't be eating!

Table 14. Ama negative imperative paradigms

Another trilled suffix *-ir* marks motion in progress.[54] It can be added to a progressive verb (*dīɟī* "is throwing" → *dīɟ-ír* "is throwing (motion in progress)"), but on several motion verbs it is documented as part of the progressive stem, as in the examples in **Table 15** below from Stevenson, Rottland, and Jakobi.[55] The motion meaning of *-ir* simply agrees with the semantics of the roots, all of which define motion along some schematic scale, so that the aspectual meaning of *-ir* assumes greater significance. Hence, *-ir* approximates a progressive stem formative for this class of verbs. The final example in **Table 15**, due to Kingston,[56] shows still another trilled suffix *-or* in the progressive stem of a caused motion verb.

FACT	PROG	Gloss
bwìg	*bugìr*	overtake
nɪfɛ̂g	*nɪfîr*	fall
tɛnɛ̀	*kɛndìr*	climb
tɪjɛ	*jeìr*	shoot
ánasa	*ánasor*	take down

Table 15. Progressive stems ending in a trill

The trill thus fuses with certain vowels that behave like theme vowels for creating extended progressive stems. As a progressive element, the trill most probably derives from the shift of pluractional → progressive, identifying it as the missing extension of the second Nyima pluractional. We then have an Ama distributive pluractional suffix *-íd̪* that resembles the Nubian distributive pluractional **-(i)ɟ*, and Ama "pseudo-pluractional" progressive suffixes of the shape *-Vr* that resemble the Nubian plural-object pluractional **-er*.

4.2.3. Innovative Dual-Participant Pluractional

A late addition to Ama's pluractional portfolio is its unique dual suffix *-ɛ̄n*.[57] The older form of the Ama dual suffix is *-ɪn*,[58] which has been noted to resemble reciprocal suffixes in other Eastern Sudanic languages, such as Kordofan Nubian *-in*, Daju *-din*, Temein *-ɛ*, and also Ik *-in* of the Kuliak group.[59] In Ama, its function has evolved to dual reciprocal and other dual participant readings, so for example *wɔ̀s-ɛ̄n* "greet DU" can refer to when two people greeted each other, or someone greeted two people, or two people greeted someone.[60] The dual suffix is regularly used in Ama folktales to link two primary characters.[61] Although such dual participant marking is extremely rare globally, it becomes possible in Nyima languages in particular where the incremental-distributive pluractional leaves a paradigmatic gap for dual subjects, as still seen in Afitti in **Table 13** above, which Ama has filled in.

5. Conclusion: Ama as a Matured Northern East Sudanic Language

Ama verbs show a number of connections to Nubian and other Eastern Sudanic languages in their clause-final syntax, CVC root shape, and certain affixes. However, these connections are more in form than meaning, as the semantics is highly innovative in such notable shifts as plural → pluractional → progressive and reciprocal → dual, and in the drive towards concretization that has moved the expression of both relative clauses and number out of noun phrases to after the verb. In addition, the movement of low-tone suffixes to the final suffix slot, while itself a formal development, has further advanced the morphologization of aspect, so that stem selection, affix selection, and affix order all vary with aspect in Ama verbs. Next to these considerable changes, Ama's stable distributive pluractional stands out as indicative of a wider Eastern Sudanic verbal category.

An explanation for the innovations found in Ama will not be found in influence from other languages of Sudan, because several of its innovations are extremely rare (adjoined relative clauses, dual verbal number, tone-driven affix order alternation). Instead of an influx of new forms, we have unusual internal evolution of existing forms, implying relative isolation. Ama then exemplifies what both Dahl and Trudgill call "mature phenomena,"[62] found in languages of isolated small communities where the language has time to evolve based on an abundance of specific shared information in a closed society of intimates. Languages spoken by isolated societies of intimates are more likely to conventionalize complex morphological paradigms, unusual categories, and unusual syntax (maturation), whereas larger, multilingual social networks encourage simpler grammars in the sense of smaller paradigms, and pragmatically well-motivated categories and syntax that are found widely in language (pidginization). Aforementioned verbal features in Ama of dual number, irregular allomorphy (in suppletive roots and in the use of a second distributive suffix), fusion (in affixes like passive and ventive that mark aspect as well), polyfunctionality (of the progressive suffix *-ar* for mirativity or long stem formation), and multiple exponence (of aspect by stem selection, affix selection, and affix order), plus the unusual syntax of adjoined relative clauses, all look like mature language phenomena.[63]

Ama nominals, similarly, are known for their relatively rich case systems, but similar case paradigms are found in Nubian and other Northern East Sudanic languages, implying that the case system largely matured at an earlier stage and the resulting complexity is retained in all these languages. Thus, it is the verb system rather than the nominal system that provides evidence of maturation in the Nyima branch in particular.

The conclusion that Ama verbs (and post-verbal syntax) have matured as a result of Nyima's isolated position, away from the river systems that hosted speakers of other languages in the Sudan region in the past, faces the possible difficulty that contacts have in fact been proposed between Nyima and other Nuba Mountain groups. Thus, it is proposed that the Niger-Congo Nuba Mountain group Heiban borrowed accusative marking and basic vocabulary from Nyima.[64] Such contact would have put a brake on maturation in Nyima, because the use of proto-Nyima for inter-group communication between first-language Nyima users and second-language Heiban users would not have supported further growth in complexity.[65] However, it is not realistic that such contacts lasted for a large proportion of Nyima history, but rather were fairly temporary periods punctuating Nyima's longer isolation. Thus, the Heiban group has now developed separately in the eastern Nuba Mountains for something approaching two millennia (given the internal diversity of the ten Heiban languages found there) since its contact with Nyima.

Some time after the contact with Heiban, Rottland and Jakobi note the likelihood of contact of Kordofan Nubian with Ama and Afitti in the north-west Nuba Mountains before the arrival of Arabic as a *lingua franca* in the Nuba Mountains.[66] Ama and Afitti are more lexically divergent than Kordofan Nubian and therefore were probably already separate communities when the Kordofan Nubians arrived. However, the innovation of dual marking on Ama verbs in the period after separation from Afitti still shows the hallmarks of maturation. It adds an extremely rare category, increases the occurrence of morphologically complex verbs by using a verbal marker in dual participant contexts that were not previously marked, and adds redundancy when agreeing with noun phrases containing two referents. This mature feature of Ama again suggests that any language contact with Kordofan Nubian occurred for only part of the time since Ama separated from Afitti.

This period nevertheless also reveals one significant example of simplification in Ama verbs that supports the idea that language contact occurred. Afitti has pronominal subject markers on the verb, seen earlier in **Table 13**, which are absent in Ama. The pronominal prefixes are not the same in form as personal pronoun words in Afitti (1SG *oi* but 1SG prefix *kə-*),[67] therefore they are not incorporated versions of the current pronoun words, but rather predate them. Some of the Afitti pronoun words (1SG *oi*, 2SG *i*)[68] are similar to Ama (1SG *àì*, 2SG *ī*) and must be retentions from proto-Nyima, hence the older pronominal prefixes must also be retentions in Afitti, but lost in Ama. Their loss in Ama is remarkable against the larger trend of growth in complexity of Ama verbs that we have examined in this paper. The predicted cause of this surprising reversal is pidginization under contact. That is, their loss is evidence that the Ama language was used for inter-group communication, presumably with the Kordofan Nubians, during which (and for which) Ama SOV sentences were simplified by dropping verbal subject marking. If Kordofan Nubians spoke Ama, then borrowing from Ama into Kordofan Nubian is also likely. In verbs, the obvious candidate for borrowing into Kordofan Nubian is the reciprocal suffix *-in*, as this is not attested elsewhere in Nubian.[69] The following two-step scenario would then account for the facts: Ama was learned and used by Kordofan Nubians, during which Ama dropped verbal subject marking and its reciprocal suffix was borrowed into Kordofan Nubian; next, Ama returned to isolation in which the reciprocal suffix developed its dual function that is unique to Ama today.

6. Abbreviations

- 1, 2, 3 – 1st, 2nd, 3rd person;
- ACC – accusative;
- DECL – declarative;
- DIR – directional;
- DISTR – distributive;
- DU – dual;
- EV – event;
- FACT – factative;
- GEN – genitive;
- IMP – imperative;
- ITR – intransitive;

› KN – Kordofan Nubian;
› LOC – locative;
› MED – mediopassive;
› MEDCAUS – mediocausative;
› PASS – passive;
› PCT – punctual;
› PF – perfect;
› PL – plural;
› PROG – progressive;
› PST – past;
› PTCP – participle;
› SA – Sudanese Arabic;
› SG – singular;
› TH – theme;
› TOP – topic;
› TR – transitive;
› VEN – ventive;
› VER – veridical

7. Bibliography

Abdel-Hafiz, Ahmed. bib/*A Reference Grammar of Kunuz Nubian.* PhD Thesis. Buffalo: State University of New York, 1988.

Bryan, Margaret A. bib/"The T/K languages: A New Substratum." *Africa* 29 (1959): pp. 1–21.

Comfort, Jade. bib/"Verbal Number in the Uncu Language (Kordofan Nubian)." *Dotawo: A Journal of Nubian Studies* 1 (2014): pp. 145–163. DOI: www/10.5070/D61110032.

Corbett, Greville G. bib/*Number.* Cambridge: Cambridge University Press, 2000.

Dahl, Östen. bib/*The Growth and Maintenance of Linguistic Complexity.* Amsterdam: John Benjamins, 2004.

Dimmendaal, Gerrit. bib/"Africa's Verb-Final Languages." In *A Linguistic Geography of Africa,* edited by Bernd Heine and Derek Nurse. Cambridge: Cambridge University Press, 2008: pp. 272–308.

Dimmendaal, Gerrit. bib/"Introduction." In *Coding Participant Marking: Construction Types in Twelve African Languages,* edited by Gerrit J. Dimmendaal. Amsterdam: John Benjamins, 2009: pp. 1–22.

Everett, Daniel. bib/"Cultural Constraints on Grammar and Cognition in Pirahã: Another Look at the Design Features of Human Language." *Current Anthropology* 46, no. 4 (2005): pp. 621–646. DOI: www/10.1086/431525.

Everett, Daniel. bib/"Pirahã Culture and Grammar: A Response to Some Criticisms." *Language* 85, no. 2 (2009): pp. 405–442. DOI: www/10.5070/D61110032.

Frajzyngier, Zygmunt. bib/"The Plural in Chadic." In *Papers in Chadic Linguistics,* edited by Paul Newman & Roxana Ma Newman. Leiden: Afrika-Studiecentrum, 1977: pp. 37–56.

Gilley, Leoma G. bib/"Katcha Noun Morphology." In *Nuba Mountain Language Studies,* edited by Thilo Schadeberg and Roger Blench. Cologne: Rüdiger Köppe,

2013: pp. 501–522.

Greenberg, Joseph. *bib/* *The Languages of Africa.* Bloomington: Indiana University Press, 1963.

Heine, Bernd & Rainer Voßen. "Sprachtypologie." In *Die Sprachen Afrikas,* edited by Bernd Heine, Thilo Schadeberg, and Ekkehard Wolff. Hamburg: Helmut Buske, 1981: pp. 407–444.

Hyman, Larry & Imelda Udoh. *bib/*"Progressive Formation in Leggbo." In *Globalization and the Study of Languages in Africa,* edited by Ozo-mekuri Ndimele. Port Harcourt: Grand Orbit Communications and Emhai Press, 2005: pp. 297–304.

Jakobi, Angelika. *Kordofan Nubian: A Synchronic and Diachronic Study.* Unpublished manuscript, 2013.

Kröger, Oliver. *bib/*"Typology Put to Practical Use: A Participatory Approach to Initial Grammar Research." In *Proceedings of the 6th World Congress of African Linguistics, Cologne 17–21 August 2009,* edited by Matthias Brenzinger & Anne-Marie Fehn. Cologne: Rüdiger Köppe, 2012: pp. 155–168.

Laca, Brenda. *bib/*"Progressives, Pluractionals and the Domains of Aspect." In *Domaines, Journées d'Études linguistiques.* Nantes: Université de Nantes, 2004: pp. 87–92.

Mufwene, Salikoko S. *bib/* *Stativity and the Progressive.* Bloomington: Indiana University Linguistics Club, 1984.

Nevins, Andrew, David Pesetsky & Cilene Rodrigues. *bib/*"Pirahã Exceptionality: A Reassessment." *Language* 85, no. 2 (2009): pp. 355–404.

Newman, Paul. *bib/*"Pluractional Verbs: An Overview." In *Verbal Plurality and Distributivity,* edited by Patricia Cabredo Hofherr and Brenda Laca. Berlin: de Gruyter, 2012: pp. 185–209.

Norton, Russell. *bib/*"Classifying the Non-Eastern-Sudanic Nuba Mountain Languages: Evidence from Pronoun Categories and Lexicostatistics." In *Nuba Mountain Language Studies: New Insights,* edited by Gertrud Schneider-Blum, Birgit Hellwig and Gerrit Dimmendaal. Cologne: Rüdiger Köppe, 2019: pp. 417–446.

Norton, Russell. "Number in Ama Verbs." *Occasional Papers in the Study of Sudanese Languages* 10 (2012): 75–94.

Norton, Russell. "The Ama Dual Suffix: An Internal Reconstruction." In *Nilo-Saharan: Models and Descriptions,* edited by Angelika Mietzner & Anne Storch. Cologne: Rüdiger Köppe, 2015: pp. 113–122.

Rilly, Claude. *Le méroïtique et sa famille linguistique.* Leuven: Peeters, 2010.

Rottland, Franz & Angelika Jakobi. "Loan Word Evidence from the Nuba Mountains: Kordofan Nubian and the Nyimang Group." *Afrikanistische Arbeitspapiere,* Sondernummer (1991): pp. 249–269.

Smits, Heleen. *A Grammar of Lumun: A Kordofanian Language of Sudan, Vol. 2* Utrecht: LOT, 2017.

Stevenson, Roland C. "A Survey of the Phonetics and Grammatical Structures of the Nuba Mountain Languages, with Particular Reference to Otoro, Katcha and Nyimaŋ." *Afrika und Übersee* 40 (1956): pp. 73–84, 93–115.

Stevenson, Roland C. "A Survey of the Phonetics and Grammatical Structures of the Nuba Mountain Languages, with Particular Reference to Otoro, Katcha and Nyimaŋ." *Afrika und Übersee* 41 (1957): pp. 27–65, 117–152, 171–196.

Stevenson, Roland. *Grammar of the Nyimang Language (Nuba Mountains).* Unpublished typescript, 1938.

Stevenson, Roland, Franz Rottland & Angelika Jakobi. "The Verb in Nyimang and Dinik." *Afrikanistiche Arbeitspapiere* 32 (1992): pp. 5–64.

Stirtz, Timothy. *A Grammar of Gaahmg: A Nilo-Saharan Language of Sudan.* Utrecht: LOT, 2011.

Trudgill, Peter. *Sociolinguistic Typology: Social Determinants of Linguistic Complexity.* Oxford: Oxford University Press, 2011.

Voogt, Alex de. "A Sketch of Afitti Phonology." *Studies in African Linguistics* 38, no. 1 (2009): pp. 35–52.

Voogt, Alex de. *bib/*"Dual Marking and Kinship Terms in Afitti." *Studies in Language* 35, no. 4 (2011): pp. 898–911. DOI: *www/*10.1075/sl.35.4.04dev.

Waag, Christine. *bib/The Fur Verb and Its Context.* Cologne: Rüdiger Köppe, 2010.

Welmers, William E. *bib/African Language Structures.* Berkeley: University of California Press, 1973.

Werner, Roland. *bib/Tìdn-áal: A Study of Midob (Darfur Nubian).* Berlin: Dietrich Reimer, 1993.

Wolff, Ekkehard. *bib/*"Patterns in Chadic (and Afroasiatic?) Verb Base Formations." In *Papers in Chadic Linguistics,* edited by Paul Newman & Roxana Ma Newman. Leiden: Afrika-Studiecentrum, 1977: pp. 199–233.

Endnotes

1. Stevenson, *Grammar of the Nyimang Language* and "A survey of the phonetics and grammatical structure of the Nuba Mountain languages with particular reference to Otoro, Katcha and Nyimaŋ," 40: p. 107. ↩

2. Rilly, *Le méroïtique et sa famille linguistique,* §4. ↩

3. De Voogt, "A Sketch of Afitti Phonology," p. 47. ↩

4. Heine & Voßen, "Sprachtypologie," cited in Kröger, "Typology Put to Practical Use," p. 159. ↩

5. Norton, "Number in Ama verbs," pp. 75–76, 85; Stevenson, "A Survey of the Phonetics and Grammatical Structure of the Nuba Mountain Languages," 41: pp. 175–176. ↩

6. Stevenson, *Grammar of the Nyimang Language,* §§2–10. ↩

7. Dimmendaal, "Africa's Verb-final Languages," §9.2.3. ↩

8. Dimmendaal, "Introduction" to *Coding Participant Marking,* pp. 6–7. ↩

9. Stevenson, "A Survey of the Phonetics and Grammatical Structure of the Nuba Mountain Languages," 41: p. 174. ↩

10. Waag, *The Fur Verb and Its Context*, p. 49; low tone is unmarked in the Fur two-tone system. ↩

11. Jakobi, *Kordofan Nubian*, p. 159. Her data from Kordofan Nubian varieties shows high tone. ↩

12. Stevenson, *Grammar of the Nyimang Language*, p. 178, shows cleft constructions with a similar core+adjoined structure, *wadang nɔ a nɛ* [*a meo tolun*] "This is the man [I saw yesterday]." ↩

13. Stevenson, *Grammar of the Nyimang Language*, p. 176, claims that "GAI gives the idea of completion, going on till an act is finished," although all his examples involve a plural subject "they." His claim suggests that this quantifier may have a collective function, over all participants and/or over all the stages in the completion of the event. It can nevertheless appear in the same clause as distributive marking *-íd̪*, as in an example shown in Norton, "Number in Ama verbs," p. 83, *wùd̪ēŋ bā dɔ̄rɛ̄ŋ t̪ɛ̀l-íd̪-ɛ̄ gàì* "the child saw each of the children [until she had seen them all]." ↩

14. Stevenson, "A Survey of the Phonetics and Grammatical Structure of the Nuba Mountain Languages," 41: p. 177. ↩

15. Welmers, *African Language Structures*, pp. 346, 348. ↩

16. Compare Mufwene, "Stativity and the Progressive," where it is argued that progressive is a stativizing category in a number of European and Bantu languages, although progressive verb forms typically have a more transient interpretation, and lexical statives a more permanent interpretation. ↩

17. Stirtz, *A Grammar of Gaahmg*, p. 40. ↩

18. Rilly, *Le méroïtique et sa famille linguistique*, annex. ↩

19. Stevenson, Rottland & Jakobi, "The Verb in Nyimang and Dinik," p. 16. By convention, *t* is dental and mid tone is left unmarked in their data. Pertinent to the present alternation, I question the phonemic status of the *w* in *t/kw* alternations before rounded vowels. ↩

20. Greenberg, *The Languages of Africa*, pp. 115, 132; Bryan, "The T/K Languages"; Gilley, "Katcha Noun Morphology," §2.5, §3, §4; *article/*Blench, this issue. ↩

21. Rilly, *Le méroïtique et sa famille linguistique,* p. 299. ↩

22. Frajzyngier, "The Plural in Chadic"; Wolff, "Patterns in Chadic (and Afroasiatic?) Verb Base Formations." ↩

23. Newman, "Pluractional Verbs" notes a separate affinity between pluractional and habitual aspect found in Niger-Congo and Chadic languages. Smits, *A Grammar of Lumun, Vol. 2,* §13, identifies habitual pluractionals in a Niger-Congo language of the Nuba Mountains. ↩

24. Hyman & Udoh, "Progressive Formation in Leggbo." ↩

25. Laca, "Progressives, Pluractionals and the Domains of Aspect." ↩

26. See, however, §4.2 below which purports to recover the missing extension. ↩

27. Rilly, *Le méroïtique et sa famille linguistique,* p. 478. ↩

28. Ibid; Old Nubian also attests the lateral in a hapax form ⲕⲁⲗ-. ↩

29. Everett, "Cultural Constraints on Grammar and Cognition in Pirahã." ↩

30. Nevins, Pesetsky & Rodrigues, "Pirahã Exceptionality"; Everett, "Pirahã Culture and Grammar." ↩

31. Stevenson, *Grammar of the Nyimang Language,* §XI; Stevenson, "A Survey of the Phonetics and Grammatical Structure of the Nuba Mountain Languages," 41: pp. 171–183; Stevenson, Rottland & Jakobi, "The Verb in Nyimang and Dinik"; Norton, "Number in Ama Verbs"; Norton, "The Ama Dual Suffix"; Norton, "Classifying the Non-Eastern-Sudanic Nuba Mountain Languages." ↩

32. The Tama plural copula *àg* is likewise listed with low tone in Rilly, *Le méroïtique et sa famille linguistique,* p. 451. ↩

33. Newman, "Pluractional Verbs." ↩

34. Norton, "Number in Ama Verbs," pp. 77, 83. ↩

35. I say the distributive is "largely" unaffected by the shift from pluractional to progressive because a dental plosive appears to have been co-opted in the progressive ventive suffix, as in *dìɟ-í-n-īg/dìɟ-íd̪-ēn-ɛ̀g* (throw-VEN-DU-DIR) "threw to"/"is throwing to" as the dental plosive is the only difference with the factative ventive suffix *-í*. ↩

36. Norton, "Number in Ama Verbs," p. 81. ↩

37. De Voogt, "Dual Marking and Kinship Terms in Afitti," p. 903, which also shows a similar plural object suffix *-to*. ↩

38. Stevenson, "A Survey of the Phonetics and Grammatical Structure of the Nuba Mountain Languages," 41: p. 187, where *ɨ* is used in the same way as contemporary *ɪ*. Tone was not recorded. ↩

39. Werner, *Tìdn-áal*, p. 52. ↩

40. Abdel-Hafiz, *A Reference Grammar of Kunuz Nubian*, p. 117. Tone was not recorded. ↩

41. Corbett, *Number*, p. 116. ↩

42. article/Jakobi, this issue ↩

43. Corbett, *Number*, pp. 115–116. ↩

44. Norton, "Number in Ama Verbs," pp. 78, 79, 91. ↩

45. De Voogt, "Dual Marking and Kinship Terms in Afitti," p. 903. ↩

46. I am grateful to Alex de Voogt for sharing this data in personal communication from his field research on Afitti. ↩

47. Stevenson, "A Survey of the Phonetics and Grammatical Structure of the Nuba Mountain Languages," 41: p. 187. ↩

48. Abdel-Hafiz, *A Reference Grammar of Kunuz Nubian*, p. 118. ↩

49. article/Jakobi, this issue. Jakobi points that the other very similar suffix *-íd* in Midob cannot be reconstructed to proto-Nubian from just one Nubian language, so appears to be an innovation, and her observation of its similarity to the Ama suffix clearly suggests borrowing into Midob from Ama's ancestor or another related language. Hence, the reconstructable pluractional **[i]ɟ* is more viable as the historic cognate of the Ama suffix. ↩

50. Rilly, *Le méroïtique et sa famille linguistique,* pp. 303–304. ↩

51. article/Jakobi, this issue. ↩

52. Comfort, "Verbal Number in the Uncu Language." ↩

53. Norton, "Number in Ama Verbs," p. 40. ↩

54. I defer description of tone on this affix to another time. ↩

55. Stevenson, Rottland & Jakobi, "The Verb in Nyimang and Dinik." ↩

56. This verb appears in unpublished data collected by Abi Kingston. ↩

57. Norton, "Number in Ama Verbs," §3. ↩

58. Stevenson, Rottland & Jakobi, "The Verb in Nyimang and Dinik," p. 28. ↩

59. Norton, "The Ama Dual Suffix," p. 121. ↩

60. Ibid., p. 120. ↩

61. Norton, "Number in Ama Verbs," pp. 84, 87. ↩

62. Dahl, *The Growth and Maintenance of Linguistic Complexity*; Trudgill, *Sociolinguistic Typology*. ↩

63. Maturity could also describe further properties of Ama verbs whose description is in preparation by the author, including further instances of allomorphy, fusion, polyfunctionality, and several kinds of tonal morphology. ↩

64. Norton, "Classifying the Non-Eastern-Sudanic Nuba Mountain Languages." ↩

65. Stevenson, “A Survey of the Phonetics and Grammatical Structure of the Nuba Mountain Languages,” 41: p. 175, notes the similarity of Ama’s nominal plural *ŋi* to a similar plural clitic *ŋi* [sic] in Heiban, which here might be interpreted as a pidginization effect in which the universally well-motivated category of nominal plurality was renewed in Nyima during inter-group communication after the earlier loss of number affixes. However, Stevenson is unusually in error in this passage as the Heiban form is actually *-ŋa* as he himself documented (ibid, p. 28). Subsequent lowering to a in Heiban cannot be ruled out (he notes Heiban’s relative Talodi has ε here), but it is also quite possible that *ŋi* was sourced internally, as the high front vowel is also the common element in the plural pronouns *àŋí/ɲí/ànί* 1PL/2PL/3PL). ↩

66. Rottland & Jakobi, “Loan Word Evidence from the Nuba Mountains.” ↩

67. Stevenson, Rottland & Jakobi, “The Verb in Nyimang and Dinik,” pp. 34–38. ↩

68. Stevenson, “A Survey of the Phonetics and Grammatical Structure of the Nuba Mountain Languages,” 41: p. 177. ↩

69. article/Jakobi, this issue. ↩

article/ Nubian Verb Extensions and Some Nyima Correspondences

author/ Angelika Jakobi

abstract/ *Having a historical-comparative approach this paper is concerned with the reconstruction of some Proto-Nubian derivational morphemes comprising two causatives, two applicatives, and two suffixes deriving verbal plural stems, as well as a now defunct causative prefix. When discussing applicatives in the Nile Nubian languages, it is argued that they involve converbs, i.e., dependent verbs, which in Old Nubian and Nobiin are marked by the suffix -a. This verbal suffix is considered to be distinct from the homophonous predicate marker -a which occurs as a clitic on various other hosts. The paper also points out that some of the Nubian verb extensions correspond to Nyima (mostly Ama) extensions, thus providing strong evidence of the genetic relationship between Nubian and Nyima. Perhaps the most striking evidence of Nubian–Ama relations and the coherence of the Nilo-Saharan phylum as a whole is provided by the archaic Nilo-Saharan *ɪ-. The reflexes of this prefix in Nubian and Ama, along with the archaic Nubian prefix *m-, which serves as verbal negation marker, supports Dimmendaal's hypothesis that these languages have undergone a restructuring process from originally prefixing to predominantly suffixing languages.*

keywords/ Nubian, comparative linguistics, Nyima, Northern East Sudanic

1. Introduction

Since Greenberg's classification of the African languages there is agreement that the Nubian languages belong to East Sudanic, the largest subgroup of the Nilo-Saharan phylum.[1] According to Bender, Dimmendaal, and Blench, East Sudanic (also known as Eastern Sudanic) is divided into a northern and a southern branch.[2] The northern branch comprises Nubian as well as the Taman languages of Darfur and Wadai, the Nyima languages[3] of the Nuba Mountains, and Nara on the Sudanese–Eritrean border. Rilly, in his historical-comparative study, argues that the extinct language of the Meroitic Empire is also part of the northern branch.[4] The southern branch consists of Berta, Jebel, Daju, Temeinian, Surmic, and Nilotic.[5] This subclassification is, however, disputed. Ehret and Starostin, for instance, suggest that Ama (referred to by the term Nyimang) is genetically closer to Temeinian and hence part of the southern – rather than the northern – branch of East Sudanic.[6]

In contrast to Ehret's and Starostin's subgrouping, the present paper will provide evidence of some verb extensions shared by Nyima and the Nubian languages. They demonstrate the genetic links between these languages and therefore support Bender's and Dimmendaal's classification of Nyima as a member of the northern East Sudanic subgroup. Although Ehret, in his historical-comparative study of Nilo-Saharan languages, tries to identify verb extensions, too, his claimed reconstructions lack corroborating evidence because he does not provide contrastive examples of extended and unextended verb stems.[7]

According to Rilly, the Nubian language family has two main branches, Nile Nubian, and western Nubian.[8] Nile Nubian comprises the medieval Old Nubian language as well as Nobiin (also known by the alternative names Mahas and Fadicca), Mattokki (Kunuz, Kunuzi, Kenzi), and Andaandi (Dongolese, Dongolawi). The western branch comprises the cluster of Kordofan Nubian languages spoken in the northern Nuba Mountains, as well as the Nubian languages of Darfur, Midob, and the nearly extinct Birgid (**Fig. 1**).

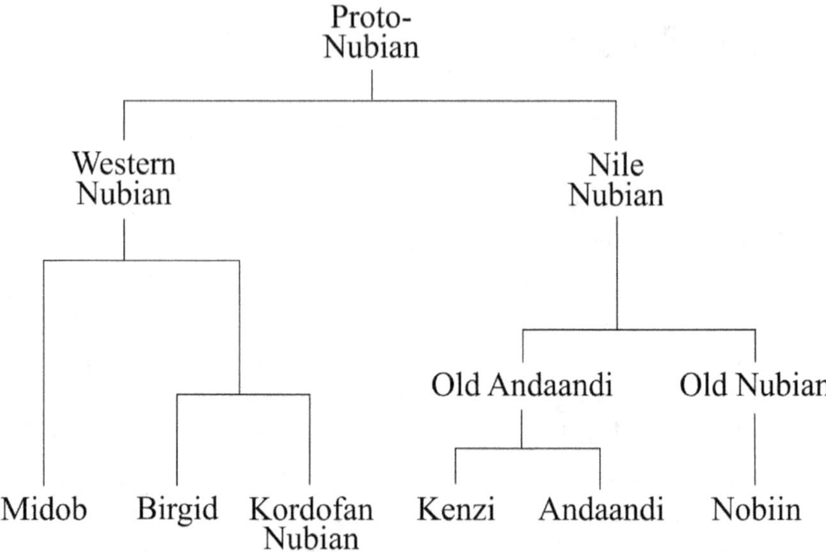

Figure 1. Family tree model of the Nubian languages[9]

Map 1 below shows the northern Nuba Mountains and the geographic distribution of the Nyima group languages, Ama, Mandal, and Afitti, and some neighboring Kordofan Nubian and non-Kordofan Nubian languages. Afitti is spoken on Jebel Dair in the northeastern Nuba Mountains. The Afitti area is adjacent to the area of Dair, a Kordofan Nubian language which occupies the southwestern part of Jebel Dair. By contrast, Ama and Mandal are spoken in the northwestern Nuba Mountains, close to the Kordofan Nubian languages Dilling, Karko, Wali, and Ghulfan.

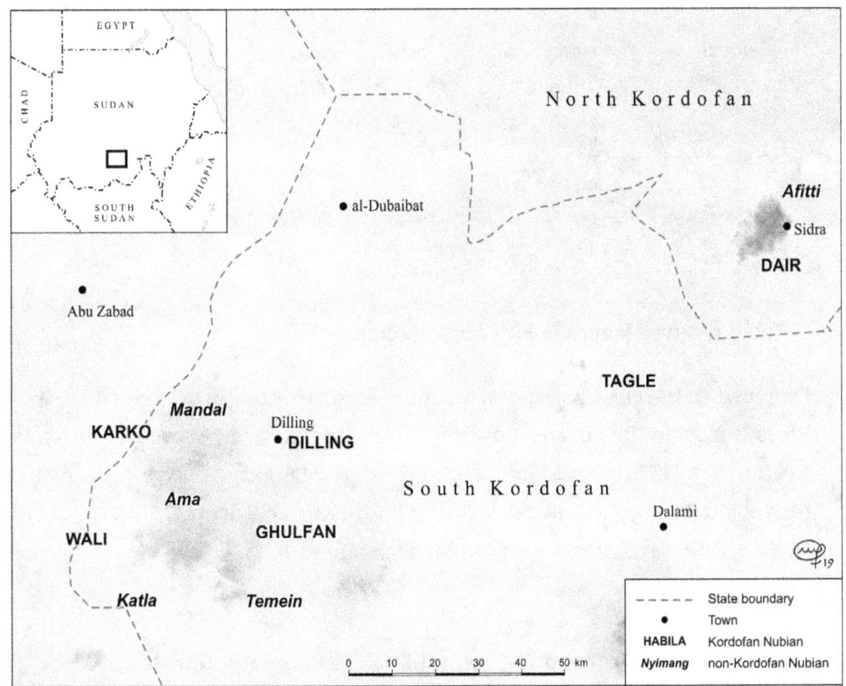

Map 1. The northern Nuba Mountains[10]

Probably due to frequent contact between speakers of Nyima and speakers of Kordofan Nubian languages, there is some lexical evidence of sound–meaning correspondences between these languages. Considering i) the close phonetic similarities between the Ama, Mandal, and Afitti items on the one hand and Kordofan Nubian items on the other; and ii) the less close resemblance between Ama, Mandal, and Afitti and the corresponding Nile Nubian (NN) items, Rottland and Jakobi have interpreted this constellation as evidence of lexical borrowing, with Kordofan Nubian as the source of the borrowings.[11] **Table 1** and **Table 2** illustrate this point: **Table 1** shows that the phonetic similarities between the Ama and Mandal items and their Proto-Kordofan Nubian (PKN) counterparts are closer than those between Ama, Mandal, and the corresponding Nile Nubian items.

Ama	Mandal	PKN	NN	Gloss
burgɔ̀l "thief"	*borgòl* "thief"	**borg-*	*maag-* (An), *mark-* (No)	steal
kwɔrʃè, kɔrʃè	*kwarʃè*	**korʃu*	*gorij* (An), *gorjo* (No)	six
tāʝò	*tāʝ*	**tɛʝ(ʝ)ɛ*	*dessi* (An, No)	green, unripe

Table 1. Ama – Mandal – PKN correspondences[12]

Examples of the close sound and meaning correspondences between Afitti and Proto-Kordofan Nubian are shown in **Table 2.** Even though a specific Kordofan Nubian variety cannot be identified as the donor language, the obvious phonetic resemblances suggest that the lexical items in Afitti originate from a Kordofan Nubian, rather than from a Nile Nubian language.

Afitti	PKN	NN	Gloss
tɔ̀rɛ	**toaɽa*	*norɛ* (An), *noree* (No)	termite
fàrsɛ·n, fàrsɛ	**farʃ-*	*barsi* (An, No)	twin
t̪ɔndɔ·	**tondo*	*dungur* (An), *dungir* (No)	blind

Table 2. Afitti–PKN correspondences

The striking Ama and Afitti similarities with the corresponding Kordofan Nubian items also indicate that borrowing into the Nyima languages has occurred rather recently, after Kordofan Nubian had split off from the other branches of the Nubian family.

However, the correspondences between the verb extensions in Nubian and Ama (**Table 3**), which are the focus of this paper, suggest a different historical interpretation, namely as evidence of their remote genetic relationship. This assumption, which will be corroborated in detail below, is based on the correspondences between the Proto-Nubian causative **u- ~ o*-prefix, which is comparable to the Ama causative *a*-prefix, and the Proto-Nubian causative suffix **-(i)gir*, corresponding to the Ama directional/causative suffix *-ɪg ~ -ɛg*. In addition, there are two pairs of phonetically and semantically very similar verb extensions, which have a limited distribution in the Nubian group. They comprise the Kordofan Nubian reciprocal *-in* vs. the Ama dual *-ɪn,* as well as Midob *-íd* vs. Ama *-íd̪*. Another set of corresponding extensions (not shown in Table 3) includes the Kordofan Nubian and Midob verbal plural *-er* as well as the Mattokki and Andaandi plural object suffix *-ir* or *-(i)r-ir* and the Ama distributional suffix *-r.*

Nubian		**Ama**	
causative prefix	PN **u- ~ o-*	causative prefix	*a-
causative	PN **-(i)g-ir*	directional, causative	*-ɪg, -ɛg*
reciprocal	KN *-in*	dual	*-ɪn*
pluractional	Mi *-íd*	distributive, pluractional	*-íd̪*

Table 3. Comparable Nubian and Ama verb extensions

Presumably, the Ama inceptive *-ɪŋ*[13] is cognate with the Nubian inchoative morphemes which comprise Old Nubian -ⲁⲅ̄,[14] Nobiin *-aŋ,*[15] Mattokki and Andaandi *-an,*[16] as well as Dilling *-ŋ.*[17] The inchoative *-an* of the Nilotic languages Bari and Lotuko is obviously related, as well.[18] As these suffixes mainly derive verbs from qualifiers and nouns, rather than from verbal bases, they are excluded from further consideration in the present paper.

Reconstructable lexical and grammatical items are indicators of a normal generational transmission.[19] They are often conceived as indicators of a continuous divergent development from the assumed proto-language to its daughter languages, the gradual divergence being depicted with a family tree model. However, such tree diagrams can account neither for diffusion or convergence between genetically related languages, nor for language contact that may have induced changes such as borrowings and other instances of interference. Evidence of contact-induced changes calls for a historical interpretation and for the identification of the donor language,[20] as illustrated by the Ama and Afitti lexical items adopted from Kordofan Nubian (**Tables 1 and 2**). Another case in point is the so-called pre-Nile Nubian substrate. It comprises several basic lexical items in Old Nubian and Nobiin which do not have cognates in the other Nubian languages. Rilly supposes that they originate from other northern East Sudanic languages.[21]

Evidence of the genetic relationship among the Nubian languages has mostly been provided by comparing lexical data.[22] In their historical-comparative studies, Zyhlarz, Bechhaus-Gerst, Jakobi, and Rilly have mainly focused on the reconstruction of Proto-Nubian lexical items and the phoneme system.[23] So far, grammatical morphemes, particularly verb extensions, have not been considered in these studies, although such bound morphemes are generally assumed to be better indicators of genetic coherence.

According to Dimmendaal, "[v]erbal derivation in the Nilo-Saharan languages commonly involves valency-changing operations such as causative, middle voice, antipassive, or pluractional and ventive marking."[24] However, the Nubian languages deviate from this pattern since dedicated markers for middle voice, antipassive, or ventive are unattested.

The present paper will show in detail that Proto-Nubian had seven verbal derivational devices: two causative suffixes (§/2.1 and §/2.2); two applicatives (§/3.3 to §/3.5); two verbal number suffixes (§/4.1 and §/4.2); and a causative prefix (§/5). The section on the applicatives (§/3) is extensive because it will show that two donative verbs can be used as independent lexical verbs and also as valency-increasing devices. I will argue that applicatives in the Nile Nubian languages are realized as converb constructions rather than as derivational suffixes, the latter being attested in the western branch of the Nubian family.

Whereas the derivational devices which are found in both branches of the Nubian language group can be reconstructed for Proto-Nubian, there are further verb extensions with a more limited distribution. The Nile Nubian languages, for instance, have passive extensions (§/6.1); Mattokki and Andaandi exhibit a plural object extension (§/6.2); and a plural stem extension is attested in Kordofan Nubian and Midob (§/6.3). A reciprocal suffix (§/6.4) as well as some plural stem extensions occur in Kordofan Nubian (§/6.5). Kordofan Nubian and Midob, meanwhile, exhibit a valency-decreasing suffix (§/6.6). Moreover, in Midob a distinct pluractional extension is found (§/6.7).

Ama, too, has a rather rich inventory of derivational extensions.[25] It has suffixes for passive, ventive, directional/causative (§/5.2); mediocausative, reciprocal, distributive (§/6.3); pluractional; and dual (§/6.4). In addition, Ama has a causative prefix (§/5.2). The range of Afitti verb extensions, however, is still little known.

The Ama data are drawn from Stevenson's survey of the Nuba Mountain languages, Tucker & Bryan's grammatical sketch of the Nyima group, which is based on Stevenson's fieldwork data, and additional work by Rottland, Jakobi, Stevenson, and Norton.[26]

The Old Nubian data mostly come from the legend of Saint Mina but also from a few other sources quoted from Van Gerven Oei's forthcoming comprehensive Old Nubian grammar.[27]

Due to their poor documentation, the nearly extinct Birgid language of Darfur and the extinct Nubian language of Jebel Haraza are not considered in the present contribution.

2. The Causative

A causative extension is a valency-increasing morphological device adding an argument with the role of causer to an intransitive or transitive clause. When the causative extension is suffixed to an intransitive verb base, it derives a transitive stem, the former intransitive subject being assigned the role of causer. When the causative suffix is attached to a transitive base, it derives a ditransitive verb. While the former transitive subject is assigned the role of causee, the former transitive object retains the role of patient. In the Nubian languages, the causative extension on a transitive verb base allows two object arguments, as shown in (7), (46), and (50).

2.1. The Causative *-(i)r-Extension

The *-*(i)r*-extension has reflexes in all Nubian languages considered in this study. However, there is ample evidence that, due to semantic bleaching, the assumed original causative function has faded away, so that reflexes of the *-*(i)r*-extension have become redundant or lexicalized features of many verbs. In the Kordofan Nubian languages, by contrast, the *-*(i)r*-extension has gained new functions, as it serves as intransitivizer and even as singular stem marker.

The initial segment of the *-*(i)r*-extension is an epenthetic vowel, which is required to prevent unadmitted consonant sequences when *-*(i)r* is attached to a consonant-final root.

PN	ON	No	Ma	An	Dil	Ta	Ka	Mi
*-(i)r	-(ⲁ)ⲣ, -ⲣ̄, -(ⲟⲩ)ⲣ	*-ir*	*-ir, -ur*	*-ir, -ur*	*-ir*	*-ir*	*-(V)r*	*-(i)r*

Table 4. The causative extension *-(i)r*

The Old Nubian *-(i)r*-extension has two variants, *-ar* and *-ur*, which are often conditioned by anticipatory assimilation to the quality of the preceding vowel(s) of the root. The extension can attach to nouns and verbs. In combination with a noun the extension derives transitive verbs.[28]

Old Nubian	Nouns		Verbs	
(1)	ⲟⲩⲗⲅ	"ear"	ⲟⲩⲗⲅ-ⲣ̄	"listen"
(2)	ⲕⲓⲧⲧ	"garment"	ⲕⲓⲧ-ⲣ̄	"clothe"
(3)	ⲥⲟⲩⲙⲡⲟⲩⲧ	"foundation"	ⲥⲟⲩⲙⲡⲟⲩⲧ-ⲣ̄	"found"

Although Van Gerven Oei conceives *-(i)r* as a "transitive" suffix which is used "to make an intransitive verb transitive,"[29] *-(i)r* can be shown to add an argument with the role of causer to the base verb. Moreover, it is not restricted to intransitive verbs but also found on transitive bases such as ⲟⲟⲕ and ⲕⲟⲩⲗⲗ deriving ditransitive stems. For this reason, *-(i)r* behaves like a typical causative extension and should be referred to by the term causative.

(4)	ⲡⲁⲗ	"come out" ITR	ⲡⲉⲗ-ⲣ̄	"release" TR
(5)	ⲟⲟⲕ	"call" TR	ⲟⲟⲕ-ⲣ̄	"cause to call" DITR, "have called"
(6)	ⲕⲟⲩⲗⲗ	"learn" TR	ⲕⲟⲩⲗⲗ-ⲣ̄	"teach" DITR

The ditransitive construction derived by the causative *-(i)r*-extension on the verb ⲕⲟⲩⲗⲗ "learn" can be illustrated by the following example. Assigning the role of causer to the addressee of the request, the causative of the transitive verb allows two accusative-marked arguments, the first being assigned the role of causee and the second the role of patient.[30]

(7) ⲁⲓ̈ⲕⲟⲛⲱ ϣⲟⲕⲕⲁ ⲕⲟⲩⲗⲗⲓⲣⲉⲥⲟ
ai-k-onō *šok-ka*
1SG-ACC-REFL book-ACC
koull-ir-e-so
learn-CAUS-IMP.2/3SG.PRED-COMM
"Teach me the book" (gr 2.4)

Browne points out that the "causative element may be weakened and become apparently redundant,"[31] that is, some verbs can occur with or without the *-(i)r-* suffix without a change in their meaning.

The Nobiin *-(i)r*-extension can derive transitive and ditransitive stems when it attaches to intransitive and transitive bases, respectively.[32]

	Nobiin			
(8)	*karj-e*	"ripen" ITR	*karj-ir-e*	"cook" TR
(9)	*naaf-e*	"be hidden" ITR	*naaf-ir-e*	"hide" TR
(10)	*jad-e*	"suck" TR	*jad-ir-e*	"suckle" DITR

Werner does not comment on Lepsius's data, nor does he provide evidence in his Nobiin grammar of such derived transitive and ditransitive verbs. However, his verb paradigms indicate that – unlike transitive verbs – intransitive verbs never take the *-(i)r*-extension in their unmarked 2SG imperative forms.[33] The absence of *-(i)r* is, no doubt, due to the original restriction of *-(i)r* to transitive and ditransitive verbs.

(11)	*nèer*	"sleep!"
(12)	*àag*	"sit!"
(13)	*kîr*	"come!"
(14)	*júù*	"go!"
(15)	*fîyy*	"lie (down)!"

2SG imperative forms of transitive verbs, by contrast, can be assigned to two groups, a group characterized by the *-(i)r*-extension and another group which does not exhibit this extension.

(16)	*tìg-ìr*	"cover!"
(17)	*fáay-ìr*	"kill!"
(18)	*úkk-îr*	"listen!"
(19)	*dèg-îr*	"tie!"
(20)	*kàb*	"eat!"
(21)	*dòllì*	"love!"
(22)	*nàl*	"see!"
(23)	*êd*	"take!"

Apparently, having ceased to be a productive derivational morpheme, Nobiin -*(i)r* has become a morphological residue of the originally causative *-*(i)r*-extension. This process in which "a morpheme loses its grammatical-semantic contribution to a word but retains some remnant of its original form and thus becomes an indistinguishable part of a word's phonological construction" can be described by Hopper's term "demorphologization."[34]

Unlike the Old Nubian and Nobiin -*(i)r*-extension, which can be attached to intransitive and transitive bases, the cognate Mattokki -*(i)r* is restricted to intransitive verb bases from which it derives transitive stems.[35] The allomorph -*ur* of -*(i)r* is conditioned by lag assimilation triggered by the root vowel.

	Mattokki			
(24)	*arub*	"be folded up" ITR	*arb-ir*	"fold up" TR
(25)	*urub*	"have a hole" ITR	*urb-ur*	"make a hole" TR
(26)	*tag*	"be covered" ITR	*tag-ir*	"cover, protect" TR

Abdel-Hafiz claims that Mattokki -*(i)r* is a "transitivizing suffix."[36] However, he overlooks the fact that it also occurs on some intransitive verbs such as "move down" and "fall,"[37] without, however, turning them into transitive verbs. These examples suggest that the functional weight of the -*(i)r*-extension is low.

(27)	*dig-ir*	"fall"
(28)	*ʃug-ur*	"move down, descend"

It is conceivable that the loss of morphological meaning observed with *-(i)r* has triggered the emergence of a reduplicated causative extension which exhibits more phonological material and more functional weight than *-(i)r.* The resulting (unattested) *-ir-ir-*suffix has presumbably undergone a phonotactic change affecting the second component of this suffix. After the metathesis of the last two segments, the resulting suffix *-ir-ri* (allomorph *-ur-ri*) has come to be realized as [iddi] or [uddi]. Massenbach accounts for this reduplicated causative suffix in her Mattokki study (29)–(30), but in Abdel-Hafiz's grammar it is not mentioned.[38]

(29) *essi* *aa-was-in*
water PROG-boil-NEUT.3SG
"the water is boiling"

(30) *essi=gi* *was-iddi*
water=ACC boil-CAUS
"boil the water!"

As in Mattokki, Andaandi *-(i)r* ~ *-(u)r* is attached to intransitive verb bases deriving transitive stems. Both the simple *-(i)r* ~ *-(u)r* and the reduplicated extension *-iddi* ~ *-uddi* are attested on these bases.[39]

	Andaandi			
(31)	*kuɲ*	"sink, get buried" ITR	*kuɲ-ur*	"bury" TR
(32)	*aag*	"squat, sit" ITR	*ag-iddi*	"cause to sit, seat" TR
(33)	*dab*	"disappear" ITR	*dab-ir*	"cause to disappear" TR

(34) *tɛn* *dungi* *dab-os-ko-n*
3SG.GEN money disappear-PFV-PT-3SG
"his/her money has disappeared"

(35) *tokkon* *dungi=gi* *dab-ir-men*
PROH money=ACC disappear-CAUS-NEG
"don't lose the money"

Regarding the *-iddi* ~ *-uddi*-extension, Armbruster claims that it is composed of *-(i)r* plus *-d(i),* the latter allegedly having a causative or intensive function.[40] However, it is difficult to corroborate his assertion, since *-d(i)* is only found after consonants where [d] may originate from [r] assimilated to a preceding consonant. Moreover, the *-(i)r*-extension may trigger the same morphophonemic changes when it is followed by *-r-i* marking the neutral[41] 1SG form. Also this morpheme sequence is realized as [iddi], e.g., *boog-ir-ri* is realized as [boogiddi] "I pour."[42] This evidence supports the analysis of the causative *-iddi*-extension as originating from *-ir-ir* → *-ir-ri* → *-iddi,* that is, as a sequence of two *-(i)r*-morphemes. Here are two Andaandi examples attesting the causative *-iddi* ~ *-uddi*-extension.

(36)	*ʃug-ur*	"move down, descend"	*ʃug-uddi*	"cause to descend"
(37)	*bowwi*	"bathe"	*boww-iddi*	"cause to bathe"

In Kordofan Nubian, the *-(i)r*-extension has gained and lost functions. In Dilling, for instance, the *-(i)r*-suffix has – apart from its causative function – adopted the function of an intransitivizer, thus both changing the valency of a verb from intransitive to transitive and, vice versa, from transitive to intransitive.[43]

	Dilling			
(38)	*dwaj*	"spoil something" TR	*dwej-ir*	"spoil" ITR
(39)	*kuj*	"hang" ITR	*kuj-ir*	"hang up" TR, OJ SG

Some transitive and intransitive verbs are always extended by the *-(i)r*-extension, thus suggesting that it has lost its valency-changing function. Noticing this loss, Kauczor refers to this extension by the German term "Stammverstärkung" – literally, "strengthening of the stem."[44]

The corresponding Tagle extension is realized as [ir] after [+ATR] root vowel(s), and as [ɪr] after [–ATR] vowels. It appears to have lost its valency-changing function, too. This is indicated by two facts. First, on some intransitive verbs, *-(i)r* ~ *-(ɪ)r* may or may not be present, as shown by the following verbs in 2SG imperative form (marked by the final *-i* ~ *-ɪ*).[45]

	Tagle	
(40)	*ʃɔ̀k-ɪ̀ ~ ʃɔ̀k-ɪ̀r-ɪ̀*	"rise!"
(41)	*dùʃ-ɪ̀ ~ dùʃ-ɪ̀r-ɪ̀*	"come out (of the ground)!"
(42)	*ɛ̀ʃ-ɪ̀ ~ ɛ̀ʃ-ɪ́r-ɪ̀*	"wake up!"

Second, Tagle *-(i)r* ~ *-(ɪ)r* is attested on some transitive verbs, but not as a causative suffix. Rather, it appears to have gained a new function in interacting with singular objects. Because of this function it contrasts with the *-er* ~ *-ɛr*-extension, which is sensitive to plural objects (see §6.3).

(43)	*ūlt-ír-ɪ̀*	"breastfeed!" OJ SG	*ūlt-ér-ɪ̀*	id. OJ PL
(44)	*ùj-ír-ɪ̀*	"put down, lay down!" OJ SG	*ùj-èr-í*	id. OJ PL

This contrast of *-(i)r* ~ *-(ɪ)r* versus *-er* ~ *-ɛr* is attested by a few Tagle verbs only. It is more common in combination with *-ig*, forming the valency-increasing extensions *-ɪg-ɪr* ~ *-ɪg-ɛr*, as shown in §2.2.

The Karko reflex of the causative *-*(i)r*-extension has an unspecified vowel *V* which adopts the quality of the root vowel, as is common in Karko suffixes having a short vowel. The causative extension can therefore be represented as *-(V)r*. It has the same segmental structure as the plural stem extension *-(V)r* discussed in §6.3 which precedes the causative suffix. In the following examples the object noun phrase *ɕə̄kə̄l* "gazelle" has the role of patient, occurring in singular form. Because of the generic reading of *ɕə̄kə̄l*, the verb requires to be realized by a plural stem.

(45) **Karko**

ɕə̄kə̄l=ə́g *fɛ̄t̪-ɛ́r*

gazelle=ACC hunt-PLR

"hunt gazelle!"

(46) *gō* *ṭǒnḍ=òg* *ɕə̄kə̄l=ə́g* *fɛ̄ṭ-r-ɛ́r*
this boy=ACC gazelle=ACC hunt-PLR-CAUS
"make this boy hunt for gazelle!"

The causative *-*(i)r* is reflected by the Midob -*(i)r*-extension. Werner provides two paired examples of -*(i)r* deriving transitive from intransitive examples.[46]

	Midob			
(47)	*tìmm-íhàm*	"we gathered" ITR	*tìmm-ír-hàm*	"we gathered" TR
(48)	*pècc-ìhêm*	"I got up" ITR	*pècc-ír-hèm*	"I woke (somebody) up" TR

In addition to deriving transitive from intransitive verbs, Midob -*(i)r* can derive ditransitive from transitive verbs. The extension -*(i)r* adds an additional argument with the role of causer and assigns the role of causee to the previous transitive subject. The patient role of the previous transitive object remains unchanged in the derived ditransitive clause. Note that the object arguments in the following two examples do not require to be overtly accusative-marked.[47] This observation confirms Werner, who points out that syntactic objects in Midob are commonly unmarked for case.[48]

(49) **Midob**
on *taa* *pacc-ihum*
3SG road deviate-PRF.3SG
"s/he deviated from the road"

(50) *on* *naa* *taa* *pacc-ir-hum*
3SG 3SG.ACC road deviate-CAUS-PRF.3SG
"s/he made him deviate from the road"

In terms of its valency-increasing function, Midob -*(i)r* is comparable to the extension -*ée-k* ~ -*èe-k* (§2.2).

2.2. The Causative *-(i)gir-Extension

As suggested by the voiced or voiceless velar stop, [g] or [k] and the close phonological similarity among the causative morphemes displayed in **Table 5**, all Nubian languages considered in this paper have retained a reflex of the causative extension *-(i)gir*. Presumably this extension originated from the lexical verb *kir* "make" which, due to grammaticalization, emerged as a valency-increasing auxiliary-like verb in a converb construction (attested in Nobiin), and finally as a causative derivational suffix on verbs. In the Kordofan Nubian languages and Midob *-(i)gir* is re-analyzed as a complex morpheme. In Dilling and Tagle it has split up into two extensions which are sensitive to a singular and a plural object, respectively.

PN	ON	No	Ma	An
*-(i)gir	-ⲅ(ⲁ)ⲣ	*-kir, -in-kir*	*-igir, -gid-di*	*-(i)gir, -(i)n-gir*

Dil	Ta	Ka	Mi
-iir < *-eg-ir* OJ.SG, *-eer* < *-ig-er* OJ.PL	*-ɪg-ɪr* OJ.SG, *-ɪg-ɛr* OJ.PL	*-ɛɛr* < *-ɛg-ɪr*	*-ée-k, -èe-k*

Table 5. The causative extension *-(i)gir*

Old Nubian -ⲅ(ⲁ)ⲣ – alternatively spelled as -ⲅⲉⲣ -ⲅⲣ̄, -ⲓⲅⲣ̄, -ⲕⲁⲣ, and -ⲕⲣ̄ – can be attached to nominals and verbs. According to Van Gerven Oei, the Old Nubian causative -ⲅ(ⲁ)ⲣ developed from an auxiliary verb, which later turned into a derivational suffix.[49]

The following examples from Browne's dictionary show that it derives transitive verb stems from an intransitive base, and ditransitive stems from a transitive base.[50]

	Old Nubian			
(51)	οκ, ωκ, οг	"stand, be (over)" ITR	οκ-κⲁρ, οκ-κρ̄	"place over, attend" TR
(52)	πλ̄λ	"shine" ITR	πλ̄λ-ιгρ̄	"reveal, illumine" TR
(53)	ιϭ, εϭ	"send, impel" TR	ιϭ-гρ̄	"cause to send" DITR

Browne points out that -(ⲁ)ρ (§2.1) and -г-(ⲁ)ρ may occasionally interchange.[51] This finding supports my claim that they have the same function.

(54)	τμ̄μ-ⲁρ ~ τμ̄μ-ιгⲁρ	"assemble"

In Nobiin, particularly in the Fadicca dialect, *kir* "make" is still used as an independent verb, as Reinisch points out.[52] In addition, *kir* has undergone a grammaticalization process which has resulted in a causative construction comprising an uninflected lexical verb marked by the converb suffix *-a* followed by *kir* serving as an auxiliary (for converb constructions see §3.2). This biverbal causative construction is very similar to the applicative construction in the Nile Nubian languages. The following examples are drawn from Reinisch.[53]

	Nobiin			
(55)	*kab*	"eat"	*kab-a kir*	"feed"
(56)	*junti*	"pregnant"	*junt-a kir*	"impregnate"

In the Nobiin variety documented by Werner, however, *kìr* is no longer part of a biverbal converb construction but rather a derivational suffix of the lexical verb root.[54] The suffix *-kèer* results from *-kir-ir,* i.e., the fusion of the causative suffix *-kir* with the 1SG present tense[55] suffix *-ir.*

(57) *ày* *tàk=kà* *kàb-kèer*
1SG 3SG=ACC eat-CAUS.IND.PRS.1SG
"I feed him," lit. "I make him eat"

In addition to *-kìr,* Nobiin exhibits the complex causative extension *-in-kir.* The etymological origin of the component *-in* is debatable. Is it the linker *-(i)n-*, as

Werner first assumed,[56] or a cognate of the Old Nubian copula verb ⲉⲓⲛ (*in*), as he has recently proposed? Werner renders *-in-kir* as "let be" or "let happen" which fits well the semantic association of *-in-kir* with permission.[57] By contrast, *-kìr* connotes with causation. This semantic distinction is confirmed by the Nobiin mother tongue speaker Isaameddiin Hasan.[58]

The inflectional suffix *-kiss* is due to anticipatory assimilation of the final consonant of *-kir* to the preterite suffix *-s.*

(58) *ày* *tàk=kà* *nàl-ìnkìss*
1SG 3SG=ACC see-CAUS.IND.PT.1SG
"I caused him to see"

The Mattokki causative extensions *-(i)gir, -kir, -giddi* (< *-gir-ri* < *-gir-ir*), and *-kiddi* (< *-kir-ri* < *-kir-ir*) derive transitive stems from intransitive bases and ditransitive stems from transitive bases.

	Mattokki			
(59)	*boor*	"be destroyed"	*boor-kiddi*	"destroy"
(60)	*soll*	"hang"	*soll-igir*	"hang up"
(61)	*kuur*	"learn"	*kuur-kiddi*	"teach"

Here is a Mattokki example of *kuur* "learn" in a causative construction with two arguments, a 1SG causee and an assumed unexpressed pronominal patient.[59]

(62) *ter* *ai=g* *aa-kuur-kiddi-mun-um*
3SG 1SG=ACC PROG-learn-CAUS-NEG-IND.PT.3SG
"he did not teach [it] to me," lit. "he did not make me learn [it]"

The Andaandi causative suffix *-(i)gir* is, as Armbruster argues,[60] morphologically composed of two morphemes, accusative marker *-g* (i.e., the "objective suffix" in Armbruster's terms) and causative suffix *-ir* discussed in §/2.1.

However, the fact that the velar stop [g] appears even in the non-Nubian Ama causative suffixes *-ɪg* and *-ɛg* (see §/5.2) indicates that this stop should be identified with the causative, rather than with the accusative morpheme.

The -*(i)gir*-extension occurs on intransitive and transitive verb stems. It is also used on borrowings from Arabic, such as *jammɛ* in (65).[61] This indicates that -*(i)gir* is highly productive.

	Andaandi			
(63)	*ɛɛʃ=ɛ*[62]	"belch"	*ɛɛʃ=ɛ-gir*	"cause or allow to belch, play with food and drink"
(64)	*ulli*	"kindle"	*ull-igir*	"cause or allow to kindle"
(65)	*jamm=ɛ*	"come together, assemble"	*jamm=ɛ-gir*	"cause or allow to come together, assemble"

Besides attaching to verbal bases, Andaandi -*(i)gir* can attach to nominal bases, too. The resulting forms are transitive verb stems.

(66)	*fɛkka*	"change, small coin" (Arabic loan)	*fekka-gir*	"convert into change"
(67)	*dolli*	"deep"	*doll-igir*	"cause or allow to be or become deep, deepen"
(68)	*owwi*	"two"	*oww-igir*	"cause or allow to be or become two, double"

In addition to the *-(i)gir*-extension, Andaandi exhibits the complex causative extension *-(i)n-gir*, realized after a vowel as [ŋgir], after a consonant as [iŋgir]. It strongly resembles the Nobiin causative *-in-kir.* Armbruster proposes to parse *-ŋ-gir* into three morphemes *-n-g-ir*, comprising the 3rd person suffix *-n* of the subjunctive present tense, the accusative marker *-g*, and the causative suffix *-ir.*[63] However, this morphological analysis is not convincing, particularly when the subject of the verb is a 2nd person addressee, as seen in the prohibitive and imperative examples below. Two alternative interpretations should be considered. Is *-(i)n-* to be identified with the linker tying the causative extension *-(i)gir* to the verb root? Or, as Werner has suggested for the Nobiin causative extension *-in-kir*,[64] should we interpret *-in* as a cognate of the Old Nubian copula ϵιɴ (*in*)? In the latter case the causative *-in-gir* may be rendered by "let be, let happen." This interpretation is supported by the notion of (negated) permission which is particularly apparent in (69).[65]

> (69) *tokkon* *dab-iŋgir-men*
> PROH get.lost-CAUS-NEG
> "don't let it get lost!"

> (70) *iig=ki* *ull-iŋgir*
> fire=ACC light-CAUS
> "cause him to light the fire!"

The Kordofan Nubian language Dilling has two causative extensions, *-iir* and *-eer.* According to Kauczor, the suffix *-iir* is a contracted realization of *-ig-ir*, cf. transitive *ʃwak-iir* "raise" and intransitive *ʃwak-ir* "rise." The suffix *-eer* is either a contracted realization of *-eg-ir* or *-ig-er.* The first is attested on the derived transitive verb *kok-eer* "split," while the latter occurs on the derived transitive verb with a plural object, *duk-eer* "bend." Some transitive verbs extended by *-eer* do not have an intransitive stem. This is true for *ʃah-eer* "mend."[66]

Dilling

(71)	*ʃwak-ir*	"rise" ITR	*ʃwak-iir*	"raise"
(72)	*duk-ir*	"bow" ITR	*duk-iir*	"bend" OJ SG
			duk-eer	"bend" OJ PL
(73)	*kok-er*	"split" ITR	*kok-eer*	"split" TR
(74)			*ʃah-eer*	"mend" TR

Similar to Dilling, Tagle uses the causative extensions *-ɪg-ɪr* and *-ɪg-ɛr,* when referring to a singular and a plural object, respectively.

Tagle

(75)	*ɛ̀ʃ-ì ~ ɛ̀ʃ-ìr-ì*	"wake up" ITR, IMP 2SG
(76)	*ɛ́ʃ-íg-ír-ì*	"wake up" TR, OJ SG, IMP 2SG
(77)	*ɛ́ʃ-íg-ɛ́r-ì*	"wake up" TR, OJ PL, IMP 2SG

The causative function of Tagle *-íg-ír* and *-íg-ɛ́r* can be demonstrated by the following examples. Note that the abbreviations SG and PL are used for glossing the number of nominal elements (e.g., nouns, agreement markers on verbs), when glossing verbal number, however, the singular and plural stems are glossed by SNG and PLR.[67]

(78) *tɔ́ɔ́ ʃɔ̀k-ìr-ì*
up rise-SNG-IMP.2SG
"rise!"

(79) *ánná ɔ́r=gí tɔ́ɔ́ ʃɔ́k-íg-ír-ì*
2SG.GEN head=ACC up raise-CAUS-SNG-IMP.2SG
"raise your head!"

(80) *ùnî=n ɔ́r-ʌ́ní=gí tɔ́ɔ́*
2PL.GEN.people=GEN head-PL=ACC up
ʃɔ́k-íg-ɛ́r-ì
raise-CAUS-PLR-IMP.2SG
"raise your people's heads!"

The Karko extension *-ɛɛr* is only found on transitive verbs. It originates from *-ɛg-ɪr*, the intervocalic velar [g] is assumed to be deleted. The extension *-ɛɛr* often expresses single events, the morphologically unmarked stem, by contrast, conveys multiple events.

(81) **Karko**
gɔ̄ hɔ̄ɔ́g kák-ɛ̀ɛ́r
this wood.ACC split-CAUS.SNG
"split this [piece of] wood!"

(82) *hɔ̄r=ɔ́g kàk*
wood.PL=ACC split
"split the [pieces of] wood!"

Midob, too, has – besides the *-(i)r*-extension discussed in § 2.1 – another valency-increasing extension. With some verb bases it is realized as high tone *-éek*, with others as low tone *-èek*. Werner's examples illustrate that *-éek* ~ *-èek* derives causative from transitive verb bases.[68] The question whether it also derives transitive from intransitive bases has yet to be answered.

	Midob			
(83)	*ètt-ìhèm*	"I crossed"	*ètt-èek-ìhèm*	"I caused to cross"
(84)	*tèey-áhèm*	"I carried"	*tèey-éek-ìhêm*	"I caused to carry"
(85)	*ètt-áhèm*	"I bought" OJ PL	*ètt-éek-ìhêm*	"I sold" OJ PL

Midob *ètt* represents the plural stem of "buy," it contrasts with the singular stem *èed*.[69] As Midob nouns are not required to be marked for number,[70] the plurality of the object is solely expressed by the plural stem *ètt*. Literally, the following example can be rendered as "I made him/her buy my goats," that is, with an unexpressed pronominal causee.[71]

(86) *ǝ́j* *ǝ́ən* *tér=g* *ett-eek-ih-èm*
1SG 1SG.GEN goat=ACC buy.PLR-CAUS-PRF-1SG
"I sold my goats"

Whereas the causative extensions in the Nile Nubian and Kordofan Nubian languages obviously originate from the Proto-Nubian **-(i)gir*-extension, it is more difficult to show this for the Midob *-éek* ~ *-èek*. The presence of the voiceless velar [k] is a first indication of the etymological relationship to **-(i)gir*, since initial Proto-Nubian **g* is regularly shifted to Midob *k*, as attested by **geel-e* > *kéelé* "red"; **gorji* > *kórcí* "six"; and **goj* > *kòcc* "slaughter."[72] Furthermore, the long vowel of *-éek* ~ *-èek* is suspected to be a realization of **-(i)r*, because syllable-final **r* is often deleted in Midob. Compare **juur* > *sóo* "go, walk"; **weer* > *pèe* "someone (indefinite pronoun)"; and **kir* > *ìi* "come." The lengthening of the *ii*-vowel in the last item, which also attests the regular loss of initial **k* in Midob, is regarded to be a compensation for the lost **r*. Compensatory lengthening does not occur in *sóo* and *pèe* because they have an originally long vowel.

As a result of the preceding considerations, the Midob causative suffix *-éek* ~ *-èek* is assumed to originate from a complex morpheme composed of **-ir* and **-(i)g*, that is, from a metathesized form of **-(i)gir*. The question what motivated this morphotactic change cannot be answered presently.

3. The Applicative

The applicative – more precisely, the benefactive applicative – is a valency-increasing morphological device which adds an object argument to the basic construction. This object argument is commonly assigned the role of beneficiary (or, depending on the semantics of the lexical verb, a semantically related role such as a recipient or addressee).

Applicative constructions in the Nubian languages are based on a grammaticalized verb "give." In the Nile Nubian languages, the grammaticalization path has led to a periphrastic applicative construction, comprising a nonfinite lexical verb and a finite donative verb. In the western branch, by contrast, the grammaticalization process has gone further, because "give" has adopted the status of a derivational applicative extension. Both the

Nile Nubian and the western Nubian applicative constructions are highly productive.

Before exploring these applicative constructions in more detail, we show in §⁄3.1 that most Nubian languages have two donative verbs serving as independent lexical verbs. In §⁄3.2 we introduce the concept of "converb," as applicatives in the Nile Nubian languages can be identified as converb constructions, see §⁄3.3 and §⁄3.5.

3.1. Two Verbs for "give"

It is assumed that originally each of the Nubian languages considered in this paper had two donative verbs. Rilly reconstructed them as **tir* and **deen*.[73] Differing in their deictic component, reflexes of **tir* refer to a 2nd or 3rd person recipient, while reflexes of **deen* are associated with a 1st person recipient. That is, **tir* can be rendered as "give to other than the speaker(s)" and **deen* as "give to the speaker(s)."

This distinction is still reflected in Nile Nubian. In the languages of the western branch, however, the system is more complex because of the morphological blending of the two donative verbs. The resulting new donative verb is employed in non-imperative applicative forms (§⁄3.4). In imperative applicative forms, by contrast, at least in Karko and Dilling, the two distinct donative verbs are used (see §⁄3.5).

Table 6 shows that the Kordofan Nubian languages exhibit some unexpected reflexes of **tir* and **deen*. Tagle *tí* and Karko *tìì* and *tèn* exhibit an initial alveolar stop. The realization of the initial consonant of Dilling *tir* and *tin* is not known, because the Dilling data are drawn from Kauczor's grammar which fails to distinguish between dental and alveolar stops – although the phonemic opposition between the dental and alveolar place of articulation is a characteristic of the Kordofan Nubian languages. For this reason, we can only assume that the two donative verbs in Dilling have an initial alveolar stop *t*, just like the Karko items and the single Tagle "give" shown in **Table 6**.[74]

Proto-Nubian word-initial **t* (as, for instance, in **toor* "enter"; **tar* "he, she"; **tossi-gu* "three"[75]) is regularly reflected by a dental *t̪* in the Kordofan Nubian languages. However, **tir* "give" is unexpectedly reflected by Karko *tìì*, i.e., with an initial alveolar, rather than with the expected dental stop ṱ. On the other hand, the shift of initial **d* (as in **deen*) to the Kordofan Nubian alveolar *t* is quite regular. It is also attested in reflexes of **duŋ(-ur)* "blind"; **diji* "five"; and **dii* "die." The fact that Karko *tìì* and *tèn* both exhibit an initial alveolar stop indicates the beginning of a morphological blending of the originally distinct donative verbs. This process of simplification is already completed in Tagle *tí*, suggesting the loss of the lexical and semantic contrast originally associated with the two verbs. As Tagle *tí* can neither be shown to be a reflex of **tir* nor of **deen*, it is considered to be the unpredictable outcome of that blending and simplification process.

In **Table 6,** the lexical items which are not regarded as reflexes of Proto-Nubian **tir* are put in parentheses.

PN	ON	No	Ma	An	Dil	Ta	Ka	Mi
**tir*	ⲧⲣ, ⲧⲣ̄	*tìr*	*tir*	*tir*	*(tir)?*	*(tí)*	*(tìì)*	*tìr*
**deen*	ⲇⲉⲛ, ⲇⲓⲛ	*dèen*	*deen*	*deen*	*tin*	*(tí)*	*tèn*	*téen*

Table 6. The two verbs for "give"

The Old Nubian reflexes of **tir* and **deen* are ⲧⲣ̄ (*tir*) and ⲇⲉⲛ (*den*), also spelled as ⲇⲓⲛ (*din*). As Proto-Nubian **deen* is reflected by *deen* in Nobiin, Mattokki, and Andaandi, one would expect the ⲉ in Old Nubian ⲇⲉⲛ to represent a long vowel as well. However, as Old Nubian does not have a standardized orthography, long vowels are sometimes spelled by doubling the corresponding vowel character but often they are just written with a single vowel in the Old Nubian texts.[76]

(87) **Old Nubian**

ⲧⲁⲕⲕⲁ ⲅⲟⲕ ⲧⲛ̄ⲛⲁⲥⲱ

tak=ka *ŋok* *tin-na-sō*

3SG=ACC glory give>2/3-IMP.2/3PL.PRED-COMM

"give him glory!"

(88) ⲁⲓ̈ⲕⲁ ⳟⲟⲕⲟⲩ ⲇⲓⲛⲉⲥⲱ

ai=ka	*ŋokou*	*din-e-sō*
1SG=ACC	glory	give>1-IMP.2/3SG.PRED-COMM

"give me glory!"

(89) **Nobiin**

tak=ka	*tir*
3SG=ACC	give>2/3

"give him/her!"

(90)

ay=ga	*deen*
1SG=ACC	give>1

"give me!"

In the following Matokki example *tir* is realized as [tij], because of the anticipatory assimilation of the root-final *r* to the following palatal *j*. The unexpressed 3PL pronominal recipient "(to) them" requires the pluractional *-(i)j-* extension combined with the plural object marker *-ir* or *-(i)r-ir*.[77]

(91) **Mattokki**

ay	*duguu=gi*	*tij-j-ir-s-im*
1SG	money=ACC	give>2/3-PLACT-PLOJ-PT2-1SG

"I gave them money"

(92)

kal	*toodek=ki*	*ay=gi*	*deen*
bread	a.little.bit=ACC	1SG=ACC	give>1

"give me a little bit of bread!"

The following Andaandi clause exhibits the plural object extension *-ir* being triggered by the plural referent of the direct object (theme). In the second example the plural referent of the indirect object (recipient) requires the pluractional *-(i)j* realized as [c] combined with the plural object extensions *-(i)r-ir*. The two examples also show that the position of the pronominal recipient may vary. In the first example the recipient precedes the theme, in the second example this sequence is reversed.[78]

(93) **Andaandi**

tɛk=ki	*in-gu=gi*	*tir-ir*
3SG=ACC	this-PL=ACC	give>2/3-PLOJ

"give these (various things) to him/her!"

(94)

in=gi	*ar=gi*	*deen-c-irir*
this=ACC	1PL=ACC	give>1-PLACT-PLOJ

"give this to us!"

Dilling and Karko distinguish two donative verbs. As pointed out in the beginning of this section, Kauczor's Dilling data do not account for the phonemic contrast between *t̪* and *t*, therefore *tir* and *tin* are spelled with the same initial character. We assume, that – similar to Tagle and Karko – the initial segment in both verbs is an alveolar *t*. The final *-en* on the uninflected donative verbs can be identified as a purposive converb marker (see §3.2).[79]

(95) **Dilling**

a=g	*waltu*	*a=tir-en*
2SG=ACC	also	2SG.ACC=give>2/3-PCNV

kol-i-a
eat.SNG-IMP.2SG-Q
"shall I give it also to you so that you eat it?"

(96)

o=g	*waltu*	*o=tin-en*
1SG=ACC	also	1SG.ACC=give>1-PCNV

kol-e-a
eat.SNG-IMP.1SG-Q
"will you give it also to me so that I eat it?"

Tagle has lost the distinction between the two donative verbs, leaving a single donative verb, *tí*. In the following examples, *tí* refers to a 3rd person and a 1SG recipient. When exchanging the 1SG accusative clitic *ò* for 2SG *à*, the verb *tí* can be shown to refer to a 2nd person recipient, as well.

(97) **Tagle**
íyí=g *tí-m-ín*
milk=ACC give-PST-3
"he gave him/them milk"

(98) *íyí=g* *ò=tí-m-ín*
milk=ACC 1SG.ACC=give-PST-3
"he gave me milk"

Like Dilling but unlike Tagle, Karko exhibits two donative verbs, *tìì* (with an irregular alveolar *t* rather than the expected dental *t̪*) and *tèn,* respectively.

(99) **Karko**
gō *t̪ēē=g* *tìì*
this cow=ACC give>2/3
"give him this cow!"

(100) *íí(g)* *t̪ēē* *tèn*
1PL.INCL.ACC cow give>1
"give us a cow!"

In Midob, the original distinction between the two donative verbs is retained as well, **tir* being reflected by the low tone verb stem *tìr* "give to you/him/them" and **deen* by the high tone verb stem *téen* "give to me/us."[80] Apparently, these stems undergo some alternations in their imperative forms, *tìr* being realized as *tìd* and *téen* as *téèm.* When they refer to a plural recipient, they require the plural stem extension *-èr* ~ *-àr* (§6.3).

	Midob			
(101)	*tìd*	"give him!"	*téèm*	"give me!"
(102)	*tìr-èr*	"give them!" 2SG	*téén-àr*	"give us!"

Parallel to their continuous use as independent verbs, the two Nubian donative verbs have undergone grammaticalization associated with applicative constructions. In the course of this process they have lost their status as lexical verbs. Due to reanalysis they have gained the status of valency-increasing elements, either as derivational suffixes or as a kind of auxiliary in a biverbal converb construction.

3.2. Converb Constructions

Before embarking on a more detailed account of these applicative constructions in §/3.3, §/3.4, and §/3.5, the present rather extensive section aims at shedding more light on the properties of the nonfinite dependent verbs. Due to their restricted occurrence and specific functions, these verbs are identified as converbs. Whereas converbs in Andaandi and Mattokki are morphologically unmarked, Old Nubian and Nobiin exhibit an *-a*-suffix as converb marker. We claim that this suffix differs from the homophone "predicate marker" *-a* which is attested as a clitic in Old Nubian and Nobiin. According to Van Gerven Oei, Old Nubian *-a* can cliticize to various hosts, including i) nominal and verbal predicates in main clauses; ii) final clauses; iii) the element preceding a universal quantifier; and iv) names and kinship terms where *-a* is used as a vocative marker.[81] A remnant of the Old Nubian predicate marker is also attested in Nobiin, where it serves as a copula.[82]

Previous scholars of Nile Nubian languages used various other terms for converbs, including "participle,"[83] "adjunctive,"[84] "verbum conjunctum,"[85] "a-Form,"[86] or "predicate marker."[87] Only in Hintze's and Smagina's studies does the term converb occur,[88] apparently because these authors were acquainted with the concept of converb in Slavic, Turkish, and Mongolian studies.

Converbs are known from various verb-final languages of Eurasia and South America. However, according to Amha & Dimmendaal, converbs are also common in the Afroasiatic and Nilo-Saharan languages of northeastern Africa.[89] In these languages, converbs share at least two typological features, one semantic and one morphological. Semantically, converbs can be used for "adverbial modification of manner" and also for combining "series of events usually anterior to or simultaneous with the event expressed by the main verb."[90] Amha & Dimmendaal also assert that converbs "are morphologically distinct from main verbs as well as dependent verb forms occurring in conditional, purposive, or reason clauses." This latter claim, however, should be restricted to conditional and reason clauses because some languages – for instance Beria (Saharan),[91] Dilling and Uncu (Kordofan Nubian)[92] – have dedicated purposive converbs (cf. Dilling examples (95) and (96)). These converbs are morphologically distinct from converbs used for conjoining a series of events or for adverbial modification.

The characteristic semantic, syntactic, and morphological properties of converbs in the Nile Nubian languages are first illustrated by three Nobiin examples. The converbs in (103) express a series of events, each of the transitive converbs being preceded by its ACC-marked object argument. The converb *joog-j-a* additionally has an INS-marked adjunct *jaaw=log*. Thus, the converb(s) and the finite main verb together with their arguments and adjuncts constitute a multiclausal construction.[93]

(103) **Nobiin**

iiw=ga	*jaaw=log*	*joog-j-a*	*issee=g*
cereals=ACC	mill=INS	grind-PLACT-CNV	dough=ACC

att-oos-a	*ittir*	*tan=ga*
knead-PFV-CNV	side.dish	3SG.GEN=ACC

niff-oos-a	*aman*	*tan=ga*	*oll-ij-a*
stir-PFV-CNV	water	3SG.GEN=ACC	draw-PLACT-CNV

id=idan	*jelli=laak*	*sukk-oos-on*
man=COM	work=towards	descend-PFV-PT.3SG

"she ground the cereals with the handmill, prepared the dough, stirred her side dish, drew her water, and went down to the work with the man"

The converb in (104) indicates an event prior to the event designated by the main verb.[94]

(104)

kaj-j-a	*tal=lo*	*juu-s-an*
come.PLR-PLACT-CNV	3SG=LOC	go-PT2-3PL

"having arrived they went to him/her"

In (105) the converb expresses an event which is simultaneous with the event designated by the main verb. In this latter case the converb can be interpreted as an adverbial modifier of the main verb.[95]

(105) *mir-a* *kir-on*
run-CNV come-PT.3SG
"s/he came running"

In the Nile Nubian languages, converbs share the same subject with the main verb.[96] Whereas main verbs are fully inflected, the range of inflectional morphemes on converbs is strongly restricted: they do not take tense, negation and cross-referencing subject markers. Derivational extensions and aspect markers, by contrast, do occur on converbs, as attested by the pluractional *-(i)j* on *kaj-j-a* in (104), and the perfective markers *-ed* and *-os* ~ *-oos*[97] illustrated in (106).

Converb constructions and serial verb constructions resemble each other because in each of them the verbs combine as a single complex predicate. However, whereas serial verbs can serve as independent verbs in simple clauses (in the same form),[98] this is not possible for converbs. Moreover, serial verbs "allow no markers of syntactic dependency on their components."[99] Converbs, in contrast, usually receive a dedicated converb marker, as attested by Old Nubian -ⲁ and the cognate Nobiin *-a*-suffix. Andaandi and Mattokki, however, do not exhibit a converb marker.[100] Its absence is considered to result from loss and hence to be a secondary historical development. Except for the lack of a converb marker, Andaandi and Mattokki converbs behave like Old Nubian and Nobiin converbs.[101]

(106) **Andaandi**
shay=gi *nii-ed* *bedd-os* *imbel* *nog-ir-an*
tea=ACC drink-PFV pray-PFV get.up go-NEUT-3SG
"they drink tea, pray, get up, and leave"

When both the converb(s) and the main verb contribute equally to the semantic expression of events, as illustrated in (106), this type of complex predicate is conceived of as a symmetrical converb construction. It differs from an asymmetrical type which comprises a converb from an open class and a main verb from a closed class.[102] These asymmetrical constructions result from specific syntactic constellations in which the converb and the main verb are immediately adjacent to each other. Such contiguous converb plus main verb sequences are subject to various grammaticalization processes in which the main verbs can turn into markers of aspect/modality, direction, or even valency change.[103] The latter, i.e., the valency-changing use of asymmetrical converb constructions, is attested by the applicative constructions in the Nile Nubian languages – and even by some causative constructions, as seen in (55) and (56).

The stative aspect marker in Nobiin, for instance, is also associated with an asymmetrical converb construction (107). It results from the collocation of a lexical verb in converb form (V1) and a finite posture verb *fiyyîr* ~ *fiir* "lie" as V2. In this bipartite construction, the posture verb renders a stative reading to V1, depicting the eating as a transient state of affairs.[104]

> (107) **Nobiin**
>
> | V1 | V2 |
> |---|---|
> | *kàb-à* | *fiir* |
> | eat-CNV | STAT.1PL |
>
> "we are eating"

Similarly, in Mattokki[105] and Andaandi, a motion verb realized by an unmarked converb (V1), plus a finite posture verb *buu* "lie, rest" (V2), is used to express a transient state of motion. Due to its grammaticalization as a stative marker, V2 has lost its status as a separable main verb. The question clitic *te,* for instance, cannot be inserted between V1 and V2.[106]

> (108) **Andaandi**
>
> | | V1 | V2 |
> |---|---|---|
> | *indo* | *juu* | *bun* |
> | here | move.along | STAT.3SG |
>
> "s/he is on his way hither"

While the preceding Nobiin and Andaandi examples illustrate the grammaticalization of an asymmetric converb construction in which the main verb has turned into an aspect marker, the following examples show another type of asymmetric converb construction. It is associated with the collocation of transfer and directed motion verbs which jointly express single directed events.[107]

(109) **Nobiin**
ay ed-a kiir > *ay ed-kiir* [ekkiir] "I bring it," lit. "I take it and come"

(110) *ay ed-a juur* > *ay ed-juur* [ejjuur] "I take it along," lit. "I take it and go"

Andaandi, too, exhibits similar converb constructions expressing directed transfer events. The verbs involved in such a construction are often synonymous or nearly synonymous.[108]

	Andaandi	
(111)	*sukk undur*	"insert it!, squeeze it in!," lit. "insert it and enter it!"
(112)	*kall undur*	"push it in!," lit. "push it and enter it!"
(113)	*kall oos*	"push it out!," lit. "push it and cause it to issue!"
(114)	*toll oos*	"pull it out!," lit. "pull it and cause it to issue!"
(115)	*tolle dukki*	"pull it out!," lit. "pull it and pull it out!"
(116)	*nog ju ind etta*	"go and bring it," lit. "go and move along and take it up and bring it!"

In Mattokki, too, such transfer events are often expressed by more than one verb. When the derived transitive verb *ʃuguddi* "bring down," for instance, is preceded by the converb *uski* "bear, give birth," the resulting construction *uski ʃuguddi* expresses the single transfer event "give birth."[109] Abdel-Hafiz considers such biverbal converb constructions as compounds and consequently writes them as one word.[110]

(117) **Mattokki**

wel	*katree=r*	*ekk-undur-s-u*
dog	wall=LOC	urinate-insert-PT2-3SG

"the dog urinated on the wall"

At least in Andaandi, however, the clitic interrogative marker *te* can be inserted between the two verbs. This indicates that they are separate verbs rather than compounds.[111]

> (118) **Andaandi**
> *ekki=te* *undur-ko-n*
> urinate=Q insert-PT1-3SG
> "did he urinate on it?"

When a directed motion or transfer event is expressed by means of two verbs, of which V1 conveys the manner of movement and V2 the path or trajectory in relation to the deictic center, this construction represents a pattern typical of verb-framed languages where "manner must be expressed in some kind of subordinate element, such as a gerund or other adverbial expression," as Slobin points out.[112] In the Nile Nubian languages, the adverbial expression is represented by a converb.

Asymmetrical converb constructions can also become fixed collocations expressing a unique and often unpredictable meaning.[113] This is illustrated by the following examples, which have become inseparable biverbal compounds.[114]

> (119) *dukk-undur* "spread rumors!," lit. "pull out and enter!"
> (120) *tull-undur* "spread lies!," lit. "blow (smoke) and enter!"

Such collocations and the grammaticalization of adjacent verbs are also manifested in asymmetric serial verb constructions, as Aikhenvald points out.[115] For this reason, these features cannot be regarded as defining properties of converbs.

The syntactic, morphological, and semantic properties of converb constructions attested in the modern Nile Nubian languages are also apparent in Old Nubian whose converbs are marked by -ⲁ. The converb(s) and the main verb, along with their respective object complements and adjuncts, form multiclausal constructions which can express a series of events, as illustrated by ⲉⲛ̀ⲉ́ⲧ-ⲁ ... ⲥⲟⲩⲕⲕ-ⲁ ⲕⲓⲥⲛⲁ in (121) and by ϭ̄ⲟⲣ-ⲁ ⲕⲓ-ⲁ̄ ... ⲕⲙ̄ⲙ-ⲁ̀ ⲟ̄ⲟ̄ⲕⲣ̄ⲥⲛⲁ in (122).[116]

(121) **Old Nubian**

ⲙⲁⲛ̀ ⲉⲧ̄ⲧⲗ̄ⲗⲟⲛ ⲕⲟⲩⲙⲡⲟⲩⲕ̀ ⲉⲛ̀ⲉ̇ⲧⲁ ⲁ̄ⲙⲁⲛⲇⲟ̀ ⲥⲟⲩⲕⲕⲁ ⲕⲓⲥⲛⲁ

man	*eitt-il=lon*	*koumpou=k*	*en-et-a*
that	woman-DET=TOP	egg=ACC	take-PFV-CNV

aman=do	*soukk-a*	*kis-n-a*
water=SUB	descend-CNV	come.PT2-2/3SG-PRED

"that woman took up the egg and went down to the water" (M 3.14–4.1)

(122) ⳟⲥⲥⲟⲩ ⲙⲏⲛⲁⲉⲓⲟⲛ ⲙⲁⲛ ⲉⲧ̄ⲧⲛ̄ ⳟⲟⲅⲗⲟ ϭⲟⲣⲁ ⲕⲓⲁ̄ ϣⲁⲁⲕⲕⲁ ⲕⲙ̄ⲙⲁ̀ ⲟ̄ⲟ̄ⲕⲣ̄ⲥⲛⲁ·

ŋissou	*mēna=eion*	*man*	*eitt=in*	*ŋog=lo*
Saint	Mina=TOP	that	woman=GEN	house=LOC

jor-a	*ki-a*	*ʃaak=ka*	*kimm-a*
go-CNV	come-CNV	door=ACC	hit-CNV

ook-ir-s-n-a
call-CAUS-PT2-2/3-PRED

"And Saint Mena went to the house of that woman, knocked on the door and had her called." (M 12.13–16)

A converb can also represent an event anterior to the event designated by the main verb, as illustrated by ⲟⲩⲕⲣⲓ ⲇⲓⲉ̇ⲅⲟⲩⲗ ⳟⲟⲕ-ⲁ ϭⲟⲣⲟⲩⲁⲛⲛⲟⲛ ... ⲕⲓⲥⲛⲁ in (123).

(123) ⲟⲩⲕⲣⲓ ⲇⲓⲉ̇ⲅⲟⲩⲗ ⳟⲟⲕⲁ ϭⲟⲣⲟⲩⲁⲛⲛⲟⲛ ⲫⲓⲗⲟⲝⲉⲛⲓⲧⲏⲛ ⲅⲁⲁⲇⲇⲱ ⲕⲓⲥⲛⲁ

oukr-i	*die-gou-l*	*ŋok-a*	*jor-ou-an=non*
day-PL	be.much-PL-DET	pass-CNV	go-PT1-3PL=FOC

philoxenitē=n	*gaad=dō*	*ki-s-n-a*
Philoxenite=GEN	shore=SUPE	come-PT2-2/3SG-PRED

"And after many days had gone by, he came to the shore of Philoxenite" (M 7.15–8.2)

When the converb expresses an event simultaneous with the event expressed by the main verb, it is used like an adverb of manner modifying the main verb, as shown by ⲇⲟⲕ-ⲁ ⲕⲛ̄ in (124).

(124) ⲙⲟⲩⲣⲧⲟⲩ ⳟⲟⲩⲗⲟⲩⲕⲁ̀ ⲇⲟⲕⲁ ⲕⲛ̄

mourtou	*ŋoulou=ka*	*dok-a*	*kin*
horse	white=ACC	ride-CNV	come.PRS.2/3SG

"[... as] he came riding a white horse" (M 11.1)

Similar to the modern Nile Nubian languages, Old Nubian converbs do not take inflectional morphemes such as tense, negation, and subject markers. In fact, the variety of aspect and derivational extensions is strongly restricted. They comprise the perfective markers, -ⲉⲓⲧ ~ -ⲉⲧ as in (121) *en-et-a* and -ⲟⲥ in (125) *aul-os-ij-a*, as well as the causative, as attested on (144) *pill-igr-a*, and the pluractional *-j* on (125) *aul-os-ij-a.*[117] These suffixes immediately precede the converb marker -ⲁ. However, in comparison to the modern Nile Nubian languages where *-os ~ -oos* is frequently found with converbs – as seen in (103) and (106) – the Old Nubian perfective marker -ⲟⲥ appears to be rather rare. Moreover, it is often attested being followed by the pluractional extension *-j*. In the modern Nile Nubian languages, by contrast, the pluractional *-(i)j* precedes *-os ~ -oos*, as in (161) *gull-ij-os-s-u*. These findings show that the position of -ⲟⲥ is not yet firmly established in the Old Nubian grammatical system. They support Van Gerven Oei's hypothesis that -ⲟⲥ and -ⲉⲓⲧ ~ -ⲉⲧ are newly developed perfective markers in Old Nubian.[118]

(125) ⲥ̄ⲧⲁⲩⲣⲟⲥⲟⲩ ⳟⲟⲕⲕⲟⲛⲁ ⲧⲱⲉⲕ ⲧⲉⲕⲕⲁ ⲁⲩⲗⲟⲥⲓⳝ[ⲁ̄]·
ⳟⲁⲗⲓ̈ⳝⲟⲩⲁⲇⲇⲛ[ⲁ]ⲉⲛⲕⲱ

istaurosou	*ŋok-ko=na*	*tōek-Ø*	*tek=ka*
cross	glory-ADJ=GEN	power-NOM	3PL=ACC

aul-os-ij-a
save-PFV-PLACT-CNV
ŋal-ijou-ad-d-n-a-enkō
save-PLACT-INTEN-PRS-2/3SG-PRED-but
"but (the) power of the glorious cross will save and rescue them" (St 15.1–9)

Asymmetric converb constructions in Old Nubian often involve two contiguous motion or transfer verbs. These collocations serve to express single directed events, as shown by (121) ⲥⲟⲩⲕⲕⲁ ⲕⲓⲥⲛⲁ "descend" plus "come," i.e., "go down to" or (122) ⳝⲟⲣⲁ ⲕⲓⲁ̄ "go" plus "come," i.e., "go to." Collocations of two nearly synonymous verbs can even turn into compound verb stems in which the converb marker is deleted.[119]

(126) ⲕⲉⲛ-ⲇⲟⲩⲕⲕ "present an offering" ← ⲕⲉⲛ "place" + ⲇⲟⲩⲕⲕ "worship" (M 6.5)

(127) ⲕⲉⲛ-ⲟⲩⲧⲟⲩⲣ "deposit" ← ⲕⲉⲛ "place" + ⲟⲩⲧⲟⲩⲣ "lay" (M 6.15)

Now, after having described the morphological, syntactic, and semantic properties of Nile Nubian converb constructions and after identifying the Old Nubian verbal suffix -ⲁ and its cognate, Nobiin *-a,* as dedicated converb markers, we will finally turn towards the applicative in the Nile Nubian and western Nubian languages.

3.3. The Applicative Based on **tir*

While Nile Nubian languages and Midob employ reflexes of **tir* in their applicative constructions, the Kordofan Nubian languages employ a new donative verb. As this verb is not a regular reflex of **tir,* it is not accounted for in this section but rather in §/3.4.

Nile Nubian applicatives are encoded by bipartite converb constructions, including a converb, which contributes to the lexical expression of the event, and an inflected donative verb as a marker of increased valence. In the western Nubian languages, however, the donative verb is a derivational extension which attaches to the stem of the lexical verb by means of the linker *-(i)n,* see Midob in **Table 7** and examples of Kordofan Nubian in §/3.4. Whereas the Midob applicative extension *-(i)n-tir* can license a 1st, 2nd, or 3rd person beneficiary, the Nile Nubian applicative based on **tir* is restricted to 2nd and 3rd person beneficiaries, thus retaining the original system.

PN	ON	No	Ma	An	Dil	Ta	Ka	Mi
**tir*	ⲧⲣ, ⲧⲣ̄	*tìr*	*tir*	*tir*	-	-	-	*-(i)n-tir*

Table 7. Applicative marker **tir*

In the bipartite Old Nubian applicative construction, the stem of the lexical verb V1 is marked for its status as dependent verb by the converb suffix -ⲁ. It is followed by V2, the finite donative verb serving as valency-increasing grammatical device.

(128) **Old Nubian**

ⲕⲟⲩⲙⲡⲟⲩⲕⲁ ⲧⲁⲛ̀ ⲉⲓⲗⲁ̀ ⲟⲩⲧⲣ̄ⲁ ⲧⲣ̄ⲥⲛⲁ

koumpou=ka	*tan*	*ei=la*	*outir-a*
egg=ACC	3SG.GEN	hand=DAT	lay-CNV

tir-s-n-a
APPL>2/3-PT2-3SG-PRED

"she placed the egg in his hand" (M 7.4–6)

Such periphrastic applicative constructions are considered to be asymmetric formations because only the converb (V1) contributes to the lexical expression of the event. The finite donative verb (V2), by contrast, provides grammatical meaning as "valence operator"[120] licensing an object argument with a beneficiary role or a semantically related role.

The following three examples illustrate an applicative construction with the utterance verb "say, tell." Because of the semantics of this verb, the applied object argument is assigned the role of addressee. When this object has a pronominal 3rd person referent as in (129), the corresponding person pronoun is not required to be overtly expressed.[121]

(129) **Nobiin**

tar	*iig-a-tir-on*
3SG	say-CNV-APPL>2/3-PT.3SG

"he told you/him/her"

(130)

talaamiidii=g	*iig-a-tij-j-on* (< *iig-a-tir-j-on*)
disciples=ACC	say-CNV-APPL>2/3-PLACT-PT.3SG

"he told his disciples"

(131) *íig-à-tèer*
say-CNV-APPL>2/3.PRS.1SG
"I tell you/him/her"

In Mattokki and Andaandi, too, the verb *tir* (with the allomorph *sir* when following *s*) has become a valency-increasing device forming applicative constructions. In (132) the pronominal object *tek=ki* has a beneficiary role, while in (133) *ek=k* has the role of addressee assigned by the utterance verb *wee* "say."

Unlike Old Nubian and Nobiin converbs, which are marked by *-a,* Mattokki and Andaandi do not have such a dedicated converb marker. Due to the lack of tone-marked data, we do not know, however, whether converbs undergo any tonal modifications.[122]

(132) **Mattokki**
tek=ki *kus-sir-sim*
3SG=ACC open-APPL>2/3-PT.1SG
"I opened [it] for him"

(133) *ai* *ek=k* *aa-wee-tir-rin*
1SG 2SG=ACC PROG-say-APPL>2/3-NEUT.1SG
"I am telling you"

Massenbach, Armbruster, Werner, and Abdel-Hafiz represent the biverbal applicative constructions as single words.[123] At least in Andaandi, however, the question clitic *te* can be inserted between the converb and the finite donative verb. This indicates that the converb and the donative verb are separable free forms. The question of whether the two verbs in the corresponding Nobiin and Mattokki applicative constructions can be separated as well has yet to be investigated.[124]

(134) **Andaandi**
kus=te *tir-kon*
open=Q APPL>2/3-PT-3
"did he open [it] for him/her?"

In Midob, the applicative construction is associated with a reflex of **tir* realized as *tir.* As in Kordofan Nubian (see §3.4) it is a bound morpheme tied to the lexical verb stem by the linker *-(i)n.* After a consonant-final lexical verb such as *əək,* the linker is realized by the allomorph *-Vn.* Apparently, due to lag assimilation, *V* adopts the quality of the stem vowel *ə.*

Although **tir* originally only referred to 3rd or 2nd person recipients/beneficiaries, as still attested in the applicative constructions of the Nile Nubian languages, this restriction does no longer hold for Midob *tir.* It can serve in applicative constructions, no matter whether the applied object has a 1st, 2nd, or 3rd person referent. Examples (135) and (136) show the directed transfer verb *əək* "send" assigning the role of recipient to a 2SG and a 1SG object pronoun.[125]

(135) **Midob**

əj	*náj=je*	*an*	*jawaab=e*
1SG	2SG=ACC	that	letter=ACC

əək-ən-tir-hem
send-LK-APPL-PRF.1SG
"I have sent that letter to you"

(136)

on	*əj=je*	*an*	*jawaab=e*
3SG	1SG=ACC	that	letter=ACC

əək-ən-tir-hum
send-LK-APPL-PRF.3SG
"s/he has sent that letter to me"

3.4. The Applicative in the Kordofan Nubian Languages

Unlike the Nile Nubian applicatives where a donative verb operates in an asymmetric converb construction, applicatives in the languages of the western branch employ a donative verb as an applicative suffix attached to the lexical verb stem by means of the linker *-(i)n.* In the introduction to §3 we have already pointed out that – except for their imperative forms – Kordofan Nubian applicative constructions exhibit a single donative verb, which is neither a regular reflex of **tir* nor of **deen.* Moreover, like *-(i)n-tir* in Midob, the applicative extension in the Kordofan Nubian languages can refer to a 1st, 2nd, or 3rd person beneficiary. This means that languages of the western branch have lost the original distinction between the two donative verbs.

Dil	**Ta**	**Ka**
-n-di < -n-ti	*-n-dì < -n-tì*	*-n-dìì < -n-tìì*

Table 8. The applicative extension in the Kordofan Nubian languages

Dilling *ti* is referred to by Kauczor as "verbum dativum."[126] When attaching to the lexical verb stem by the linker *-(i)n,* the resulting morpheme sequence is realized as *-(i)n-di.* It is assumed to originate in the innovative *t*-initial donative verb which is employed in Tagle and Karko. The utterance verb in (137) assigns the role of addressee to the unexpressed 3rd person object pronoun. In (138) the verb "hit" assigns to the 1st person object clitic the role of a "maleficiary," rather than beneficiary.[127]

(137) **Dilling**
fe-n-di-re
say-LK-APPL-PRS.1SG
"I tell him"

(138) *or=gi* *o=bod-n-di-m* [obo:num]
head=ACC 1SG.ACC=hit-LK-APPL-PST.3
"he hit me (on my) head"

In Tagle, too, the linker *-(i)n* connects the applicative extension *-tì* with the lexical verb stem. The *-tì*-extension is realized as [dì] after adopting the [+voice] feature of the nasal in *-(i)n.* Although Tagle suffixes mostly take the same ATR value as the root vowel, the applicative suffix retains the [+ATR] value of the donative verb *tì.* This suggests that the applicative extension *-n-dì* has not yet acquired the phonological properties of "regular" bound morphemes, whose vowels commonly harmonize with the root vowel. As applicative extension, Tagle *tì* has a low tone. When used as independent verb, it has a high tone, as seen in (97) and (98). Examples (139) and (140) show the applicative extension referring to a 3rd person and a 1st person beneficiary.[128]

(139) **Tagle**

t̪ɛ́nd̪ò *íd̪ó=gí* *kʌt̪ò=ò* *ʃó-n-dì-m*
girl.SG woman=ACC field=ACC weed-LK-APPL-PST.3
"the girl weeded the field for the woman"

(140) *t̪ɛ́nd̪ò* *kʌt̪ò=g* *ɔ̀=ʃó-n-dì-m*
girl.SG field=ACC 1SG.ACC=weed-LK-APPL-PST.3
"the girl weeded the field for me"

Applicative extentions may attach to an intransitive or transitive verb stem, as illustrated by the Karko verbs *ɓīj* "descend (ITR)" and *kɛɛ* "make sth. good (TR)," respectively, shown in (141)–(143). The applicative extension *-n-dìì* (*-dìì* after *l*) is a realization of *-n-tìì*. It licenses both a 3rd person, a 1st person, and a 2nd person beneficiary. The pronominal 3SG beneficiary *t̪éě* is not required to be overtly expressed. The position of the locative-marked adjunct is variable, preceding or following the verb phrase.[129]

(141) **Karko**

t̪óóɲē (*t̪éě*) *kóld* *ɓīj-īk-n-dìì*
child.DIM.PL 3SG.ACC well.LOC descend-PLR-LK-APPL
"the children go down for him into the well"

(142) *t̪óóɲē* *ɔ̀=ɓīj-īk-n-dìì* *kóld*
child.DIM.PL 1SG.ACC=descend-PLR-LK-APPL well.LOC
"the children go down for me into the well"

(143) *ɓwàr* *ɔ̀=nàà* *ûúg* *t̪ɔ́ɔ́*
existence 1SG=GEN 2PL.ACC place
kɛ̀ɛ̀-ŋgàl-dìì
make.good-TR.PST-APPL
"my existence made your life good."/ lit. "... made the place good for you" (This is said to children to remind them that they are dependent of their parents and that they have to pay them respect.)

As shown in this section, applicative constructions in the Kordofan Nubian languages use a single donative verb, which adds an object argument whose referent may be a 1st, 2nd, or 3rd person beneficiary. This simplification of the original system is also attested in Midob (§/3.3).

3.5. The Applicative Based on *deen

Reflexes of *deen* "give to 1st person" are attested in all Nile Nubian applicative constructions. However, in Kordofan Nubian, more precisely in Dilling and Karko, reflexes of **deen* are restricted to applicative imperative forms, as shown at the end of this section. Tagle, by contrast, no longer exhibits a reflex of **deen*. These are indicators of a restructuring process associated with the weakening and the final loss of the function of **deen*. Due to the lack of data, we do not know whether Midob applicative imperative forms are also affected by this process.

PN	ON	No	Ma	An
**deen*	ⲇⲉⲛ	*dèen*	*deen*	*deen*

Table 9. Nile Nubian applicative marker *deen

When Old Nubian ⲇⲉⲛ "give to 1st person" is employed as a valence operator, the resulting applicative is a bipartite construction composed of V1 – a lexical verb stem marked by the converb marker -ⲁ – plus the finite ⲇⲉⲛ as V2. The plural number of a 1st person beneficiary is reflected by the pluractional extension -ⲟ̄ (see §/4.1). Example (144) also shows that the values of the inflectional suffixes on the main verb – with -ⲉ-ⲥⲟ marking the imperative form in a command – have scope over the preceding converb, which means that it is also conceived as an imperative form, even though it does not show the corresponding inflectional suffixes.[130]

(144) **Old Nubian**
ⲙⲩⲥⲧⲏⲣⲟⲩ ⲉⲕ̄ⲕⲁ ⲉ̄ⲅⲓⲇⲣⲟⲩⲕⲁ ⲟⲩⲕⲁ ⲡⲗ̄ⲗⲓ̈ⲅⲣⲁ̄ ⲇⲉⳟϭⲉⲥⲟ
mustērou *eik=ka* *egid-r-ou=ka* *ou=ka*
mystery 2SG=ACC ask-PRS-1/2PL=ACC 1PL.EXCL=ACC
pill-igr-a *deñ-j-e-so*
shine-CAUS-CNV APPL>1-PLACT-IMP.2/3SG.PRED-COMM
"reveal to us the mystery which we ask you" (St 5.3–7)

The position of the pronominal beneficiary appears to be variable. In (144) the pronominal beneficiary ⲟⲩⲕⲁ immediately precedes the converb, whereas in Nobiin example (145) the theme precedes the converb, the pronominal beneficiary occupying clause-initial position.[131]

(145) **Nobiin**
ay=ga *an-gi* *gelabije* *uwo=ga*
1SG=ACC 1SG.GEN-uncle jellabiya two=ACC
V1 V2
jan-a *deen-on*
buy-CNV APPL>1-PT.3SG
"my uncle bought me two jellabiyas"

Most commonly, applicative constructions assign a beneficiary role to the applied object, as seen in (144) and (145). However, when interacting with an utterance verb like "say, tell," the applied object is assigned the role of addressee.[132]

(146) *ànn-ùu* *ày=g*
1SG.GEN-grandfather 1SG=ACC
íig-a-dèn-ô
tell-CNV-APPL>1-PT.3SG
"my grandfather told me"

Unlike Old Nubian and Nobiin, which employ the converb marker *-a*, the converbs in Mattokki and Andaandi are unmarked.[133]

(147) **Mattokki**

een	*kadee=g*	*sukki-deen-s-u*
woman	dress=ACC	wash-APPL>1-PT2-3

"the woman washed the dress for me"

Studies of the modern Nile Nubian languages mostly represent the periphrastic applicative constructions as a single word. This may be due to the realization of these biverbal forms as a single prosodic phrase. However, at least in Andaandi, the question clitic *te* can be inserted between the dependent verb and the finite donative verb, thus providing clear evidence of the bipartite character of the applicative constructions.[134]

(148) **Andaandi**

er	*ay=gi*	*iʃin=te*	*deen-ko-n*
2SG	1SG=ACC	send=Q	APPL>1-PT-3SG

"did you send it to me?"

As for Kordofan Nubian, only Dilling and Karko have retained reflexes of **deen*. They appear in two grammatical contexts: i) when employed as lexical transfer verbs, as shown in §3.1; and ii) when used as applicative extensions in imperative forms. Tagle, by contrast, has preserved no reflex of **deen*.

Dil	**Ta**	**Ka**
-nin < *-n-tin* IMP	–	*-nVn* < *-n-tèn* IMP

Table 10. Kordofan Nubian applicative markers in imperatives based on *deen

The Dilling applicative extension *-nin* is assumed to originate from the fusion of the linker *-(i)n* plus the regular reflex of **deen* "give to 1st person," *-tin*. In the imperative forms *-nin* stands in paradigmatic contrasts with *-(i)n-di* stemming from the linker *-(i)n* plus the irregular donative verb *ti* referring to a 3rd person beneficiary.

The directed transfer verbs *kuʃ* "take to" and *kwata* "bring" assign the role of recipient to the applied object. In (149) both the pronominal recipient and the pronominal theme are unexpressed.[135]

(149) **Dilling**
kuʃ-in-di
take.to-LK-APPL>2/3.IMP.2SG
"take it to him!"

(150) *oti* *o=kwata-n(i)n-(i)*
water 1SG.ACC=bring-APPL>1-IMP.2SG
"bring me water!"

Similar to Dilling *-nin,* Karko exhibits with *-nVn* a realization of the linker *-(i)n* fused with *tèn* "give to 1st person," the latter being a regular reflex of **deen.* The applicative extension *-nVn* contrasts with *-n-dìì* (after *b* realized as the allomorph *-m-bìì*) which originates from the linker plus the irregular donative verb *tìì* and refers to a 3rd person beneficiary.

Interestingly, in Kordofan Nubian applicative constructions the morphosyntactic behavior of the two objects differs from the behavior of the corresponding objects in the Nile Nubian languages. In the Kordofan Nubian languages, it is the number of the theme argument that triggers the selection of a singular or plural verb stem. In Karko, for instance, a singular theme selects the singular verb stem *ɓùù* (151), while a plural theme selects the plural stem *ɓùb* (152). In the Nile Nubian languages, by contrast, it is the number of the beneficiary which interacts with the verb stem, as seen in (144), where the 1st person plural beneficiary selects the *-(i)j*-marked plural verb stem.

(151) **Karko**
kèṯ=èg *ɓùù-m-bìì*
cloth.SG=ACC wash.SNG-LK-APPL>2/3
"wash the cloth for him/them!"

(152) *kèn=ég* *ɓùb-n-dìì*
cloth.PL=ACC wash.PLR-LK-APPL>2/3
"wash the clothes for him!"

(153) *áǎ* *kèn=ég* *ɓùb-nùn*
1PL.EXCL.ACC cloth.PL=ACC wash.PLR-LK.APPL>1
"wash the clothes for us!"

Summarizing §/3, we recognize that the reflexes of the donative verbs **tir* and **deen* continue to be employed as lexical verbs of transfer. Parallel to this use and bleached of their original semantic content, they have come to serve as valency-increasing grammatical elements in applicative constructions – at least in the Nile Nubian languages. In Kordofan Nubian, however, a simplification process has begun which is associated with the emergence of a new verb *ti* which is replacing the original donative verbs and is considered to result from a morphological blending of both. The initial consonant of *ti* appears to be a reflex of the initial of **deen,* while the high front vowel of *ti* stems from the vowel of **tir.* In Karko, such CV-shaped lexical items are realized with a long vowel, as confirmed by Karko *tìì* "give," in Tagle with a short vowel, *tí.* This contrast is also attested by Karko *dìì* "drink" corresponding to Tagle *dì,* and Karko *tìì* "die" corresponding to Tagle *tì.* Note that Karko *tìì* "die" and *tìì* "give" are homophones.

4. Verbal Number

Verbal number is a grammatical category which "can reflect the number of times an action is done or the number of participants in the action."[136] That is, it can be sensitive to event number conveying aspectual notions such as intense, repetitive, distributed, or even single actions. It can also interact with the number of intransitive subjects or transitive objects. As verbal number is insensitive to transitive agents, however, this pattern of grammatical relations is a realization of an ergative alignment system.

The Nubian languages exhibit several verbal number marking extensions. Two of them, **-(i)j* (§/4.1) and **-(i)k* (§/4.2) are reconstructable because they are attested in both branches of the Nubian family. Other extensions have a more restricted distribution. This is true for the plural object extension *-ir* and *-(i)r-ir* in Mattokki and Andaandi (§/6.2), the plural stem extension *-er* attested in the Kordofan Nubian languages and Midob, and also for further plural stem suffixes in the Kordofan Nubian languages (§/6.5).

4.1. Pluractional *-(i)j

Reflexes of the *-(i)j-extension are attested in all Nubian languages where it operates as a highly productive morpheme with a wide range of semantic and morphosyntactic properties. Because of its frequent occurrence in these languages, it is suggested that it should be referred to by the term pluractional (glossed as PLACT) to distinguish it from other plural stem extensions.

While the western Nubian languages reflect the *-(i)j-extension by -j, -c, -ʃ, or even -ɕ, the Nile Nubian languages reflect it by -j, this consonant being realized as voiced palatal stop [ɟ] which has several allomorphs depending on the preceding or following consonant. When the pluractional extension is attached to a consonant-final verb stem, it is predictably preceded by the epenthetic high front vowel *i* to prevent certain unadmitted consonant sequences.

PN	ON	No	Ma	An	Dil	Ta	Ka	Mi
*-(i)j	-(ι)ϭ	-(i)j	-(i)j	-(i)j	-j ~ -c	-c	-ɕ ~ -j	-j ~ -c

Table 11. The pluractional extension *-(i)j

Browne points out that Old Nubian -ϭ "refers to a plural object (either direct or indirect) and occasionally to a plural subject [...] it may also refer to a plural object not specifically identified in the text."[137] The first example illustrates how -(ι)ϭ interacts with a transitive plural object, the second shows the interaction of -(ι)ϭ with an intransitive plural subject.

(154) **Old Nubian**
ⲕⲁⲡⲟⲡⲓⲅⲟⲩⲕⲁ ⲇⲟⲗⲓϭⲛⲓⲁ̄
kapop-igou=ka *dol-ij-ni-a*
pearl-PL=ACC gather-PLACT-PURP-QUOT
"in order to gather pearls" (SC 4.19)

(155) ⲇⲓϭⲟⲗⲅⲟⲩⲛⲁ
di-j-ol-gou=na
die-PLACT-PST1-PL=GEN
"of those who are dead" (SC 8.12–13)

While Lepsius refers to the *-(i)j*-extension in Nobiin as "verbum plurale,"[138] Werner uses the term "Pluralobjekt-Erweiterung" (plural object extension).[139] This latter designation is, however, not quite adequate, because *-(i)j* is not confined to interacting with plural objects; it can also be triggered by an intransitive plural subject and by event plurality.[140]

	Nobiin			
(156)	*ày kàb-ìr*	"I eat" OJ SG	*ày kàb-j-ir*	"I eat (a lot or several times)" OJ PL
(157)	*ày nèer-ìr*	"I sleep"	*ày nèer-j-ìr*	"I sleep (several times)"

Because of the wide range of functions covered by *-(i)j*, Khalil uses the term "verbal plural marker."[141] Apart from interacting with plural participants and event plurality, the *-(i)j*-extension is also used to signal respect when addressing a person, as Khalil shows.

As for *-(i)j* in Mattokki, Massenbach highlights the fact that it expresses the intensity of an action.[142]

(158) **Mattokki**
man ʃibir urub-buu-n
that basket have.hole-STAT-3SG
"that basket has a hole"

(159) *man ʃibir urub-ij-buu-n*
that basket have.hole-PLACT-STAT-3SG
"that basket is thoroughly perforated"

(160) *ter gulud=ki aa-toog-ij-mun-um*
3SG jar=ACC PROG-break-PLACT-NEG-NEUT.3SG
"he does not smash the jar"

Abdel-Hafiz, in turn, chooses the term "distributive" to refer to the Mattokki *-(i)j*-extension because it "has the effect of spreading the action over time and space."

He also points out that the -*(i)j*-suffix "can indicate the intensity with which an action is performed,"[143] as illustrated in (162).

(161) *duguu=g* *gull-ij-os-s-u*
money=ACC throw-PLACT-PFV-PT2-3SG
"s/he threw the money here and there"

(162) *gur* *baab=ki* *toog-is-s-u*
bull door=ACC break-PLACT-PT2-3SG
"the bull broke the door"

In (162) the -*(i)j*-extension is realized as [is], due to regressive assimilation when followed by the preterite suffix -*s*.

As for the Andaandi suffix -*(i)j*, Armbruster notes that it "usually has an intensive or repetitive force."[144]

	Andaandi			
(163)	*war*	"jump"	*war-ij*	"jump continually"
(164)	*or*	"tear"	*or-ij*	"tear to pieces"
(165)	*aaw*	"do"	*aw-ij*	"do repetitively"

(166) *tinn-ɛssi=n* *dilti=g* *aw-ij-in*
her-sister=GEN hair=ACC do-PLACT-3SG
"s/he plaits her sister's hair"

The Dilling reflex of *-*(i)j* is -*j*. Kauczor's examples suggest that it can refer to a plural object but it can also express the intensity or frequency of an event.[145]

	Dilling			
(167)	*mon*	"dislike"	*mon-j-i*	"hate (intensely)"
(168)	*bel-er*	"throw OJ SG to the ground (in wrestling)"	*bel-j-i*	"throw to the ground OJ PL or frequently"

The Tagle reflex of *-(i)j is realized as the voiced palatal stop [ɟ] or after /l/ as the voiceless palatal stop [c]. It expresses repetitive or multiple events. The examples are provided in the 2nd singular imperative form.

Tagle

(169)	*áŋ-ír-ì*	"catch, seize!" OJ SG	*áŋ-c-í* [áɲcí]	id. RPT
(170)	*kìŋ-ír-ì*	"repair!" OJ SG	*kíŋ-c-í* [kíɲcí]	id. RPT

(171) *kòn-ú-nù=gì* *kákár=kò* *jìl-ì*
bird-SG-DIM.SG=ACC stone=INS throw-IMP.2SG
"throw a stone at the bird!"

(172) *kòn-ú-nù=gì* *kákár-í=kò*
bird-SG-DIM.SG=ACC stone-PL=INS
jíl-c-í
throw-PLACT-IMP.2SG
"continue to throw stones at the bird!"

In Karko, the *-(i)j-extension is realized as voiced palatal plosive [ɟ] after a vowel, and as [Vɟ] after a consonant (except for /n/ and /l/). Following these consonants, *-(i)j is realized as voiceless alveopalatal fricative [ɕ]. In this case, [ɕ] is difficult to identify as a suffix because the preceding /l/ and /n/ are deleted. The following (unmarked) imperative forms refer to a singular or plural object.

Karko

(173)	*ɕàn*	"buy/sell!" OJ SG	*ɕàɕ*	id. OJ PL
(174)	*kìl*	"jump over!" OJ SG	*kìɕ*	id. OJ PL
(175)	*t̪ōl-ór*	"swallow!" OJ SG[146]	*t̪òɕ*	id. OJ PL

(176) *kwàt̪* *t̪ōl-ór*
pebble.SG swallow-PLR
"swallow the pebble!"

(177) *kwǎr* *t̪òɓ*
pebble.PL.ACC swallow.PLACT
"swallow the pebbles!"

In the Kordofan Nubian languages like Karko, the pluractional extension is selected by the plural object (patient) in a transitive clause like (177) and by the plural direct object (theme) in a ditransitive clause, as shown in (179). This patterning of the transitive patient with the ditransitive theme – but not with the indirect object, the beneficiary – is known as the indirect-object construction.[147]

(178) *kə̄k-ə̄nd̪=ə́g* *ə̀g=ɛ̄g-nɛ̀n*
stone-SG=ACC 1SG.ACC=roll-LK.APPL>1
"roll the stone for me!"

(179) *kə̄k-ə̄r=ə́g* *ə̀g=ɛ̄g-ɛ̄j-nɛ̂n*
stone-PL=ACC 1SG.ACC=roll-PLACT-LK.APPL>1
"roll the stones for me!"

Proto-Nubian **-(i)j* is reflected by Midob *-c* (allomorph *-j*). According to Werner, this extension marks participant and event plurality, the latter expressing "repetitivity, intensity."[148] However, he provides only two pairs of contrastive examples. Examples (180) and (181) show that *-c* is sensitive to the plural number of the intransitive subject.

(180) **Midob**
ìi-hêm
come-IND.PRF.1SG
"I came"

(181) *ìi-c-áhàm*
come-PLACT-IND.PRF.3PL
"they came"

The other pair of examples raises the question whether the *-j*-extension is required by an unexpressed pronominal plural object or even by event plurality.[149]

(182) *éeg-ìr-wà*
answer-CAUS-IND.CONT.1SG
"I answer"

(183) *éeg-ìr-j-wà*
answer-CAUS-PLACT-IND.CONT.1PL
"we answer"

In addition to its event plurality and participant plurality marking function, Midob *-c* has come to serve as the marker of the 2nd person imperative plural form. The corresponding singular form is morphologically unmarked.[150]

(184)	*kóod*	"see" IMP 2SG	*kóod-íc*	"see" IMP 2PL
(185)	*sô*	"go" IMP 2SG	*sóo-íc* [sówíc]	"go" IMP 2PL

This development of the pluractional extension adopting the additional function of a 2PL imperative marker is an innovation which is unattested in the other Nubian languages.

4.2. The Plural Stem Extension *-(i)k

Probably because the *-(i)k extension is mainly attested on ideophonic verbs, which often play a marginal role in grammars, the plural stem extension *-(i)k has been overlooked in most Nubian grammars. Compared to the other extensions *-(i)k is less productive and more lexicalized. Moreover, as far as I can see, it is unattested in Old Nubian and Midob. Despite these deficiencies *-(i)k has reflexes in both branches of the Nubian language family. For this reason, it is considered to be a reconstructable Proto-Nubian extension.

PN	ON	No	Ma	An	Dil	Ta	Ka	Mi
*-(i)k	–	-k	-k	-k	-k	-(i)k	-(V)k	–

Table 12. The plural stem extension *-(i)k

As Armbruster was the first to provide evidence of the -*(i)k*-extension, this section considers Andaandi data first.[151] Listing a few pairs of verbs Armbruster identifies -*k* as a suffix with "perhaps intensive or factitive" meaning. While it is obvious that the geminate velar stop *kk* results from the regressive assimilation of the root-final consonant to the following -*k*, it is not clear why the long root vowel is shortened in case of (186) *jak-k-i* and (187) *jok-k-i* but unchanged in the case of (188) *uuk-k-i*.

	Andaandi			
(186)	*jaag*	"knead"	*jak-k-i*	"compress"
(187)	*joog*	"grind"	*jok-k-i*	"chew (food)"
(188)	*uuw*	"call"	*uuk-k-i*	"bark"

Armbruster provides a list of some twenty Andaandi verbs exhibiting -*k*. Most of them do not have an underived counterpart, though. This suggests that -*k* is no longer a productive morpheme and that it has become lexicalized. In addition to Armbruster, El-Guzuuli has compiled many Andaandi ideophonic verbs, several of them exhibiting the -*k*-extension.[152]

(189) *loori* *weer* *udud-k-in*
lorry IDF rumble-PLR-3SG
"a lorry rumbles"

(190) *iig* *aag* *habab-k-in*
fire PROG blaze-PLR-3SG
"the fire is blazing"

Although Massenbach does not address the -*k*-extension in her Mattokki grammar sketch, her dictionary contains some verbs which exhibit -*k*, e.g., *jok-k(i)* "chew"; *kil-ik(i)* "chirp"; *tos-k(i)* "cough"; and *wak-k(i)* "yelp (fox)." The fact that -*k* often occurs on verbs depicting inherently repetitive events like rumble, blaze, chew, chirp, cough, and yelp indicates that it reflects event plurality.

This is also true for Nobiin. Werner's compilation of Nobiin ideophones contains a list of sixteen "ideophonic verbs imitating animal sounds," all sharing a low-high tone pattern.[153] Among these verbs are nine which exhibit the *-k*-extension. Here we present just two examples.

(191) **Nobiin**
áadíi ùu-k-ín
hyena howl-PLR-3SG
"the hyena howls"

(192) *kùglúul kìik-k-ín*
rooster crow-PLR-3SG
"the rooster crows"

As for Old Nubian, there is no evidence of the stem extension *-k*, not even in combination with the reduplicated stems of apparently onomatopoeic or ideophonic verbs,[154] to which *-k* is often attached in the modern Nile Nubian languages.

The *-k*-extension in the Nile Nubian languages is assumed to be cognate to *-k* in Dilling, *-(i)k* in Tagle and *-(V)k* in Karko. As it is often combined with other plural stem extensions, it is also considered in §6.5. Here a few examples may suffice. They suggest that *-(V)k* is often associated with repetitive events but the examples also show that, due to semantic extension, *-(V)k* can also reflect the number of participants in the action. Both properties are typical of verbal number markers.

	Dilling[155]			
(193)	*ir*	"bear child" TR, OJ SG	*ir-k*	id. OJ PL, RPT
	be	"get lost" ITR, SJ SG	*be-k*	id. SJ SG, RPT
	Tagle			
(194)	*ònḓ*	"sip, absorb" TR, OJ SG	*ónḓ-ík*	id. OJ SG, RPT
	ḓáḓḓ	"cross, pass" ITR, SJ SG	*ḓáḓḓ-ík*	id. SJ SG, RPT
	Karko			
(195)	*kúʃ-ɛ́ɛ́r*	"hang up" TR, OJ SG	*kùj-ùk*	id. OJ PL
	ʃíl-ɛ̀ɛ́r	"kindle" TR, OJ SG	*ʃil-ìk*	id. OJ PL

As Midob is still comparatively poorly documented, there is presently no clear evidence of the *-(i)k-extension.

5. Traces of the Archaic Causative Prefix

According to Dimmendaal's typological study, the archaic causative *i-prefix (allomorph *ɪ-) is a historically stable feature, since it is attested in several distinct Nilo-Saharan subgroups, including different branches of the East Sudanic group, i.e., Me'en, Majang, and Southern Nilotic, as well as Central Sudanic, represented by Ma'di.[156]

(196)	Me'en	-dibis	"be full"	-i-dibis	"fill"
(197)	Majang	-paak	"be hot"	-ɪ-paak	"heat"
(198)	Kipsigiis	-nér	"be fat"	-ì-nɛ́ɛ̂r	"fatten"
(199)	Ma'di	tū	"climb up"	ī-tú	"make climb up, promote"

5.1. The Causative Prefix in the Nubian Languages

Me'en, Majang, Kipsigiis, and Ma'di have retained reflexes of the causative prefix with the original high front vowel *i* ~ *ɪ*. This V-shaped prefix is retained both in Nubian and Ama although it has undergone vowel shifts. In the Nubian languages, this shift has resulted in the emergence of an *u- ~ o-prefix, in Ama the shift has led to the prefix *a-* (see §5.2). The reconstructed Nubian vowels **u* ~ *o* can be identified as prefixes because they are all associated with transitive verb stems which contrast with the phonologically and semantically similar intransitive verb stems that do not exhibit an initial vowel. The small number of these derived transitive verbs and the lack of productivity of the vowel prefix suggest that they are a remnant of the archaic causative *i-prefix.

Prefixes are rare in the Nubian languages. Another instance of a petrified prefix is the verbal negation marker **m-*,[157] which is attested in all Nubian languages:

e.g., Old Nubian ⲙ-ⲟⲛ, ⲙ-ⲟⲩⲛ "hate, reject, be reluctant" vs. ⲟⲛ, ⲟⲩⲛ "love," Nobiin *m-éskìr* "be unable" vs. *éské* "be able." In Dilling, **m-* has regularly shifted to /b/: *b-or-di* "barren" vs. *ir* "give birth." In Midob, **m-* has regularly shifted to /p/: *p-óon-hèm* "I hated, refused, rejected" vs. *óo-hêm* (< *óonhèm*) "I loved." As the prefixing pattern strongly deviates from the predominantly suffixing pattern, which is now typical of all Nubian languages, it suggests that a restructuring process has taken place.

A closer look at the examples below reveals that when the causative prefix is attached to a verb root, it tends to adopt the quality of the root vowel. The root vowel, in turn, often adopts the quality of the original high front vowel prefix **i-*. This process is known as paradigmatic displacement,[158] which is probably motivated by the canonical (C)V(V)(C) shape of Nubian roots. When they are followed by another syllable, this second syllable tends to be reanalyzed as a suffix. Such a syllabic suffix is usually realized with an epenthetic high front vowel *i*.

PN	ON	No	Ma	An	Dil	Ta	Ka	Mi
**u- ~ o-*	ⲟⲩ-	*u-*	*u-*	*u-*	*u-, o-*	*u-, e-*	*ə-, ɔ-, u-*	*u-*

Table 13. The archaic causative prefix **u- ~ o-*

In Old Nubian,[159] for instance, there is evidence of an ⲟⲩ-prefix on transitive verb stems, whereas this prefix is absent on the cognate intransitive stems.

	Old Nubian	
(200)	ⲧⲟⲣ, ⲧⲟⲩⲣ, ⲧⲟ(ⲣ)ⲁⲣ	"enter" ITR
	ⲟⲩ-ⲧⲣ̄, ⲟⲩ-ⲧⲟⲩⲣ, ⲟⲩ-ⲧⲁⲣ	"lay, put, hold, deposit" TR

Another intransitive verb root, ⲥⲟⲩⲕⲕ "descend," attests two derived stems with increased valency: one stem is derived by the ⲟⲩ-prefix plus the causative -(ⲁ)ⲣ- ~ -ⲟⲩⲣ-suffix; the other stem is extended by the causative -ⲕⲣ̄-suffix but without the ⲟⲩ-prefix. Presumably the absence, i.e., loss of the ⲟⲩ-prefix and the suffixation of the productive -ⲕⲣ̄-suffix (see §/2.2) was triggered by the semantic fading of the causative function of the ⲟⲩ-prefix.

(201)	ⲥⲟⲩⲕⲕ, ⲥⲟⲅⲅ	“descend” ITR
	ⲟⲩ-ⲥⲕ-(ⲁ)ⲣ, ⲟⲩ-ⲥⲕ-ⲟⲩⲣ	“place” TR
	ⲥⲟⲩⲕ-ⲕⲣ̄	“cause to descend” TR

The *u*-prefix attested in Old Nubian is also found on cognate verbs in the modern Nile Nubian languages: e.g., *u-dir* (Nobiin); *u-ndur* (Mattokki and Andaandi); and *u-skir* (Nobiin, Mattokki, Andaandi). Lepsius recognizes that Andaandi *u-ndire, u-ndure* is a cognate of Nobiin *u-dire.*[160] The addition of the nasal attested in *u-ndir(e)* and *u-ndur(e)* is due to epenthesis.[161] It is conceivable that the derived unattested stem *u-toor* underwent a number of phonological and morphological changes, including vowel assimilation, the insertion of the epenthetic *n,* which has triggered the voicing of the following original root-initial *t,* and the re-analysis of the root-final *Vr* sequence as the causative *-ir*-suffix (see §2.1). Two distinct developments are assumed: *utoor* > *utor* > *utur* > *untur* > *undur,* as attested in Mattokki and Andaandi, and *utoor* > *utur* > *udur* > *udir* in Nobiin.

(202)	**An, Ma**	too(r)[162]	“enter” ITR
	No	*toor-e*	“enter” ITR
	No	*u-dir-e*	“take to, lay down, put into, insert” TR
	Ma	*u-ndur-e*	“put in, name, dress” TR
	An	*u-ndur-e*	“put in, introduce, insert” TR

The extension of the verb stem *u-sk* with the causative *-ir* results from a secondary process that started when the causative prefix lost its productivity.

(203)	**No**	*sukk-e*	“descend” ITR
	No, Ma, An	*u-sk-ir-e*	“put down, lay down” TR
	Ma, An	*u-sk-ir-e*	“give birth” TR

As for Kordofan Nubian, Kauczor was the first to recognize the extension of verb stems by means of prefixes (“Stammbildung durch Präfixe”).[163] As they introduce a causer, the Dilling *u*- and *o*-prefixes are assumed to be reflexes of the archaic *i-causative.

Dilling

(204)	*jir*	"lie down" ITR	*u-jir*	"lay down" TR
(205)	*tor*	"enter" ITR	*o-tir*	"insert, put into" TR

These two verb pairs have cognates in Tagle. A native speaker, however, would not perceive the verb root *jèr* to be the base of *ù-jír* or *ù-jèr,* nor *ṯór* to be the base of *è-ṯír,* since the initial vowel no longer operates as a productive prefix.[164] Tagle examples (206) and (207) are given in the 2SG imperative form, marked by an *-i-* suffix.

Tagle

(206)	*jèr-í*	"lie down!" ITR
	ù-jír-ì	"put down, lay down!" TR, OJ SG
	ù-jèr-í	"put down, lay down!" TR, OJ PL
(207)	*ṯór-í*	"enter, begin!" ITR
	è-ṯír-ì[165]	"insert, put in, start!" TR

Cognates of the Tagle intransitive/transitive verb pairs "lie down"/"put down" and "enter"/"insert" exist in Karko as well. The archaic Nilo-Saharan **i*-prefix is reflected by the initial vowel of the transitive items, which is associated with a particular form of vowel harmony in which the quality of the root vowel is adopted by the short suffix vowel due to lag assimilation: e.g., *ɔ̀k-ɔ́ṯ* "bean" SG; *ūk-ūnḏ* "fire" PL; *ɓə̀t-ə̀d* "closed" PTC SG. The imperative forms *ə̄-ṯə́r, ɔ̄-ṯɔ́r, ū-júr* suggest that the initial vowels of these verbs are re-analyzed as root vowels and that the verb-final *Vr* sequence is conceived of as a *-Vr*-suffix (see §2.1). Karko imperatives are marked by a low tone when the verb stems are underived: e.g., *ṯɔ̀r* and *jɛ̀r*. The imperative forms of verbs derived by *-Vr,* however, can have different tone patterns depending on the tone class to which the verbs belong. The contrast between singular and plural imperative forms is unmarked by dedicated suffixes but often expressed by vowel alternation, as (208) *ə̄-ṯə́r* vs. *ɔ̄-ṯɔ́r* illustrate.

Karko

(208)	*t̪òr*	"enter!" ITR, IMP 2SG
	ə̄-t̪ə́r	"enter, insert, start, cause!" TR, IMP 2SG
	ɔ̄-t̪ɔ́r	"enter, insert, start, cause!" TR, IMP 2PL
(209)	*jɛ̀r*	"lie down, go to sleep!" ITR, IMP 2SG
	ū-júr	"put down!" TR, IMP 2SG

(210) *kám-m-bíl* *jɛ̀r*
eat.PLR-LK-first lie.down.SNG
"eat first then go to sleep!"

(211) *ɓǎnt̪àà=g* *kúrɛī=ét̪* *ū-júr*
bag=ACC chair=LOC CAUS-put.down
"put the bag on the chair!"

Because of their phonological and semantic similarities, the Midob verb stems *súkk* "descend" and *ú-kk* "give birth" can be identified as cognates of Nile Nubian *sukk-* "descend" and *u-skir-* "put down, lay down, give birth"; see examples (201) and (203) above.

Midob

(212)	*súkk-ihèm*	"I descended"
	ú-kk-áhèm	"I gave birth"

The initial vowel of the Midob verb stem *ú-kk* is assumed to reflect the archaic causative prefix. It is conceivable that due to this prefix and the preferred monosyllabic structure of lexical roots, the unattested bisyllabic verb stem *ú-súkk* has undergone some changes involving the deletion of the second vowel and the fricative /s/. The deletion of /s/ before /k/ is also observed in other Midob lexical items: e.g., *ùkúdí* "dust, sand" < PN **Vskidi*; and *úfúdí* ~ *úkúdí* < PN **VskVdi.*[166] The fact that the geminated velar of *súkk* is retained in *ú-kk* corroborates the assumed derivational relationship between these two stems.

5.2. The Causative Prefix and Causative Suffixes in Ama

Ama and Afitti verbs commonly exhibit two bases which used to be referred to as "definite" and "indefinite" aspect stems.[167] In recent studies by Rilly and Norton, the definite and indefinite are recognized as perfective and imperfective aspect stems, respectively.[168]

As in the Nubian languages, verbal derivational extensions in Ama are usually suffixed to the verb. Therefore, a prefixed extension such as the causative *a-* is a remarkable deviation from the suffixing pattern.[169]

	Ama			
(213)	*a-t̪os/a-kwos*	"suckle"	*t̪os/kwos*	"suck"
(214)	*a-mɔ*	"raise"	*mɔ*	"rise"

Stevenson points out that the *a*-marked causative may "also be combined with the *ɪg* form,"[170] which apparently has a causative function as well. Tucker & Bryan, too, note that the causative *a*-prefix is sometimes combined with the *-ɪg-* and *-ɛg*-extensions and that, in addition to the causative function, these suffixes express the meaning of "action directed towards."[171] For this reason, Norton uses the term "directional" rather than causative.[172] For the *-ɪd*-suffix on *tam* see §⁄6.7.

(215)	*a-t̪al-ɪg*	"feed"	*t̪al*	"eat"
(216)	*a-tam-ɪd-ɛg*	"feed"	*tam*	"eat"

Interestingly, Stevenson, Rottland & Jakobi have documented another form of the causative verb "suckle" in Ama.[173] Its two causative stems do not exhibit the *a*-prefix but only the causative *-ìg*-suffix.

(217)	*t̪ɔʃ-ìg/kwɔʃ-ìg*	"suckle"	*t̪os-o/kwoʃ-ì*	"suck"

Thus, in Ama there are three alternative patterns of causative marking:

› the causative stems are solely marked by the *a*-prefix, as attested by (213) *a-t̪os/a-kwos* and (214) *a-mɔ*;

› the causative is simultaneously marked by the *a*-prefix and the *-ɪg-* or *-(ɪd-)ɛg*-suffix, as in (215) *a-t̪al-ɪg* and (216) *a-tam-ɪd-ɛg*; and
› the causative is only marked by the *-ìg*-suffix, as (217) *t̪ɔʃ-ìg/kwɔʃ-ìg* show.

It is quite conceivable that the three patterns reflect three stages in the historical development from a prefixing pattern to a suffixing pattern. The coincidence of the causative being marked by both the *a*-prefix and the *-ɪg-* or *-ɛg*-suffix, as found in *a-t̪al-ɪg* and *a-tam-ɪd-ɛg*, represents an intermediate step in that restructuring process.

The velar consonant of the Ama suffix *-ɪg* or *-ɛg* is strongly reminiscent of the velar consonant that is part of the Nubian causative suffixes, Nobiin *-kìr*, Mattokki *-igir*, Andaandi *-(i)gir*, Dilling *-eg-ir* and *-ig-er*, and Midob *-éek* and *-èek* (see §⁄2.2). Since bound morphemes are not easily borrowed, these Nubian causative suffixes are considered to be cognates of the Ama *-ɪg* and *-ɛg* causative suffixes. At present, this assumption cannot be corroborated by data from Afitti, since the Afitti verb stems documented so far do not show any evidence of an *-ɪg-* or *-ɛg*-suffix.

Concluding this section, we recognize that both Nubian and Ama exhibit a petrified causative prefix. Since remnants of this prefix are also found in Central Sudanic and several branches of East Sudanic, they provide comparative evidence of the genetic relationships between these languages. Along with the prefixed Nubian negation marker **m-* (see §⁄5.1), the causative prefixes in Nubian and Ama suggest that these languages have undergone a typological change from prefixing to suffixing languages. These prefixes in Nubian and Ama corroborate Dimmendaal's hypothesis, which assumes "that the common ancestor of Central Sudanic and Northeastern Nilo-Saharan was typologically more similar to the Moru-Madi languages within the Central Sudanic branch than to any other Nilo-Saharan subgroup found today."[174]

6. Verb Extensions with a Restricted Distribution

Some verbal extensions have a restricted distribution because they occur only in a single Nubian language or in a subgroup of the Nubian family.

6.1. Nile Nubian Passive Extensions

Unlike the languages of the western branch, the Nile Nubian languages have dedicated passive extensions. They comprise Old Nubian -(ι)ⲧⲁⲕ, Nobiin *-dakk* ~ *-takk* ~ *-daŋ*, Mattokki *-takk*, and Andaandi *-katt*. Nobiin and Matokki *-dakk* ~ *-takk* suggest that Old Nubian -ⲧⲁⲕ (although spelled with a single ⲕ), used to be realized with a geminate *kk*, too.

(218) **Old Nubian**
ⲁ̇ⲉ̄ⲧⲧⲁⲕⲁⲧⲁⲙⲏ
aeit-tak-a-ta-mē
insult-PASS-PRED-NEG-JUS.SG
"don't you be insulted!" (M 6.11)

Apart from *-dakk* ~ *-takk*, Nobiin has another passive extension, *-daŋ*, which, according to Reinisch, is restricted to the Fadicca variety.[175] As far as we know today, it is unattested in Old Nubian.[176] Both Reinisch and Lepsius provide examples of *-daŋ* being attached to original Nobiin items and even to borrowings from Arabic as in (220),[177] which attest the productivity of the extension. Due to the phonetic similarities of *-daŋ* and the inchoative *-aŋ*, Reinisch and Lepsius conceive of *-daŋ* as being composed of a *d*-prefix plus *-aŋ*. According to Reinisch, *d*- has a "reflexive-passive" function.[178]

	Nobiin			
(219)	*nuluu-aŋ*	"become white"	*nuluu-d-aŋ*	"be whitened"
(220)	*nadiif-aŋ*	"become clean"	*nadiif-d-aŋ*	"be cleaned"

However, this hypothesis is not convincing unless we can corroborate the existence of a *d-prefix. Moreover, (221), a translation of Mark 2:27, suggests that *-dakk* and *-daŋ* are simply variants of the same extension. A more literal translation of this example should read: "The Sabbath was made because of man, man was not made because of Sabbath."[179]

(221)	*santee-l*	*aadem=in=doorro*	*aaw-dakk-on*
	sabbat-DET	man=GEN=because.of	do-PASS-PT.3SG
	aadem	*santee=n=doorro*	*aaw-daŋ-kum-mun*
	man	sabbat=GEN=because.of	do-PASS-PT-NEG

"the Sabbath was made for man, not man for the Sabbath"

As for Mattokki, Massenbach points out that the passive extension is realized as [takk] or, more rarely, as [katt].[180]

(222) **Mattokki**

buuwe-tákk-imn-um

call-PASS-NEG-PRS.3SG

"he is not called"

Abdel-Hafiz only mentions the *-takk* variant and its allomorph *-cakk* which is used after *c*. It can be used with transitive verbs, but also with intransitive verbs such as *neer* "sleep."[181]

(223)	*indo*	*neer-takk-is-u*
	here	sleep-PASS-PT-3SG

"it was slept here"

(224) **Andaandi**

goraan	*kuur-katt-in*
Qur'an	learn-PASS-3SG

"the Qur'an is learnt / the Qur'an can be learnt"

Both Matokki *-takk* and Andaandi *-katt* are productive extensions, as shown by their use with Arabic loanwords.[182]

Mattokki

(225) *gaffir-takk* "be forgiven"

Andaandi

(226) *hamd=ee-katt*[183] "be praised"

As for the origin of the passive extensions various suggestions have been advanced. Reinisch proposes two rather vague hypotheses:[184]

1. *katt* has developed from *k-att*, i.e., from the accusative marker plus the verb *att* "bring."
2. Andaandi *katt* "wrap, role (cigarette)" corresponds to Nobiin *kand* "wrap, dress" or *takk* with the same meaning.

Reinisch's second hypothesis is supported by Armbruster, who suggests, too, that the Andaandi passive suffix *-katt* originates from the verb *katt* "wrap."[185] Smagina, in turn, argues that Old Nubian *tak(k)* derives from the short form of the 3SG pronoun accusative, the long form being *takka.*[186] Although the incorporation of a pronoun as part of a passivizing strategy is conceivable, as Van Gerven Oei points out,[187] the presence of Nobiin *-daŋ* as a variant of *-dakk* ~ *-takk* does not support the assumption of the Old Nubian *-tak(k)* passive extension originating in the 3SG pronoun.

Given the fact that Nobiin *-daŋ* and Old Nubian -ⲧⲁⲕ have a CVC-shape suggests that they originate from a verb root, similar to the CVC-shaped causative and applicative extensions, **-(i)gir* and **-tir,* which stem from the verbs *gir* ~ *kir* "make" and *tir* "give to 2nd or 3rd person." The Nobiin and Mattokki extensions *-dakk* ~ *-takk* may owe their final geminated *kk* and their CVCC-shape to a lexical CVC-shaped root incremented by a velar stop. Perhaps this stop can be identified as the plural stem extension *-k.* Its function in this context is, however, unclear (§⁄4.2).

Passive markers often have a verbal origin, as shown by the English *be-* and *get-* passives and the German *werden*-passive. Therefore, we follow Reinisch's and Armbruster's suggestions assuming that the passive extensions originate from two semantically related verbs, "wrap, wind" and "be covered." It is conceivable that Andaandi *-katt* originates from *kant* "wrap, wind," a verb attested both in Nobiin and Andaandi,[188] particularly because the gemination of *tt* resulting from the regressive assimilation of *n* to *t* is also attested in the lexical variants *sunti* and *sutti* "hoof, fingernail."[189]

It is also possible that Nobiin *-daŋ* and *-dakk* ~ *-takk* as well as Matokki *-takk* are based on *tag* "get covered"[190] incremented by the extension *-k,* i.e., *-tag-k* > *-takk.* In the course of grammaticalization the initial *t* may have undergone weakening, i.e., *t* > *d* which has led to the realization of *-takk* as *-dakk.* It is also conceivable that during the assumed grammaticalization process, one of the Nobiin varieties retained *tag* without extending it by *-k.* Considering that the initial and final consonant of *tag* may have been weakened, i.e., *t* > *d* and *g* > *ŋ,* it is possible that this variant of the passive extensions has come to be realized as *-daŋ.*

Of course, we cannot exclude that Andaandi *-katt* does not originate from *kant* but rather from the metathesis of *-takk* > *-katt* (even though the motivation for this phonotactic change is as yet unclear). That suggestion has the advantage of conceiving the passive extensions in the Nile Nubian languages to have a common origin in a single verb, *tag* "get covered." The semantic notions of this intransitive verb fit well with its grammaticalization as a passive marker.

Unlike the Nile Nubian languages, the Kordofan Nubian languages do not have a dedicated passive extension. Rather, as Comfort and Jakobi have shown,[191] the passive and other non-basic intransitive constructions are based on verbal plural stems (see §/6.5).

As for Midob, Werner denies that there is "a real passive."[192] He points out that semantically passive notions are either expressed by a stative or a 3PL active verb form. The latter option is cross-linguistically quite common, it also exists in Old Nubian and Nobiin.[193] As the 3PL element "is not understood to refer to any specific group of individuals,"[194] it is known as "generalized subject" or "impersonal."[195]

6.2. The Mattokki and Andaandi Plural Object *-ir-* and *-(i)r-ir-*Extensions

The plural object extensions *-ir* and *-(i)r-ir* are restricted to Mattokki and Andaandi. Unlike the pluractional **-(i)j* (§/4.1) and the *-er*-extension §/6.3, these extensions have a strongly restricted function because they are only selected when the referent of the transitive object is plural. That is, they do not interact with plural subjects of intransitive clauses. Both Massenbach and Armbruster account for this productive suffix, but Abdel-Hafiz does not mention it in his Mattokki grammar.[196]

(227) **Mattokki**

ai *toog-s-im*
1SG break-PT2-1SG
"I smashed it"

(228) *ai* *toog-ir-s-im*
1SG break-PLOJ-PT2-1SG
"I smashed them"

(229) *ar* *el-r-un* [ellun]
1PL find-NEUT-1PL
"we find it"

(230) *ar* *el-ir-r-un*
1PL find-PLOJ-NEUT-1PL
"we find them"

Armbruster observes that Andaandi *-ir*, which is sometimes reduplicated and realized as [irir], additionally has distributive connotations since it is "used when the verb's object is a plural that is regarded as a series of singulars."[197] But when discussing (231) and (232), mother tongue speaker El-Shafie El-Guzuuli pointed out that he does not perceive a semantic difference between them.[198]

(231) **Andaandi**

in-gu=gi *sokke-rir*
this-PL=ACC take-PLOJ
"take (each of) these away!"

(232) *in-gu=gi* *sokke*
this-PL=ACC take
"take (each of) these away!"

Unlike the reduplicated causative *-ir-ir-*extension, which is realized as [iddi], the reduplicated plural object extension *-(i)r-ir* is never pronounced as [iddi]. This finding supports Armbruster's assumption that the plural object extension is not identical in origin with the causative **-(i)r*-extension (see §2.1).[199]

6.3. The Kordofan Nubian and Midob Plural Stem Extension *-er*

Another verbal number marking device is represented by the highly productive extension *-er* (glossed as PLR). It is confined to the Kordofan Nubian languages and Midob. Kauczor was not only the first to recognize the Dilling prefixes *u-* and *o-* (§/5.1), he also noticed that the Dilling *-er*-extension is used in four distinct grammatical contexts:[200]

- when a transitive verb refers to a plural object;
- when an intransitive verb refers to a plural subject;
- when a transitive verb is used without a syntactic object; and
- when a transitive verb has passive meaning.

The first two contexts indicate that the interaction of *-er* with an intransitive plural subject and a transitive plural object represents an ergative alignment pattern. In this respect, the plural stem extension *-er* is comparable to the pluractional **-(i)j* (§/4.1), which is associated with the same pattern of grammatical relations. The last two contexts suggest that *-er* is associated with a low degree of transitivity (in the sense of Hopper & Thompson's concept of transitivity as a scalar value[201]).

Kauczor also points out that some verbs are always extended by *-er.* This finding has been confirmed in recent studies of other Kordofan Nubian languages, particularly Uncu, Tagle, and Tabaq where verbs with a lexicalized *-er*-extension often express inherently repetitive events, such as "stutter" and "bark."[202] Some examples from Tagle may suffice to illustrate how the plural stem extension is used. In an intransitive clause, *-er* refers to the plural subject.[203]

(233) **Tagle**
ìyì *ékk-é*
1SG urinate-PST.1SG
"I urinated"

(234) *àyì ékk-ér-ó*
1PL urinate-PLR-PST.1PL
"we urinated"

In a transitive clause, *-er* refers to the plural object.

(235) *àyì kér=gì kíl-ó*
1PL fence.SG=ACC jump-PST.1PL
"we jumped the fence"

(236) *àyì kér-nd̪ú=gí kíl-ér-ó*
1PL fence-PL=ACC jump-PLR-PST.1PL
"we jumped the fences"

The *-er*-extension also occurs in transitivity alternations. Compare the transitive clause in (237) to the agent-preserving clause in (238) and to the patient-preserving non-basic intransitive clause in (239).

(237) *íyé-t̪ù ēg-ī=gī túy-é-n*
shepherd-SG goat-PL=ACC milk-PLR-3
"the shepherd milks the goats" / "the shepherd milks goats"

(238) *íyé-t̪ù túy-é-n*
shepherd-SG milk-PLR-3
"the shepherd milks"

(239) *ōd̪-d̪ū túy-é-n*
goat-SG milk-PLR-3
"the goat milks, i.e., produces milk" / "a goat milks, i.e., produces milk"

Depending on the semantics of the verb and the semantic properties of its arguments, non-basic intransitivity constructions may even have a facilitative or passive reading.[204]

(240) *ì-t̪ɔ̀* *dʌ̄ɲɲ-ɛ̄-n*
baobab-SG climb-PLR-3
"the baobab is easy to climb" / "the baobab gets climbed"

Some transitive and intransitive verbs expressing inherently repetitive events are always marked by the *-er*-extension, as shown by the following 2SG/2PL imperative forms of Tagle. On these verbs the *-er*-extension has become lexicalized.

(241) *t̪ʊ́m-ɛ́r-í* SG/*t̪ʊ́m-ɛ́r-ɛ́* PL "stutter!"

(242) *bóg-ér-ì* SG/*bóg-ér-è* PL "bark!"

(243) *ùr-ér-ì* SG/*ùr-ér-è* PL "light a fire!"

The morphologically unmarked imperative examples from Karko show that the *-er*-extension is realized with an unspecified vowel which adopts the quality of the root vowel. Segmentally, it resembles the causative extension -*Vr* (see §2.1).

Karko

(244) *hə̄ɲ-ə́r* "greet!"

(245) *ūl-úr* "breastfeed!"

(246) *ɓàb-àr* "wipe off!"

(247) *ɛ̀b-ɛ̀r* "wash (hands, body)!"

The *-er*-extension is often found combined with other verbal number marking devices, most frequently with the alternation of the root vowel. Tabaq examples (248)–(250) also show that *-er* may occur in paradigmatic contrast with the singular stem extension *-ɪr* ~ *-ʊr*. This indicates that extensions which mark verbal number are not exclusively employed to express plurality; they can also refer to single participants and events.[205] Extensions marking singular verb stems have exclusively been documented in the Kordofan Nubian branch.[206]

Tabaq

	SNG	PLR	Gloss
(248)	*dóṯ-òr*	*dʷáṯ-ὲr-*	"cut across"
(249)	*ʃɔ́ɲk-ír*	*ʃʷáɲk-ɛ́r*	"dry"
(250)	*kʷɔ́ɔ́k-ír ~ kʷɔɔk-ór*	*kʷáák-ɛ́r*	"hide"

Midob *-er* is obviously a cognate of the Kordofan Nubian *-er*-extension. Werner claims that it is "no longer operative and can neither be clearly identified with plurality of object only."[207] The examples below show that *-er* is, in fact, sensitive to the plural subject of an intransitive verb, as shown by "sit" and "stop," and to the plural indirect object (i.e., the recipient) of the ditransitive "give" verb.[208]

Midob

(251)	*tèl-ér-hàm*	"they sat down" (several people)
(252)	*tèkk-ér-íc*	"stop!" ITR IMP 2PL
(253)	*tìr-îc*	"give to him!" IMP 2PL
(254)	*tìr-èr-îc*	"give to them!" IMP 2PL

Interestingly, the Kordofan Nubian and Midob *-er*-extension is phonetically and semantically comparable to the Ama *-r*-suffix, which, according to Norton, has distributive connotations, i.e., it distributes the event either over several object referents or over a series of sub-events.[209] It is always preceded by another distributive suffix, *-Vd̪*, and the theme vowel *a*. The resulting complex *-Vd̪-a-r*-suffix in Ama corresponds to the Afitti verbal plural suffix *(-tə)-r*. As distributivity is closely associated with plurality, it is quite conceivable that the Kordofan Nubian and Midob plural stem extension *-er* is a cognate of Ama *(-Vd̪-a)-r* and Afitti *(-tə)-r*. Moreover, these extensions may be related to the Mattokki and Andaandi extensions *-ir* and *-(i)r-ir*, which are sensitive to plural objects and distributive events (see §6.2). The different but semantically related functions of these extensions – verbal plural, distributive, plural object – indicate that this extension is of considerable age.

6.4. The Kordofan Nubian Reciprocal *-in*-Extension

Whereas the Nile Nubian languages and Midob express reciprocal notions lexically, the Kordofan Nubian languages exhibit a productive reciprocal extension which is attached to plural verb stems. Reciprocal constructions are intransitive; for this reason, in Tagle the intransitive past marker is required, *-(ì)bὲl,* which contrasts with the transitive past marker *-(í)nàl.*

(255) **Tagle**

ínì *kòn-nú-nù=gì* *ìcí=kɔ̀*

people bird-SG-DIM.SG=ACC hand=INS

áŋ-ínàl-à-m [áŋàlàm]

seize-TR.PST-PL-PST.3

"the people seized the bird by hand"

(256) *ínì* *àɲ-c-ìn-ìbὲl-ʌ̀-m*

people seize-PLR-RCP-ITR.PST-PL-PST.3

"the people seized each other"

In Karko the reciprocal extension has several allomorphs. Because of its underspecified vowel the extension *-Vn* adopts the quality of the stem vowel. As in Tagle, the reciprocal is attached to the plural verb stem, which signals low transitivity. In the past it requires the intransitive past marker *-ɲj.*

(257) **Karko**

ín *kwɛ̌ɛ̀=g* *fɛ́t̪-ɛ́n-ɲj-ɛ̀ɛ̀*

people spear.PL=ACC throw.PLR-RCP-ITR.PST-3PL

"the people threw spears at each other"

The Kordofan Nubian reciprocal *-in*-suffix looks strikingly similar to the Ama dual suffixes *-īn* and *-ēn.* According to Norton's internal reconstruction, Ama *-īn* is the older form, which originates from an old reciprocal suffix.[210] He also points out that similar reciprocal extensions are attested in several East Sudanic languages. For these reasons, Kordofan Nubian *-in* and Ama *-īn* can be considered cognates, providing another piece of evidence for the genetic relationship between these languages. So far, we do not know whether Afitti exhibits a comparable extension.[211]

6.5. Further Plural Stem Extensions in the Kordofan Nubian Languages

The Kordofan Nubian languages are rich in verbal number marking devices. In addition to the reflexes of the productive pluractional **-(i)j* and plural stem marker *-er* there are several further less productive extensions as well as alternations of the root vowel, tonal alternations, and reduplication of the root. Some verbs have a single marked plural stem which is sensitive both to repetitive events and plural objects, other verbs have two distinct plural stems, one interacting with event number, the other one interacting with the intransitive plural subject or transitive plural object.

	Dilling			
(258)	*bur*	"get solid" ITR, SJ SG	*bur-k-iɲ*	id. SJ PL
(259)	*ʃoɲ*	"get dry" ITR, SJ SG	*ʃwaɲ-c-iŋ*	id. SJ PL
(260)	*dil*	"gather" ITR, SJ PL	*dil-t-ig*	id. SJ PL, RPT

The stacking of plural stem extensions (i.e., the use of more than one suffix) is a common phenomenon in the Kordofan Nubian languages, as attested by Dilling (258) *bur-k-iɲ,* (259) *ʃwaɲ-c-iŋ,* and (260) *dil-t-ig,* as well as Tagle (261) *èl-t-ìg-ì,* (262) *éṯ-íŋ-k-í,* and (264) *dɛ́-k-ɛ́r-ɛ́.* While (261) and (262) display 2SG imperative forms marked by a final *-i,* (263) and (264) represent the 2SG/2PL imperative forms, marked by *-i/ -e ~ -ɛ.*

Tagle

(261)	*él-ír-ì*	"reach!" TR, OJ SG	*èl-t-ìg-ì*	id. OJ SG, RPT
(262)	*èt̪-ír-ì*	"enter!" TR, OJ SG	*ét̪-íŋ-k-í*	id. OJ PL, RPT
(263)	*nòm-èr-í*	"run!" ITR, SJ SG	*nòm-k-é*	id. SJ PL, RPT
(264)	*dí*	"stand up, get up!" ITR, SJ SG	*dɛ́-k-ɛ́r-ɛ́*	id. SJ PL, RPT

Karko, too, uses various plural stem extensions, including *-t-Vg*, *-kVn*, and *-(V)k*, which are often combined with other formal devices such as tonal alternation and the reduplication of the verb root. The examples also illustrate that some verbs exhibit more than one plural stem, one stem interacting with participant number and the other with event number. The "fact that there is usually more than one formal strategy" for marking verbal number suggests "that this grammatical domain is subject to a high degree of communicative dynamism."[212]

Karko

(265)	*kūg-úr*	"fix, connect!" TR, OJ SG	*kùg-t-ùg*	id. OJ PL, RPT		
(266)	*dìí-r*	"sink!" ITR, SJ SG	*dìì-kìn*	id. SJ PL	*dīī-dìì-k*	id. RPT
(267)	*nwàá-r*	"run!" ITR, SJ SG	*nwàà-kàn*	id. SJ PL	*dòɓ*	id. RPT

Like the *-er*-extension (§6.3), the suffixes introduced in the present section can mark plural verb stems which are required in transitivity alternations. For this reason, they are glossed just like *-er* by PLR. Here are two pairs of Karko examples contrasting transitive and non-basic intransitive clauses. The latter are illustrated by the agent-preserving clause (269) and the patient-preserving clause (271).

(268) *ín* *wèè=g* *díg-t-ìg*
people sorghum=ACC gather-PLR-PLR
"the people gather the sorghum (ears)"

(269) *ín* *kùld=ūt* *díg-t-ìg*
people mountain=LOC gather-PLR-PLR
"the people gather on the mountain"

(270) *īīḓ* *ṯóóɲéè=g* *fɛ̀j-ɛ́k*
man children=ACC wake.up-PLR
"the man wakes the children up"

(271) *ṯóóɲē* *fɛ̀j-ɛ́k*
children wake.up-PLR
"the children wake up"

6.6. The Kordofan Nubian *-aḓ-* and Midob *-át-*Extensions

These productive extensions, Kordofan Nubian *-aḓ* and Midob *-át,* are assumed to be cognates, first, because non-initial Kordofan Nubian *ḓ* can correspond to Midob alveolar *t,*[213] and second, because these suffixes have similar functions, since they are both associated with decreased valency. However, *-át* and *-aḓ* differ in that the first is a verbal extension which does not trigger a change of the word category, while the latter turns the verb into a "verbal adjective," as Kauczor suggests,[214] or rather a resultative participle. When the morpheme *-aḓ* attaches to verbal stems, the outcome is a resultative participle expressing states that result from previous events which have affected or changed the entity whose properties are designated by the participle.

The *-aḓ*-extension is a portmanteau morpheme since it cumulatively expresses decreased valency and singular number. The corresponding plural morphemes, Dilling *-e,* Tagle *-an-i* ~ *-ʌn-ɪ,* and Karko *-Vn* are portmanteau morphemes too, as they cover both decreased valency and plural number. However, only Tagle *-an-i* ~ *-ʌn-ɪ* and Karko *-Vn* are etymologically related to each other, while Dilling *-e* appears to have a different origin.[215]

Dilling

(272)	*bar/bar-k-iɲ*	"be tired"	*bar-k-ad/bar-k-e*	"tired"
(273)	*beʃ-ir/bej*	"damage"	*beʃ-ig-ad/bej-ig-e*	"damaged"
(274)	*em*	"wash"	*em-ad/em-e*	"washed"

The Tagle participles are regularly associated with a low tone pattern. The singular forms are marked by complex suffixes composed of the participle marker plus a vowel suffix marking number, *-aḏ-u ~ -ʌḏ-ʊ* and the plural forms by *-an-i ~ -ʌn-ɪ*. This means that Tagle participles are double marked for number. The participles can serve as attributive adjectives modifying a noun phrase or as predicative adjectives in copula clauses.

(275a) **Tagle**
kí-ṯó *èṯ-ìŋk-àḏ-ù*
door-SG enter-PLR-PTC.SG-SG
"the closed door"

(275b) *kí-ní* *èṯ-ìŋk-àn-ì*
door-PL enter-PLR-PTC.PL-PL
"the closed doors"

(276a) *kì-ṯò* *dùy-àḏ-ù-ní* [dùyàdùní]
cloth-SG sew-PTC.SG-SG-COP
"the cloth is sewn"

(276b) *kì-nì* *dùy-àn-ì-ní*
cloth-PL sew-PTC.PL-PL-COP
"the clothes are sewn"

Similar to Tagle, Karko participles are characterized by a low tone pattern. They are inflected for singular by *-Vḏ* and for plural by *-Vn,* the vowel *V* adopting the quality of the stem vowel.

Karko

(277)	*kàm-àd̪/kàm-àn*	"eaten"
(278)	*t̪ə̀f-ə̀d̪/t̪ə̀f-ə̀n*	"killed"

Interestingly, most of the participles illustrated here exhibit a marked plural stem: e.g., Dilling *bar-k-ad/bar-k-e* "tired," *beʃ-ig-ad/bej-ig-e* "damaged"; Tagle *èt̪-ìŋk-àd̪-ù/èt̪-ìŋk-àn-ì* "closed." The corresponding singular stems are Dilling *bar, beʃ-ir* and Tagle *èt̪-ír,* respectively. The Karko examples *kàm-àd̪/kàm-àn* "eaten" and *tə̀f-ə̀d̪/tə̀f-ə̀n* "killed," however, exhibit suppletive plural stems, the corresponding singular stems being *kə̀l* and *fúr,* respectively. The plural verb stems are selected because they are associated with low transitivity (which is also addressed in §6.3).

As for the Midob *-át*-extension, we suggest an analysis different from Werner's. On first sight, (279)–(281) support his claim that *-(r)ati* derives reflexive verbs.[216]

Midob

(279)	*èeb-àh-êm*	"I washed" TR	*èeb-árát-ìh-èm*	"I washed myself" REFL
(280)	*tə̀g-ə̀n-dóo-h-èm*	"I covered" TR	*tə̀g-rát-ìh-èm*	"I covered myself" REFL
(281)	*pìss-ìr-h-êm*	"I have sprinkled" TR	*pìss-ìrát-íh-èm*	"I sprinkled myself" REFL

However, his Midob grammar also contains a few counter examples which do not express reflexive notions.[217] They suggest that *-r-at* is a complex morpheme composed of *-(i)r ~ -(a)r* plus *-át.* Whereas the first component looks like a reflex of the causative **-(i)r,* the second component *-át* can be identified as a valency-decreasing device deriving intransitive from transitive verbs.

(282)	*òss-ír-hèm*	"I soaked" TR	*òss-ìr-át-ùm*	"it is soaking"
(283)	*tə̀g-ə̀r-hèm*	"I closed, covered" TR	*tə̀g-r-át-òn-ûm*	"it was covered"[218]

It is still conceivable that *-at* can also trigger a reflexive interpretation, especially when it is attached to verbs with an animate and agentive subject such as "wash," "cover," and "sprinkle."

If Kordofan Nubian *-ad̪* and Midob *-át* are cognate valency-decreasing morphemes, are they related to the passive extensions, Old Nubian *-tak* and Nobiin *-dakk* ~ *-takk* ~ *-daŋ*? Although the metathesis of *-ad̪* > *-d̪a* and *-át* > *-tá* is conceivable, none of these suffixes exhibits a velar which would match the final consonants of *-tak* and *-dakk* ~ *-takk* ~ *-daŋ*. For this reason, there is too little evidence supporting the assumption of a common origin of these extensions.

6.7. The Midob *-íd*-Extension

Tucker & Bryan identify a *-Vda*-suffix which expresses "plural action."[219]

(284)	*ʊkk-a*	"bear"	*ʊkk-ʊda*	"bear often"
(285)	*ökk-a*	"bear twins"	*ökk-ʊda*	"bear twins often"
(286)	*acc-a*	"bite"	*acc-ida*	"bite often"

Werner, in turn, recognizes this suffix as *-íd*, ending in an alveolar [d].[220] His examples suggest that the final *-a* on *-Vda* is not part of this suffix. Similarly to Tucker & Bryan, he describes this suffix as expressing "plurality of action."[221]

(287)	*úkk-ánònùm*	"she has given birth"	*úkk-íd-ánònùm*	"she has given birth (to many children)"

A phonetically and semantically similar VC-shaped extension is attested in Ama by *-íd̪*. According to Norton, the Ama extension *-íd̪* has a distributive function.[222] It is sensitive to a plural object participant, as shown in (289) or to a plural subject participant as in (290). Moreover, it can express an event distributed in time over a series of sub-events, as in (291). Norton considers *-íd̪*, with these distributional functions, as a type of pluractional.[223]

(288) **Ama**

əŋí bā wùd̪ēŋ dɛ̄ɛ́í
1PL VER child hit
"we hit the child"

(289) *əŋí bā dɔ̄rɛŋ dɛ̄-íd̪-í*
1PL VER children hit-DSTR-TH
"we hit the children"

(290) *əŋí bā tūɽ-íd-è*
1PL VER cry-DSTR-TH
"we (three or more) each cried"

(291) *əŋí bā dɔ̄rɛŋ mɔ̄l dɛ̄-íd̪-í*
1PL VER children five hit-DSTR-TH
"we hit until we had hit five children"

Midob is spoken in Darfur and Ama in the Nuba Mountains. In view of the geographical distance between these languages today, (recent) direct borrowing is unlikely. Considering that the non-initial dental *d̪* and the non-initial alveolar *d* may correspond to each other,[224] the striking semantic and phonetic resemblances between Ama *-íd̪* and Midob *-íd* suggest that these suffixes are cognates. They represent another piece of evidence for the common genetic origins of Ama and the Nubian languages. Unfortunately, as in the case of the causative *-ɪg-* or *-ɛg-*suffix and the reciprocal/dual suffix *-ɪn,* corroborating evidence from Afitti is (still) missing.

7. Conclusions

If we disregard the predicable epenthetic vowel, we recognize that six of the seven reconstructable derivational extensions either consist of a single consonant C or of a CV(V)C pattern. While the C-shaped extensions include **-(i)r,* the pluractional **-(i)j,* and the plural stem extension **-(i)k,* the CV(V)C pattern is represented by the causative morpheme **-(i)gir* and the applicative morphemes **tir* and **deen.* The latter pattern coincides with the canonical syllable pattern of

Nubian lexical roots, thus corroborating the assumed origin of **(i)gir, *tir,* and **deen* from lexical items, or, more precisely, from lexical verbs.

Whereas **-(i)r, *-(i)j, *-(i)k, *-(i)gir, *tir,* and **deen* can be traced back to Proto-Nubian, the causative **u- ~ o*-prefix and its cognate, the Ama *a*-prefix, are assumed to originate from the archaic Nilo-Saharan **i-*. As reflexes of this prefix are also attested in several branches of Eastern Sudanic and in Central Sudanic, they prove to be historically stable derivational morphemes which corroborate the assumed genetic coherence of the Nilo-Saharan phylum, as Dimmendaal argues.[225] Moreover, the prefixes suggest that these languages have changed from an originally prefixing to a predominantly suffixing type. Another indicator of this conversion process is the archaic Nubian **m*-prefix, which used to serve as a negation marker.

The comparative perspective on the Nubian verb extensions reveals language change motivated by various instances of grammaticalization, including semantic bleaching, the weakening and loss of functions, blending, the adoption of new grammatical functions, and even the emergence of new morphemes.

A manifestation of language change is the grammaticalization of the causative extension **-(i)r.* The Old Nubian and Nobiin *-(i)r*-suffix tends to become redundant and therefore appears as a lexicalized element on some verbs. In Mattokki and Andaandi the gradual loss of the causative function of the *-ir*-extension has motivated the development of a reduplicated suffix. The resulting new *-ir-ir*-extension, realized as [iddi], is considered to be a compensation for the nearly defunct *-ir.* In the Kordofan Nubian languages the weakening of the causative function has resulted in *-(i)r* serving as a transitivizer on some Dilling verbs and on other verbs as an intransitivizer. On some Tagle verbs, in turn, *-ir* is even used in paradigmatic contrast to *-er,* thus differentiating singular from plural stems. Such morphologically marked singular stems only occur in Kordofan Nubian languages, whereas in the Nile Nubian languages they are unattested.

Another instance of grammaticalization is the assumed morphological blending of the two donative verbs, resulting in the emergence of the innovative verb *ti.* In the Kordofan Nubian languages *ti* has begun to replace the original donative verbs, particularly in applicative constructions. These distinct stages of grammaticalization indicate that the western Nubian languages have undergone more morphological and syntactic changes than the Nile Nubian languages which have retained the two original verbs.

Suggesting that the Old Nubian and Nobiin *-a*-suffix is a converb marker and therefore different from the Old Nubian clitic predicate marker *-a*, we have highlighted some syntactic, morphological, and semantic properties of converbs in the Nile Nubian languages. They can express chains of successive events or even events prior or simultaneous to the event expressed by the main verb. Converbs are also employed as adverbial modifiers of main verbs. In these contexts, converbs are used in symmetric formations, i.e., the converb(s) and the main verb of a clause contribute equally to the expression of two or more events. In an asymmetric converb construction, by contrast, the converb and the adjacent main verb jointly express a single event. Such asymmetric formations are often associated with directed motion or transfer events or with the grammaticalization of the main verb as an aspect-marking or even valency-changing device. The latter is attested by the biverbal applicative construction in the Nile Nubian languages where the second verb is represented by a finite donative verb. This serves as a valence operator commonly licensing an additional argument with the role of a beneficiary.

Unlike the biverbal applicative construction in the Nile Nubian languages, applicatives in the Kordofan Nubian and Midob form monoverbal constructions, since "give" has become a derivational morpheme being suffixed to the stem of the lexical verb by means of the linker *-(i)n*. This means that in Kordofan Nubian applicative constructions the development of "give" as a bound derivational morpheme has reached a further stage on the grammaticalization path than "give" in the Nile Nubian converb constructions. At least in Andaandi, the auxiliary-like "give" verb is a free form which can be separated from the preceding lexical verb by means of the question clitic *te*.

Verbal number plays an important role, as it can express event number and participant number. The pluractional **-(i)j*, for instance, conveys event plurality associated with various aspectual notions. In Andaandi, Dilling, and Midob it expresses intensive and repetitive actions, in Tagle repetitive and continued actions, and in Mattokki distributive events. It also has morphosyntactic functions, as indicated by the interaction between the *-*(i)j*-marked verb stems and the plural subject in intransitive clauses or the plural object in transitive clauses. In ditransitive applicative constructions the reflex of **-(i)j* is selected by the plural indirect object (i.e., the beneficiary), as attested in the Old Nubian example (144). In Kordofan Nubian ditransitive applicative constructions, however, it is the plural direct object (i.e., the theme) which selects a reflex of *-(i)j, as shown in the Karko example (179). In transitive clauses *-(i)j is sensitive to the plural object (patient), as shown in the Old Nubian example (154) and Karko example (177). Thus, the selection of the *-(i)j-extension provides evidence of two patterns of alignment. Whereas the patient aligns with the beneficiary in Old Nubian, in Karko the patient aligns with the theme. These two patterns are known as secondary-object construction and indirect-object construction, respectively.[226]

Verbal number marking in the Kordofan Nubian languages is far more complex than in the Nile Nubian languages. It is carried out by means of several formal strategies, including a variety of suffixes which may be combined with each other and with the alternation of the stem vowel and tone pattern. The morphological complexity of this system suggests that it is rather instable.[227] In addition to expressing event number and participant number, Kordofan Nubian plural stems can even serve as valency-decreasing devices in agent-preserving and patient-preserving clauses which may convey facilitative and passive meanings.

In addition to reconstructing several Proto-Nubian verb extensions, the present paper also shows striking phonetic and semantic resemblances between several Nubian and Nyima (mostly Ama) verb extensions. The Nubian causative suffix *-(i)gir, for instance, exhibits a velar stop. A velar [g] is also found in the Ama directional/causative extensions *-ɪg* and *-ɛg*. The Ama causative verbs "feed" and "suckle" addressed in §5.2 suggest that the *-ɪg-* and *-ɛg*-extensions have come to replace the now defunct causative *a*-prefix, the latter being a cognate of the Proto-Nubian **u-* ~ *o*-prefix.

The Kordofan Nubian reciprocal extension *-in* is comparable to the Ama dual *-ɪn*, which, according to Norton, originates from a reciprocal extension.[228]

When we consider that the Proto-Nubian liquid **r* is retained in most of its daughter languages, as attested by **ur* "head," **m-iir* "barren," and **tir* "give to 2nd or 3rd person,"[229] it is quite conceivable that the Kordofan Nubian and Midob verbal plural suffix *-er* and the Mattokki and Andaandi plural object *-ir-* or *-(i)r-ir*-extension are cognates. They also appear to correspond to the Ama distributive extension *-r* and to the *-r* component of the complex Ama and Afitti extensions *(-Vḓ-a)-r* and *(-tə)-r*, respectively. In addition to the shared *-r*-suffix, all of these extensions convey the semantic notion of plurality.

The Midob plural stem extension *-íd-* ~ *-ʊd* and the Ama distributive *-íḓ* share several features, such as a VC-shaped structure, a high vowel, and high tone. Moreover, they are both semantically associated with plurality. Therefore, it seems likely that they have a common genetic origin.

As bound morphemes are less often subject to borrowing than free morphemes, these corresponding verb extensions point to a remote genetic relationship between Nubian and Nyima, rather than to contact-induced similarities.

However, in addition to the suggestive evidence of their old genetic links, there are also indicators of recent convergence between Nubian and Nyima, as attested by lexical borrowings (**Tables 1 and 2**). Since the phonetic similarities of the Ama, Mandal, and Afitti items to the Kordofan Nubian items is stronger than to the corresponding Nile Nubian items, they indicate that Kordofan Nubian is the donor language of these borrowings. It is assumed that Ama and Afitti adopted Kordofan Nubian lexical items due to contact with the ancestors of the present Kordofan Nubian language speakers, after they had migrated to and settled in the Nuba Mountains.

8. Abbreviations

- 1, 2, 3 – 1st, 2nd, 3rd person;
- ACC – accusative;
- An – Andaandi;
- APPL – applicative;
- CAUS – causative;
- CNV – converb;
- COM – comitative;
- COMM – command;
- CONT – continuous;
- DET – determiner;
- Dil – Dilling;
- DIM – diminutive;
- DISTR – distributive;

› DITR – ditransitive;
› GEN – genitive;
› EXCL – exclusive;
› IMP – imperative;
› INCL – inclusive;
› IND – indicative;
› INTEN – intentional;
› INS – instrumental;
› ITR – intransitive;
› JUS – jussive;
› Ka – Karko;
› Ma – Mattokki;
› LK – linker;
› LOC – locative;
› Mi – Midob;
› NEG – negation;
› NEUT – neutral;
› NN – Nile Nubian;
› No – Nobiin;
› OJ – object;
› ON – Old Nubian;
› PASS – passive;
› PCNV – purposive converb;
› PL – plural of nominal;
› PLACT – pluractional;
› PLR – plural verb stem;
› PN – Proto-Nubian;
› PKN – Proto-Kordofan Nubian;
› PLOJ – plural object;
› PRED – predicate;
› PRF – perfect;
› PROG – progressive;
› PFV – perfective;
› PRS – present tense;
› PST – past;
› PT – preterite;
› PTC – participle;

- PROG – progressive;
- PROH – prohibitive;
- Q – question;
- REFL – reflexive;
- RCP – reciprocal;
- RPT – repetitive;
- SJ – subject;
- SG – singular of nominal;
- SGT – singulative;
- SNG – singular verb stem;
- STAT – stative;
- SUB – subessive;
- SUPE – superessive;
- Ta – Tagle;
- TH – theme;
- TOP – topic;
- TR – transitive;
- VER – veridical;
- VET – vetitive.

9. Bibliography

Abdel-Hafiz, Ahmed S. bib/ *A Reference Grammar of Kunuz Nubian.* PhD Thesis, State University of New York at Buffalo, 1988.

Abel, Hans. bib/ *Eine Erzählung im Dialekt von Ermenne (Nubien).* Abhandlungen der philologisch-historischen Klasse der Gesellschaft der Wissenschaften 29, no. 8. Leipzig: Teubner, 1913.

Almkvist, Herman N. bib/ *Nubische Studien im Sudān 1877–78.* Edited by K.V. Zetterstéen. Uppsala: Almkvist & Wiksell; Leipzig: Harrassowitz, 1911.

Aikhenvald, Alexandra Y. bib/ *Serial Verbs.* Oxford: Oxford University Press, 2018.

Ameka, Felix K. "Ewe Serial Verb Constructions in Their Grammatical Context." In *Serial Verb Constructions: A Cross-linguistic Typology,* edited by Alexandra Y. Aikhenvald & Robert M.W. Dixon. Oxford: Oxford University Press, 2006: pp. 124–143.

Amha, Azeb & Gerrit J. Dimmendaal. "Converbs in an African Perspective." In *Catching Language,* edited by Felix A. Ameka, Alan Dench & Nicholas Evans. Berlin & New York: Mouton de Gruyter, 2006: pp. 393–440.

Amha, Azeb & Gerrit J. Dimmendaal. bib/ "Verbal Compounding in Wolaitta." In *Serial Verb Constructions: A Cross-Linguistic Typology,* edited by Alexandra Y. Aikhenvald & Robert M.W. Dixon. Oxford & New York: Oxford University Press, 2006: pp. 319–337.

Armbruster, Charles H. bib/ *Dongolese Nubian: A Grammar.* Cambridge: Cambridge University Press, 1960.

Armbruster, Charles H. bib/ *Dongolese Nubian: A Lexicon.* Cambridge: Cambridge University Press, 1965.

Bechhaus-Gerst, Marianne. bib/ "'Nile-Nubian' Reconsidered." In *Topics in Nilo-Saharan Linguistics,* edited by M. Lionel Bender. Hamburg: Buske, 1989: pp. 85–96.

Bechhaus-Gerst, Marianne. bib/ "Sprachliche und historische Rekonstruktionen im Bereich des Nubischen unter besonderer Berücksichtigung des Nilnubischen."

Sprache und Geschichte in Afrika 6 (1984/85): pp. 7–134.

Bechhaus-Gerst, Marianne. bib/*The (Hi)story of Nobiin: 1000 Years of Language Change.* Frankfurt: Peter Lang, 2011.

Bender, M. Lionel. "Nilo-Saharan." In *African Languages: An Introduction,* edited by Bernd Heine & Derek Nurse. Cambridge: Cambridge University Press, 2000: pp. 43–75.

Bender, M. Lionel. bib/*The Nilo-Saharan Languages: A Comparative Essay.* Munich: Lincom Europa, 1996.

Blench, Roger M. "Morphological Evidence for the Coherence of East Sudanic." *Dotawo: A Journal of Nubian Studies* 7 (2020): article/this issue.

Browne, Gerald M. bib/*Old Nubian Dictionary.* Leuven: Peeters, 1996.

Browne, Gerald M. bib/*Old Nubian Grammar.* Munich: Lincom Europa, 2002.

Browne, Gerald M. bib/*The Old Nubian Miracle of Saint Menas.* Vienna-Mödling: Verein der Förderer der Sudanforschung, 1994.

Comfort, Jade. bib/"Converbs in Uncunwee (Kordofan Nubian)." In *Nuba Mountain Language Studies,* edited by Thilo C. Schadeberg & Roger M. Blench. Cologne: Rüdiger Köppe, 2013: pp. 381–400.

Comfort, Jade. bib/"Verbal Number in the Uncu Language (Kordofan Nubian)." *Dotawo: A Journal of Nubian Studies* 1 (2014): pp. 145–163. DOI: www/10.5070/D61110032.

Comfort, Jade & Angelika Jakobi bib/"The Verb 'to give' as a Verbal Extension in Uncunwee (Kordofan Nubian)." In *Afrikanische Sprachen im Fokus,* edited by Raija Kramer, Holger Tröbs & Raimund Kastenholz. Cologne: Rüdiger Köppe, 2011: pp. 27–35.

Creissels, Denis. bib/"Benefactive Applicative Periphrases: A Typological Approach." In *Benefactives and Malefactives: Typological Perspectives and Case Studies,* edited by Fernando Zúñiga & Seppo Kittilä. Amsterdam & Philadelphia: John Benjamins, 2010: pp. 29–69.

Dimmendaal, Gerrit J. "Comparative African Linguistics." In *The Cambridge Handbook of African Linguistics,* edited by H. Ekkehard Wolff. Cambridge: Cambridge University Press, 2019: pp. 139–165.

Dimmendaal, Gerrit J. "Eastern Sudanic and the Wadi Howar and Wadi El Milk Diaspora." *Sprache und Geschichte in Afrika* 18 (2007): pp. 37–67.

Dimmendaal, Gerrit J. *Historical Linguistics and the Comparative Study of African Languages.* Amsterdam: John Benjamins, 2011.

Dimmendaal, Gerrit J. "Nilo-Saharan." In *The Oxford Handbook of Derivational Morphology,* edited by Rochelle Lieber & Pavol Štekauer. Oxford: Oxford University Press, 2014: pp. 591–607.

Dimmendaal, Gerrit J. "On Stable and Unstable Features in Nilo-Saharan." In *Nilo-Saharan Issues and Perspectives,* edited by Helga Schröder & Prisca Jerono. Cologne: Rüdiger Köppe, 2018: pp. 9–23.

Dimmendaal, Gerrit J. "Pluractionality and the Distribution of Number Marking across Categories." In *Number – Constructions and Semantics: Case Studies from Africa, Amazonia, India and Oceania,* edited by Anne Storch & Gerrit J. Dimmendaal. Amsterdam: John Benjamins, 2014: pp. 57–75.

Dimmendaal, Gerrit J., Colleen Ahland, Angelika Jakobi & Constance Kutsch Lojenga. "Linguistic Features and Typologies in Languages Commonly Referred to as 'Nilo-Saharan'." In *The Cambridge Handbook of African Linguistics,* edited by H. Ekkehard Wolff. Cambridge: Cambridge University Press, 2019: pp. 326–381.

Ehret, Christopher. *A Historical-Comparative Reconstruction of Nilo-Saharan.* Cologne: Rüdiger Köppe, 2001.

Gerven Oei, Vincent W.J. van. "A Note on the Old Nubian Morpheme -ⲁ in Nominal and Verbal Predicates." In *Nubian Voices II: New Texts and Studies on Christian Nubian Culture,* edited by Adam Łajtar, Grzegorz Ochała, and Jacques van der Vliet. Warsaw: Raphael Taubenschlag Foundation, 2015: pp. 313–334.

Gerven Oei, Vincent W.J. van. *A Reference Grammar of Old Nubian.* Leuven: Peeters, forthcoming.

Greenberg, Joseph H. bib/*Studies in African Linguistic Classification.* New Haven: Compass, 1955.

Greenberg, Joseph H. bib/*The Languages of Africa.* 3rd edition. Bloomington: Indiana University Press, 1970.

Grüning, Manfred. bib/*A Sketch of the Midob Verbal Morphology.* MA Thesis, Redcliffe College, 2014.

Hashim, Mohamed El-Hadi Hassan. bib/*Nobiiguun Kummaanchii – Shoo Urragi. Nobiin Stories, Vol. 1.* Edited and translated by Roland Werner. Berlin: Nubian Press, 2005.

Haspelmath, Martin. bib/"The Grammaticization of Passive Morphology." *Studies in Language* 14, no. 1 (1990): pp. 25–72. DOI: www/10.1075/sl.14.1.03has.

Haspelmath, Martin. bib/"Ditransitive Constructions: The Verb 'Give'." In *The World Atlas of Language Structures Online,* edited by Matthew S. Dryer & Martin Haspelmath. Leipzig, Max Planck Institute for Evolutionary Anthropology, 2013. www/http://wals.info/chapter/105.

Hintze, Fritz. bib/"Beobachtungen zur altnubischen Grammatik I und II." *Berliner Beiträge zur Ägyptologie und Sudanarchäologie* 20, no. 3 (1971): pp. 287–293.

Hopper, Paul J. bib/"Where Do Words Come From?" In *Studies in Typology and Diachrony: Papers Presented to Joseph H. Greenberg on His 75th Birthday,* edited by William Croft, Keith M. Denning & Suzanne Kemmer. Amsterdam: John Benjamins, 1990: pp. 151–160.

Hopper, Paul J. & Sandra A. Thompson. bib/"Transitivity in Grammar and Discourse." *Language* 56, no. 2 (1980): pp. 251–299. DOI: www/10.2307/413757.

Jakobi, Angelika. bib/"The Loss of Syllable-final Proto-Nubian Consonants." In *Insights into Nilo-Saharan Language, History and Culture,* edited by Al-Amin Abu-Manga, Leoma Gilley & Anne Storch. Cologne: Rüdiger Köppe, 2006: pp. 215–228.

Jakobi, Angelika. bib/"Verbal Number and Transitivity in Karko (Kordofan Nubian)." *Sprachtypologie und Universalienforschung* 70, no. 1 (2017): pp. 117–142. DOI: www/10.1515/stuf-2017-0007.

Jakobi, Angelika & Joachim Crass. bib/ *Grammaire du beria (langue saharienne).* Cologne: Rüdiger Köppe, 2004.

Jakobi, Angelika & El-Shafie El-Guzuuli. bib/ "Perception Verbs and Their Semantics in Dongolawi (Nile Nubian)." In *Perception and Cognition in Language and Culture,* edited by Anne Storch & Alexandra Aikhenvald. Leiden: Brill, 2013: pp. 193–215.

Jakobi, Angelika & Ali Ibrahim. bib/ "Labile Verbs in Tagle (Kordofan Nubian)." In *Nuba Mountain Language Studies: New Insights,* edited by Gertrud Schneider-Blum, Birgit Hellwig & Gerrit J. Dimmendaal. Cologne: Rüdiger Köppe, 2018: pp. 99–127.

Jakobi, Angelika, Ali Ibrahim & Gumma Ibrahim Gulfan. "Verbal Number and Grammatical Relations in Tagle." *Faits de Langues/Journal of Language Diversity* 51, no. 1 (2020): pp. 99–116.

Kauczor, P. Daniel. bib/ *Die bergnubische Sprache (Dialekt von Gebel Deleń).* Vienna: Alfred Hölder, 1920.

Keenan, Edward L. & Matthew S. Dryer. "Passive in the World's Languages." In *Language Typology and Syntactic Description,* Vol. 1: *Clause Structure,* edited by Timothy Shopen. Cambridge: Cambridge University Press, 2007: pp. 325–361.

Khalil, Mohamed K. "The Verbal Plural Marker in Nobiin (Nile Nubian)."}bib:d49f8a89-7fff-4de7-bab6-b8ce57cb6db6not found *Dotawo: A Journal of Nubian Studies* 2 (2015): pp. 59–71.

Lepsius, C. Richard. bib/ *Nubische Grammatik. Mit einer Einleitung über die Völker und Sprachen Afrikas.* Berlin: Wilhelm Hertz, 1880.

Massenbach, Gertrud von. bib/ "Wörterbuch des nubischen Kunûzi-Dialektes mit einer grammatischen Einleitung." *Mitteilungen des Seminars für Orientalische Sprachen* 36 (1933): pp. 99–227.

Mufwene, Salikoko S. bib/ *Stativity and the Progressive.* Bloomington: Indiana University Linguistics Club, 1984.

Norton, Russell. "Ama Verbs in Comparative Perspective." *Dotawo: A Journal of Nubian Studies* 7 (2020): article/ this issue.

Norton, Russell. bib/"Number in Ama Verbs." *Occasional Papers in the Study of Sudanese Languages* 10 (2012): pp. 75–93.

Norton, Russell. bib/"The Ama Dual Suffix: An Internal Reconstruction." In *Nilo-Saharan: Models and Descriptions,* edited by Angelika Mietzner & Anne Storch. Cologne: Rüdiger Köppe, 2015: pp. 113–122.

Noonan, Michael. bib/"Genetic Classification and Language Contact." In *Handbook of Language Contact,* edited by Raymond Hickey. Malden: Wiley-Blackwell, 2010: pp. 48–65.

Pointner, Lena. bib/"Verbal Number in Tabaq." In *Nuba Mountain Language Studies: New Insights,* edited by Gertrud Schneider-Blum, Birgit Hellwig & Gerrit J. Dimmendaal. Cologne: Rüdiger Köppe, 2018: pp. 77–97.

Rapold, Christian J. bib/"Defining Converbs Ten Years On – A Hitchhikers' Guide." In *Converbs, Medial Verbs, Clause Chaining and Related Issues,* edited by Sascha Völlmin, Azeb Amha, Christian J. Rapold & Silvia Zaugg-Coretti. Cologne: Rüdiger Köppe Verlag, 2012: pp. 7–30.

Reinisch, Leo. bib/*Die Nuba-Sprache.* 2 vols. Vienna: Wilhelm Braumüller, 1879.

Reinisch, Leo. bib/*Die sprachliche Stellung des Nuba.* Vienna: Hölder, 1911.

Rilly, Claude. bib/*Le méroïtique et sa famille linguistique.* Leuven: Peeters, 2010.

Rilly, Claude. bib/"The Linguistic Position of Meroitic: New Perspectives for Understanding the Texts." *Sudan & Nubia* 12 (2008): pp. 2–12.

Rottland, Franz & Angelika Jakobi. bib/"Loan Word Evidence from the Nuba Mountains: Kordofan Nubian and the Nyimang Group." *Afrikanistische Arbeitspapiere,* Sondernummer (1991): pp. 249–269.

Slobin, Dan I. bib/"What Makes Manner of Motion Verbs Salient? Explorations in Linguistic Typology, Discourse and Cognition." In *Space in Languages. Linguistic Systems and Cognitive Categories,* edited by Maya Hickmann & Stéphane Robert. Amsterdam: John Benjamins, 2006: pp. 59–81.

Smagina, Eugenia B. bib/*The Old Nubian Language.* Translated by José Andrés Alonso de la Fuente. Dotawo Monograph 3. Earth: punctum books, 2017.

Starostin, George. bib/"Lexicostatistical Studies in East Sudanic I: On the Genetic Unity of Nubian–Nara–Tama." *Journal of Language Relationship* 15, no. 2 (2017): pp. 87–113.

Stevenson, Roland C. bib/"A Survey of the Phonetics and Grammatical Structures of the Nuba Mountain Languages, with Particular Reference to Otoro, Katcha and Nyimaŋ." *Afrika und Übersee* 40 (1956): pp. 73–84, 93–115.

Stevenson, Roland C. bib/"A Survey of the Phonetics and Grammatical Structures of the Nuba Mountain Languages, with Particular Reference to Otoro, Katcha and Nyimaŋ." *Afrika und Übersee* 41 (1957): pp. 27–65, 117–152, 171–196.

Stevenson, Roland, Franz Rottland & Angelika Jakobi. bib/"The Verb in Nyimang and Dinik." *Afrikanistische Arbeitspapiere* 32 (1992): pp. 5–64.

Thelwall, Robin. bib/"Lexicostatistical Relations between Nubian, Daju and Dinka." In *Etudes Nubiennes, Colloque de Chantilly, 2–6 Juillet 1975,* edited by Jean Leclant and Jean Vercouttier. Cairo: IFAO, 1978: pp. 265–286.

Thelwall, Robin. bib/"Meidob Nubian: Phonology, Grammatical Notes and Basic Vocabulary." In *Nilo-Saharan Language Studies,* edited by M. Lionel Bender. East Lansing: African Studies Center, Michigan State University, 1983: pp. 97–113.

Tucker, Archibald N. & Margaret A. Bryan. bib/*Linguistic Analyses: The Non-Bantu Languages of North-Eastern Africa.* London: Oxford University Press, 1966.

Veselinova, Ljuba N. bib/"Verbal Number and Suppletion." In *The World Atlas of Language Structures Online,* edited by Matthew S. Dryer & Martin Haspelmath. Leipzig: Max Planck Institute for Evolutionary Anthropology, 2013. www/ http://wals.info/chapter/80.

Voogt, Alex de. bib/"Dual Marking and Kinship Terms in Afitti." *Studies in Language* 35, no. 4 (2011): pp. 898–911. DOI: www/10.1075/sl.35.4.04dev.

Werner, Roland. bib/*Grammatik des Nobiin (Nilnubisch). Phonologie, Tonologie und Morphologie.* Hamburg: Helmut Buske, 1987.

Werner, Roland. "Ideophones in Nobiin," unpublished ms presented as hand-out at the 9th Nilo-Saharan Linguistics Colloquium at Khartoum, 2004.

Werner, Roland. bib/*Tìdn-áal: A Study of Midob (Darfur-Nubian).* Berlin: Dietrich Reimer, 1993.

Zyhlarz, Ernst. bib/"Die Lautverschiebungen des Nubischen." *Zeitschrift für Eingeborenen-Sprachen* 35 (1949/50): pp. 1–20, 128–146, 280–313.

Endnotes

1. This paper is partly based on data drawn from published sources, partly collected in collaboration with mother tongue speakers. I am deeply indebted to the unflagging commitment of El-Shafie El-Guzuuli who contributed examples of Andaandi, to Ali Ibrahim of Tagle, Ahmed Hamdan of Karko, and Ishaag Hassan of Midob. Isaameddiin Hasan provided advice on Nobiin. ↩

2. Bender, *The Nilo-Saharan Languages: A Comparative Essay*; Bender, "Nilo-Saharan"; Dimmendaal, "Eastern Sudanic and the Wadi Howar and Wadi El Milk Diaspora"; article/Blench, this issue. ↩

3. In the present paper I will use the term Nyima to refer to the language group comprising Ama, Mandal, and Afitti. Afitti is also known as Dinik (Stevenson, Rottland & Jakobi, "The Verb in Nyimang and Dinik."). ↩

4. Rilly, *Le méroïtique et sa famille linguistique.* ↩

5. For a recent sub-classification of East Sudanic, see Dimmendaal et al., "Linguistic Features and Typologies in Languages Commonly Referred to as 'Nilo-Saharan'." ↩

6. Ehret, *A Historical-Comparative Reconstruction of Nilo-Saharan,* p. 141; Starostin, "Lexicostatistical Studies in East Sudanic I." Both Ehret and Starostin use Ama (but no Afitti) data. ↩

7. Ehret, *A Historical-Comparative Reconstruction of Nilo-Saharan,* chap. 5. ↩

8. Rilly, *Le méroïtique et sa famille linguistique.* ↩

9. Adapted from Rilly, "The Linguistic Position of Meroitic." ↩

10. I would like to thank the cartographer at the Institute of African Studies and Egyptology, University of Cologne, Monika Feinen, for designing the map. ↩

11. Rottland & Jakobi, "Loan Word Evidence from the Nuba Mountains." ↩

12. For the purpose of clarity, the different spelling conventions adopted for writing the various modern Nubian languages in the Latin script have been unified in this paper. Thus, the following digraphs are replaced by single IPA symbols: *sh* → *ʃ*; *ch* → *c*; *ny* → *ɲ*; and *ng* → *ŋ*. Consonantal characters with diacritics are replaced as follows, *š* → *ʃ*; *ğ*, *ǵ* → *j*; *ń*, *ñ* → *ɲ*; *ṅ* → *ŋ*. The IPA symbol *ɟ*, however, is replaced by *j*. Long vowels are rendered by two identical vowel symbols, e.g., *ii*, rather than by a vowel plus colon (e.g., *iː*) or a vowel with a macron (e.g., *ī*). To facilitate the comparison of the language data from different sources, alveolar stops are rendered by *t* and *d*; the corresponding dentals being represented by *t̪* and *d̪*. ↩

13. Tucker & Bryan, *Linguistic Analyses,* p. 245. ↩

14. Van Gerven Oei, *A Reference Grammar of Old Nubian,* §14.1.3. ↩

15. Werner, *Grammatik des Nobiin,* pp. 204–205. ↩

16. Massenbach, "Wörterbuch des nubischen Kunûzi-Dialektes," pp. 121–122, Armbruster, *Dongolese Nubian: A Grammar,* §§3888–3889. ↩

17. According to Kauczor (*Die bergnubische Sprache,* §§445–448), the inchoative is realized by the complex singular suffix *-n-er* and the plural suffix *-ŋ*. It is the plural suffix which looks like a cognate of the corresponding Nile Nubian inchoative suffixes. ↩

18. Greenberg, *The Languages of Africa,* p. 93. ↩

19. Noonan, "Genetic Classification and Language Contact." ↩

20. Dimmendaal, "Comparative African Linguistics." ↩

21. Rilly, *Le méroïtique et sa famille linguistique,* pp. 285–288. ↩

22. Thelwall, "Lexicostatistical Relations Between Nubian, Daju and Dinka." ↩

23. Zyhlarz, “Die Lautverschiebungen des Nubischen”; Bechhaus-Gerst, “Sprachliche und historische Rekonstruktionen im Bereich des Nubischen”; Bechhaus-Gerst, “‘Nile-Nubian’ Reconsidered”; Jakobi, “The Loss of Syllable-final Proto-Nubian Consonants”; Rilly, *Le méroïtique et sa famille linguistique.* ↩

24. Dimmendaal, “Nilo-Saharan,” p. 52. ↩

25. Stevenson, “A Survey of the Phonetics and Grammatical Structure of the Nuba Mountain Languages” and article/Norton, this issue. ↩

26. Stevenson, “A Survey of the Phonetics and Grammatical Structure of the Nuba Mountain Languages”; Tucker & Bryan, *Linguistic Analyses,* pp. 243–252; Rottland & Jakobi, “Loan Word Evidence from the Nuba Mountains”; Stevenson, Rottland & Jakobi, “The Verb in Nyimang and Dinik”; article/Norton, this issue. ↩

27. Browne, *The Old Nubian Miracle of Saint Menas*; Van Gerven Oei, *A Reference Grammar of Old Nubian.* ↩

28. The examples are drawn from Browne, *Old Nubian Dictionary.* ↩

29. Van Gerven Oei, *A Reference Grammar of Old Nubian,* §13.2.1. ↩

30. Example from Van Gerven Oei, *A Reference Grammar of Old Nubian,* §10.2.1. ↩

31. Browne, *Old Nubian Grammar,* p. 47. ↩

32. Lepsius, *Nubische Grammatik,* p. 152. ↩

33. Werner, *Grammatik des Nobiin,* pp. 220–273. ↩

34. Hopper, “Where Do Words Come From?” p. 154. ↩

35. Examples drawn from Massenbach, “Wörterbuch des nubischen Kunûzi-Dialektes,” pp. 132–133, 215. ↩

36. Abdel-Hafiz, *A Reference Grammar of Kunuz Nubian,* pp. 105–106. ↩

37. Massenbach, “Wörterbuch des nubischen Kunûzi-Dialektes,” pp. 157, 214. ↩

38. Examples from Massenbach, “Wörterbuch des nubischen Kunûzi-Dialektes,” p. 132. ↩

39. Examples from Armbruster, *Dongolese Nubian: A Grammar,* §§3670–76 and §3722; Armbruster, *Dongolese Nubian: A Lexicon,* p. 44. ↩

40. Armbruster, *Dongolese Nubian: A Grammar,* §2865 and §3718. ↩

41. "Neutral" is a tentative term for a (non-preterite, non-negative) suffix which in previous studies has been called "present tense." The term "imperfective" is probably more appropriate. ↩

42. Armbruster, *Dongolese Nubian: A Grammar,* §3708. ↩

43. Examples drawn from Kauczor, *Die bergnubische Sprache,* §253. ↩

44. Ibid. ↩

45. All Tagle examples are provided by Ali Ibrahim (p.c.). ↩

46. Werner, *Tìdn-áal,* p. 53. Werner translates (48) with English infinitives, "to get up" and "to get/wake (somebody) up." He does not provide morpheme glossing. Due to the inflectional suffix *-(i)hem,* they can be identified as 1st person perfect indicative forms. ↩

47. Examples provided without tone marks by Ishaag Hassan, p.c., January 2019. ↩

48. Werner, *Tìdn-áal,* p. 29. ↩

49. Van Gerven Oei, *A Reference Grammar of Old Nubian,* §13.2.2. ↩

50. Browne, *Old Nubian Dictionary,* pp. 81, 124, 152. ↩

51. Browne, *Old Nubian Grammar,* p. 48. ↩

52. Reinisch, *Die sprachliche Stellung des Nuba,* p. 37. ↩

53. Ibid. ↩

54. Werner, *Grammatik des Nobiin,* p. 178. ↩

55. "Present tense" is a preliminary term for a category that is probably more adequately described as imperfective aspect. ↩

56. Werner, *Grammatik des Nobiin,* p. 179. ↩

57. Werner, p.c., October 2020. ↩

58. Isaameddiin Hasan, p.c., 2017. ↩

59. Massenbach, "Wörterbuch des nubischen Kunûzi-Dialektes," p. 132. ↩

60. Armbruster, *Dongolese Nubian: A Grammar,* §§3665ff. ↩

61. Borrowed Arabic verbs are integrated into the Andaandi verbal system by means of the clitic verb ɛ which is more frequently realized with a long vowel as ɛɛ "say," cf. Armbruster, *Dongolese Nubian: A Grammar,* §2879 and §§3602–3607. ↩

62. ɛɛʃ belongs to the class of onomatopoeia or ideophones. They are not used as free forms but are turned into verbs by means of the clitic verb ɛ "say," cf. Armbruster, *Dongolese Nubian: A Grammar*, §§2870–2877. ↩

63. Armbruster, *Dongolese Nubian: A Grammar,* §3688. ↩

64. Werner, p.c., October 2020. ↩

65. Examples provided by E. El-Guzuuli, p.c. June 2019. ↩

66. Examples from Kauczor, *Die bergnubische Sprache,* §269 and §270. ↩

67. In (78) *ʃɔ̀k-ìr-ì* can be replaced by *ʃɔ̀k-ì*. ↩

68. Examples from Werner, *Tìdn-áal,* pp. 54, 89. ↩

69. Ibid., p. 86. ↩

70. Ibid., p. 27. ↩

71. Example from Grüning, *A Sketch of the Midob Verbal Morphology,* p. 41. ↩

72. The reconstructed PN lexical items are drawn from Rilly, *Le méroïtique et sa famille linguistique,* p. 273, the corresponding Midob items from Werner's Midob–English vocabulary in *Tìdn-áal,* pp. 75–143. ↩

73. Rilly, *Le méroïtique et sa famille linguistique,* p. 443. ↩

74. The alveolar *t* as an initial segment of the two donative verbs is also attested in Uncunwee, as seen in Comfort & Jakobi, "The Verb 'to give' as a Verbal Extension in Uncunwee." ↩

75. See the sets of cognates in the appendix of Rilly's *Le méroïtique et sa famille linguistique*, p. 518, no. 182. ↩

76. Cf. Van Gerven Oei, *A Reference Grammar of Old Nubian*, §2.2. Nobiin examples from Werner, p.c., October 2020. ↩

77. Examples from Massenbach, "Wörterbuch des nubischen Kunûzi-Dialektes," p. 128. ↩

78. Examples from Armbruster, *Dongolese Nubian: A Lexicon*, pp. 48, 200. ↩

79. Examples from Kauczor, *Die bergnubische Sprache*, p. 346. ↩

80. Werner, *Tìdn-áal*, pp. 56, 130, 132. ↩

81. Van Gerven Oei, *A Reference Grammar of Old Nubian*. chap. 7. ↩

82. Werner, *Grammatik des Nobiin*, pp. 167–170. ↩

83. Lepsius, *Nubische Grammatik*, p. 292; Reinisch, *Die sprachliche Stellung des Nuba*, p. 25. ↩

84. Browne, *Old Nubian Grammar*, p. 64; Hintze, "Beobachtungen zur altnubischen Grammatik I und II," p. 287; Bechhaus-Gerst, *The (Hi)story of Nobiin*, p. 137ff. ↩

85. Massenbach, "Wörterbuch des nubischen Kunûzi-Dialektes," p. 126. ↩

86. Werner, *Grammatik des Nobiin*, pp. 167–170. Werner's term "a-Form" covers both the converb marker and the copula. ↩

87. Van Gerven Oei, "A Note on the Old Nubian Morpheme -ⲁ in Nominal and Verbal Predicates." ↩

88. Hintze, "Beobachtungen zur altnubischen Grammatik I und II," p. 287; Smagina, *The Old Nubian Language*. ↩

89. Amha & Dimmendaal, "Converbs in an African Perspective." ↩

90. Ibid., p. 394. ↩

91. Jakobi & Crass, *Grammaire du beria,* pp. 168f. ↩

92. Comfort, "Converbs in Uncunwee (Kordofan Nubian)." ↩

93. Example from Hashim, *Nobiiguun Kummaanchii,* p. 54. ↩

94. Example from Lepsius, *Nubische Grammatik,* p. 345. Lepsius's German translation reads: "angekommen gingen sie zu ihm." ↩

95. Example from Lepsius, *Nubische Grammatik,* p. 364. ↩

96. Unlike the Nile Nubian languages, which solely use same subject converbs, the Kordofan Nubian languages exhibit same subject, different subject, and purposive converbs; see, for example, Comfort, "Converbs in Uncunwee (Kordofan Nubian)." ↩

97. The Nobiin perfective marker is realized with a long [o:], while the corresponding marker in Mattokki and Andaandi has a short [o]. ↩

98. Ameka, "Ewe Serial Verb Constructions in their Grammatical Context," p. 128. ↩

99. Aikhenvald, "Serial Verb Constructions in Typological Perspective," p. 6. ↩

100. Massenbach, "Wörterbuch des nubischen Kunûzi-Dialektes," p. 126 points out that the converb ("Verbum conjunctum") is realized i) without a suffix; ii) with the suffix *-ka*; and iii) with the suffix *-rgi ~ -rigi.* It is unclear, however, which criteria trigger the selection of one of these converb forms. ↩

101. Jakobi & El-Guzuuli, "Perception Verbs and their Semantics in Dongolawi," erroneously refer to converbs as serial verbs, thus disregarding the fact that Andaandi (Dongolawi) converbs cannot function as independent verbs in simple clauses, as serial verbs can do. ↩

102. Amha & Dimmendaal, "Verbal Compounding in Wolaitta," p. 327. ↩

103. Rapold, "Defining Converbs Ten Years On," p. 13. ↩

104. Mufwene, *Stativity and the Progressive.* Example from Werner, *Grammatik des Nobiin,* p. 185. ↩

105. Abdel-Hafiz, *A Reference Grammar of Kunuz Nubian,* pp. 115–117. ↩

106. Example from Armbruster, *Dongolese Nubian: A Lexicon,* p. 38. ↩

107. Examples from Lepsius, *Nubische Grammatik,* p. 292. ↩

108. Examples provided by El-Shafie El-Guzuuli, p.c. ↩

109. Massenbach, "Wörterbuch des nubischen Kunûzi-Dialektes," p. 214. According to El-Shafie El-Guzuuli, p.c., this expression is not used in Andaandi. ↩

110. Abdel-Hafiz, *A Reference Grammar of Kunuz Nubian,* pp. 123–125. Example from ibid., p. 125. ↩

111. Example provided by El-Shafie El-Guzuuli, p.c. ↩

112. Slobin, "What Makes Manner of Motion Salient," p. 62. ↩

113. Amha & Dimmendaal, "Verbal Compounding in Wolaitta," p. 327. ↩

114. Examples provided by El-Shafie El-Guzuuli, p.c. ↩

115. Aikhenvald, "Serial Verb Constructions in Typological Perspective," p. 30f. ↩

116. Examples from Browne, *The Old Nubian Miracle of Saint Menas,* pp. 12, 7. Glossing is taken from Van Gerven Oei, *A Reference Grammar of Old Nubian,* §15.1.3 and §7. Unlike Van Gerven Oei, I consider *-ir* in *ook-ir-s-n-a* to be a causative, rather than a transitive extension (see §/2.1). ↩

117. Browne, *Old Nubian Grammar,* p. 65; Bechhaus-Gerst, *The (Hi)story of Nobiin,* p. 148. ↩

118. Van Gerven Oei, *A Reference Grammar of Old Nubian,* §11.1.2. Example from ibid., §11.1.1.1. ↩

119. Browne, *The Old Nubian Miracle of Saint Menas,* p. 35 describes the unmarked converb in these collocations as "desinenceless adjunctive." ↩

120. Creissels, "Benefactive Applicative Periphrases." ↩

121. Examples from Lepsius, *Nubische Grammatik,* pp. 135, 136; Werner, *Grammatik des Nobiin,* p. 187. ↩

122. Examples from Massenbach, "Wörterbuch des nubischen Kunûzi-Dialektes," p. 134. ↩

123. Massenbach, "Wörterbuch des nubischen Kunûzi-Dialektes"; Armbruster, *Dongolese Nubian: A Grammar,* §3998; Werner, *Grammatik des Nobiin,* p. 272; Abdel-Hafiz, *A Reference Grammar of Kunuz Nubian.* ↩

124. Example provided by El-Guzuuli, p.c., November 2013. ↩

125. Examples provided by Ishaag Hassan, p.c., January 2019. ↩

126. Kauczor, *Die bergnubische Sprache,* §§374–377. ↩

127. Examples from ibid., §380f. ↩

128. Tagle examples provided by Ali Ibrahim, p.c. ↩

129. Karko examples provided by Ahmed Hamdan, p.c. For the plural stem extension *-(V)k* on *ɓīj-īk-n-dìì* see §4.2 and §6.5. ↩

130. Example from Van Gerven Oei, *A Reference Grammar of Old Nubian,* §7.2.3.1. Old Nubian ⲇⲉⲛ is here written with a final ⳡ rather than ⲛ, thus mirroring its realization as palatal [ɲ] when followed by the palatal stop [ɟ] (i.e., Old Nubian ϭ). ↩

131. Example from Abel, *Eine Erzählung im Dialekt von Ermenne,* ex. 69. ↩

132. Example from Werner, *Grammatik des Nobiin,* p. 188. Werner's glossing of *-a* as "a(-Form)" is here replaced by the glossing CNV. Note that we would expect the vowel of *-dèn* to be long rather than short. ↩

133. Example from Abdel-Hafiz, *A Reference Grammar of Kunuz Nubian,* p. 114. ↩

134. Example provided by El-Shafie El-Guzuuli, p.c. The 3SG pronominal direct object is unexpressed. ↩

135. Examples from Kauczor, *Die bergnubische Sprache,* §375 and §378. ↩

136. Veselinova, "Verbal Number and Suppletion." ↩

137. Browne, *Old Nubian Grammar,* p. 49. ↩

138. Lepsius, *Nubische Grammatik,* p. 127. ↩

139. Werner, *Grammatik des Nobiin,* p. 173. ↩

140. Examples from Werner, p.c., October 2020. ↩

141. Khalil, "The Verbal Plural Marker in Nobiin." ↩

142. Examples from Massenbach, "Wörterbuch des nubischen Kunûzi-Dialektes," p. 132. ↩

143. Abdel-Hafiz, *A Reference Grammar of Kunuz Nubian,* p. 117f. ↩

144. Armbruster, *Dongolese Nubian: A Grammar,* §2881. Examples from ibid., §2883f. ↩

145. Kauczor, *Die bergnubische Sprache,* §262. ↩

146. The singular stem *tōl-ór* is extended by the plural stem marker *-Vr* (see §6.3). ↩

147. Haspelmath, "Ditransitive Constructions." ↩

148. Werner, *Tìdn-áal,* pp. 50, 52. ↩

149. Examples from ibid., pp. 49 and 86. Werner erroneously translates them as "I answered" and "we answered." However, as the Midob *-wa*-suffix marks the 1SG and 1PL of the "continuous indicative," they should be rendered by "I answer" and "we answer." ↩

150. Ibid., p. 58f. ↩

151. Armbruster, *Dongolese Nubian: A Grammar,* §§2852–2855. ↩

152. El-Shafie El-Guzuuli, p.c., October 2020. ↩

153. Werner, "Ideophones in Nobiin." ↩

154. Van Gerven Oei, *A Reference Grammar of Old Nubian,* §18.2. ↩

155. Examples from Kauczor, *Die bergnubische Sprache,* p. 128. ↩

156. Dimmendaal, "Nilo-Saharan," p. 395f. ↩

157. The "verbal negative in m" is a feature of several Eastern Sudanic languages; see Greenberg, *Studies in African Linguistic Classification,* p. 76. ↩

158. Dimmendaal, *Historical Linguistics and the Comparative Study of African Languages,* p. 107. ↩

159. Due to the lack of a standard orthography, the ON lexical items commonly exhibit several spelling variants. ↩

160. Lepsius, Nubische Grammatik, pp. 405, 141f. Lepsius regards the verb-final *-e* on *undire, undure, udire, sukke, uskire* as the infinitive suffix. ↩

161. Epenthesis involving a consonant is specifically known as excrescence. The insertion of a nasal before another consonant, as attested by *undur,* has also occurred in English *messenger* and *passenger,* which are loanwords originating from the French nouns *messager* and *passager.* ↩

162. In Mattokki and Andaandi, some lexical items with a root-final *r* delete this *r* in the citation form. However, when followed by a suffix, the *r* shows up again, e.g., *toor-os-ko-r-an* "they have entered"; *toor-iid* "entrance." ↩

163. Kauczor, *Die bergnubische Sprache,* p. 137. ↩

164. Ali Ibrahim, a native speaker of Tagle, rejects the proposed analysis: "this is not the transitive verb opposite to 'lie down,' it just means to 'put down.' [...] Also the two verbs, 'enter' and 'insert,' are different roots in Tagle." ↩

165. The initial /e/ vowel in Tagle *ètírì* regularly corresponds to /o/ in other Kordofan Nubian cognates (Ali Ibrahim, p.c.). ↩

166. Jakobi, "The Loss of Syllable-final Proto-Nubian Consonants," p. 220. ↩

167. E.g., Stevenson, "A Survey of the Phonetics and Grammatical Structure of the Nuba Mountain Languages," 41: pp. 177f. and Tucker & Bryan, *Linguistic Analyses,* p. 249. ↩

168. Rilly, *Le méroïtique et sa famille linguistique*; Norton, "Number in Ama Verbs." ↩

169. Apart from Stevenson and Tucker & Bryan, the causative prefix is also identified by Norton ("Number in Ama Verbs," p. 84), as suggested by his morpheme glossing of the verb form *á-cì-ɛ̄n* as CAUS-happen-DU. Examples from Stevenson, "A Survey of the Phonetics and Grammatical Structure of the Nuba Mountain Languages," 41: p. 179. ↩

170. Stevenson, "A Survey of the Phonetics and Grammatical Structure of the Nuba Mountain Languages," 41: 179. ↩

171. Tucker & Bryan, *Linguistic Analyses,* p. 245. ↩

172. article/Norton, this issue. ↩

173. Stevenson, Rottland & Jakobi, "The Verb in Nyimang and Dinik," p. 16. The corresponding Afitti stems *tòsù/kosìl* "suck" and "suckle" lack an overtly marked distinction between the transitive and the causative stems. ↩

174. Dimmendaal, "On Stable and Unstable Features in Nilo-Saharan," p. 19. ↩

175. Reinisch, *Die Nuba-Sprache,* vol. 1, p. 64; Reinisch, *Die sprachliche Stellung des Nuba,* p. 41. ↩

176. Van Gerven Oei, p.c., September 2020. ↩

177. Lepsius, *Nubische Grammatik,* pp. 100f. ↩

178. Reinisch, *Die sprachliche Stellung des Nuba,* p. 41, fn. 1. ↩

179. Example from Werner, p.c., October 2020. ↩

180. Massenbach, "Wörterbuch des nubischen Kunûzi-Dialektes," p. 134. ↩

181. Abdel-Hafiz, *A Reference Grammar of Kunuz Nubian,* p. 111f. ↩

182. Examples from Massenbach, "Wörterbuch des nubischen Kunûzi-Dialektes," p. 122; Armbruster, *Dongolese Nubian: A Grammar,* §4099. ↩

183. The clitic *-ee* can be identified as the verb "say." Here it is used as a finite "light verb" following a coverb represented by a lexical item borrowed from Arabic. Such coverb plus light verb constructions are widely attested in the languages of northeastern Africa, as Dimmendaal ("Eastern Sudanic and the Wadi Howar and Wadi El Milk Diaspora") has shown. In Ama they are common, too (article/ Norton, this issue). ↩

184. Reinisch, *Die Nuba-Sprache,* vol. 1, p. 62. ↩

185. Armbruster, *Dongolese Nubian: A Grammar,* §4093. ↩

186. Smagina, *The Old Nubian Language,* p. 43. ↩

187. Van Gerven Oei, p.c., September 2020. ↩

188. Almkvist, *Nubische Studien im Sudān 1877–78,* p. 223. ↩

189. Lepsius, *Nubische Grammatik,* p. 388. ↩

190. This verb is attested in all Nile Nubian languages: Browne, *Old Nubian Dictionary,* p. 163; Massenbach, "Wörterbuch des nubischen Kunûzi-Dialektes," p. 215; Armbruster, *Dongolese Nubian: A Lexicon,* p. 192. Almkvist, *Nubische Studien im Sudān 1877–78,* p. 249 lists the transitive counterpart *tag-ir* "cover," German "bedecken." ↩

191. Comfort, "Verbal Number in the Uncu Language"; Jakobi, "Verbal Number and Transitivity in Karko (Kordofan Nubian)." ↩

192. Werner, *Tìdn-áal,* p. 55. ↩

193. Van Gerven Oei, *A Reference Grammar of Old Nubian,* §13.2.3.2; Lepsius, *Nubische Grammatik,* p. 102. ↩

194. Keenan & Dryer, "Passive in the World's Languages," p. 329. ↩

195. Haspelmath, "The Grammaticization of Passive Morphology," p. 49. ↩

196. Armbruster, *Dongolese Nubian: A Grammar,* §3031ff. Examples from Massenbach, "Wörterbuch des nubischen Kunûzi-Dialektes," pp. 127–128. ↩

197. Armbruster, *Dongolese Nubian: A Grammar,* §5456. ↩

198. El-Guzuuli, p.c., September 2020. ↩

199. Armbruster, *Dongolese Nubian: A Grammar,* §3668. ↩

200. Kauczor, *Die bergnubische Sprache,* §252. ↩

201. Hopper & Thompson, “Transitivity in Grammar and Discourse.” ↩

202. Comfort, “Verbal Number in the Uncu Language”; Jakobi & Ibrahim, “Labile Verbs in Tagle”; Pointner, “Verbal Number in Tabaq.” ↩

203. In Tagle, the extension is realized as [er] or [ɛr], depending on the ATR feature of the stem vowel. ↩

204. Jakobi & Ibrahim, “Labile Verbs in Tagle.” ↩

205. Jakobi, “Verbal Number and Transitivity in Karko.” ↩

206. Examples from Pointner, “Verbal Number in Tabaq,” p. 83. ↩

207. Werner, *Tìdn-áal,* p. 52. ↩

208. Werner’s grammar lacks explicit information on the marking of imperative forms. However, from the glossing of the examples ending in *-ec* ~ *-ic,* such as *òtt-éc* “enter!” PL (ibid., p. 111) and *péesir-íc* “leave, go out!” PL (p. 115), one can conclude that *-ec* ~ *-ic* is the 2PL imperative marker. It is assumed to be a reflex of the pluractional **-(i)j*-extension (see §/4.1). ↩

209. *article/*Norton, this issue. ↩

210. Norton, “The Ama Dual Suffix.” ↩

211. De Voogt, “Dual Marking and Kinship Terms in Afitti,” p. 903. Being mainly concerned with dual possessive pronouns attested on Afitti kinship terms, De Voogt provides little insight into dual extensions on the verb. He claims that “Afitti has singular and plural subject marking in the verbal system, but an unmarked subject dual,” but he also admits that “the un-marked dual form has an uncertain status and meaning.” ↩

212. Dimmendaal, “Pluractionality and the Distribution of Number Marking across Categories,” p. 73. ↩

213. Rilly, *Le méroïtique et sa famille linguistique,* p. 480, no. 114. ↩

214. Kauczor, *Die bergnubische Sprache,* §462. ↩

215. Examples from Kauczor, *Die bergnubische Sprache,* §§462f. ↩

216. Werner, *Tìdn-áal,* p. 53. This suffix is *-r-at,* rather than *-rati,* because the final *-i* is an epenthetic vowel which is part of the following morpheme. The vowel prevents the unadmitted sequences of *-h* preceded by a consonant. ↩

217. Ibid., pp. 110 and 136. ↩

218. Ibid., p. 136 renders this example by "it is covered." However, the presence of the past marker *-òn* suggests that the example should be rendered by "it was covered." ↩

219. Tucker & Bryan, *Linguistic Analyses,* p. 317. ↩

220. Thelwall, "Meidob Nubian," p. 100, asserts that "t, d, n are alveolar." ↩

221. Werner, *Tìdn-áal,* p. 52. ↩

222. Norton, "Number in Ama Verbs." ↩

223. *article/*Norton, this issue. Examples from Norton, "Number in Ama Verbs," pp. 77 and 78. ↩

224. Rilly, *Le méroïtique et sa famille linguistique,* p. 327. ↩

225. Dimmendaal, "Nilo-Saharan." ↩

226. Haspelmath, "Ditransitive Constructions," Jakobi, Ibrahim & Ibrahim Gulfan, "Verbal Number and Grammatical Relations in Tagle." ↩

227. Dimmendaal, "Pluractionality and the Distribution of Number Marking across Categories," p. 130. ↩

228. Norton, "The Ama Dual Suffix." ↩

229. Rilly, *Le méroïtique et sa famille linguistique,* pp. 230, 231, 244. ↩

article/

Restoring "Nile-Nubian": How to Balance Lexicostatistics and Etymology in Historical Research on Nubian Languages

author/ *George Starostin*

abstract/ *The paper offers a critical analysis of the proposal to dismantle the genetic unity of the so-called Nile-Nubian languages by positioning one of its former constituents, the Nobiin language, as the earliest offshoot from the Common Nubian stem. Combining straightforward lexicostatistical methodology with more scrupulous etymological analysis of the material, I argue that the evidence in favor of the hypothesis that Nobiin is the earliest offshoot may and, in fact, should rather be interpreted as evidence for a strong lexical substrate in Nobiin, accounting for its accelerated rate of change in comparison to the closely related Kenuzi-Dongolawi (Mattokki-Andaandi) cluster.*

keywords/ comparative linguistics, Nilo-Saharan, glottochronology, lexicostatistics, Nubian, West Nilotic

1. Introduction

Although there has never been any serious disagreement on which languages constitute the Nubian family, its internal classification has been continuously refined and revised, due to such factors as the overall complexity of the processes of linguistic divergence and convergence in the "Sudanic" area of

Africa; constant influx of new data that forces scholars to reevaluate former assumptions; and lack of scholarly agreement on what types of data provide the best arguments for language classification.

Traditionally, four main units have been recognized within Nubian[1]:

- Nile-Nubian, consisting of the closely related Kenuzi–Dongolawi (Mattokki–Andaandi) dialect cluster and the somewhat more distant Nobiin (= Fadidja–Mahas) cluster;
- Kordofan Nubian, or Hill Nubian, consisting of numerous (and generally poorly studied, although the situation has significantly improved in the past decade) languages such as Dilling, Karko, Wali, Kadaru, etc.;
- Birgid (Birked, Birged), now-extinct , formerly spoken in Darfur;
- Midob (Meidob), also in Darfur.

This is, for instance, the default classification model adopted in Joseph Greenberg's general classification of the languages of Africa,[2] and for a long time it was accepted in almost every piece of research on the history of Nubian languages.

More recently, however, an important and challenging hypothesis on a re-classification of Nubian has been advanced by Marianne Bechhaus-Gerst.[3] Having conducted a detailed lexicostatistical study of a representative batch of Nubian lects, she made the important observation that, while the percentage of common matches between the two main components of Nile-Nubian is indeed very high (70%), Kenuzi–Dongolawi consistently shows a much higher percentage in common with the other three branches of Nubian than Nobiin (**Table 1**).

	Midob	**Birgid**	**Kadaru**	**Debri**	**Dilling**	**K/D**
K/D	54%	48%	58%	57%	58%	
Nobiin	40%	37%	43%	41%	43%	70%

Table 1. Part of the lexicostatistical matrix for Nubian[4]

In Bechhaus-Gerst's view, such a discrepancy could only be interpreted as evidence of Kenuzi–Dongolawi and Nobiin not sharing an intermediate common "Nile-Nubian" ancestor (if they did share one, its modern descendants should be expected to have more or less the same percentages of matches with the other Nubian subgroups). Instead, she proposed independent lines of development for the two dialect clusters, positioning Nobiin as not just a separate branch of Nubian, but actually the earliest segregating branch of Nubian. Consequently, in her standard historical scenario described at length in two monographs, there was not one, but two separate migrations into the Nile Valley from the original Nubian homeland (somewhere in South Kordofan/Darfur) — one approximately around 1,500 BCE (the ancestors of modern Nobiin-speaking people), and one around the beginning of the Common Era (speakers of Kenuzi–Dongolawi). As for the multiple exclusive similarities between Nobiin and Kenuzi–Dongolawi, these were explained away as results of "intensive language contact."[5] The lexicostatistical evidence was further supported by the analysis of certain phonetic and grammatical peculiarities of Nobiin that separate it from Kenuzi–Dongolawi; however, as of today it is the lexical specificity of Nobiin that remains at the core of the argument.

Bechhaus-Gerst's classificatory model, with its important implications not only for the history of Nubian peoples, but also for the theoretical and methodological development of historical and areal linguistics in general, remains somewhat controversial. While it has been embraced in the recent editions of such influential online language catalogs as www/Ethnologue and www/Glottolog and is often quoted as an important example of convergent linguistic processes in Africa,[6] specialists in the field often remain undecided,[7] and it is concluded in the most recent handbook on African linguistics that "the internal classification of Nubian remains unclear."[8] One of the most vocal opponents of the new model is Claude Rilly, whose research on the reconstruction of Proto-Nubian (in conjunction with his work on the historical relations and genetic affiliation of Meroitic) and investigation into Bechhaus-Gerst's evidence has led him to an even stronger endorsement of the Nile-Nubian hypothesis than ever before.[9]

While in theory there is nothing impossible about the historical scenario suggested by Bechhaus-Gerst, in practice the idea that language A, rather distantly related to language B, could undergo a serious convergent development over an approximately 1,000-year long period (from the supposed migration of Kenuzi–Dongolawi into the Nile Valley and up to the attestation of the first texts in Old Nubian, which already share most of the important features of modern Nobiin), to the point where language A can easily be misclassified even by specialists as belonging to the same group as language B, seems rather far-fetched. At the very least, it would seem to make perfect sense, before adopting it wholeheartedly, to look for alternate solutions that might yield a more satisfactory explanation to the odd deviations found in the data.

Let us look again more closely (**Table 2**) at the lexicostatistical evidence, reducing it, for the sake of simple clarity, to percentages of matches observed in a "triangle" consisting of Kenuzi–Dongolawi, Nobiin, and one other Nubian language that is universally recognized as belonging to a very distinct and specific subbranch of the family — Midob. Comparative data are given from the older study by Bechhaus-Gerst and my own, more recent examination of the basic lexicon evidence.[10]

	Nobiin	**Midob**
K/D	70%	54%
Nobiin		40%

Table 2a. Lexicostatistical relations between Nile-Nubian and Midob (Bechhaus-Gerst)[11]

	Nobiin	**Midob**
K/D	66%	57%
Nobiin		51%

Table 2b. Lexicostatistical relations between Nile-Nubian and Midob (Starostin)[12]

The significant differences in figures between two instances of lexicostatistical calculations are explained by a number of factors (slightly divergent Swadesh-type lists; different etymologizations of several items on the list; exclusion of transparent recent loans from Arabic in Starostin's model). Nevertheless, the obvious problem does not go away in the second model: Midob clearly shares a significantly larger number of cognates with K/D than with Nobiin — a fact that directly contradicts the K/D–Nobiin proximity on the Nubian phylogenetic tree. The situation remains the same if we substitute Midob with any other non-Nile-Nubian language, such as Birgid or any of the multiple Hill Nubian idioms.

The important thing is that there are actually two possible reasons for this discrepancy in the lexicostatistical matrix. One, endorsed by Bechhaus-Gerst, is that the K/D–Nobiin number is incorrectly increased by the addition of a large number of items that have not been inherited from a common ancestor, but actually borrowed from Nobiin into K/D. An alternate scenario, however, is that the active recipient was Nobiin, except that the donor was not K/D — rather, a certain percentage of Nobiin basic lexicon could have been borrowed from a third, possibly unidentified source, over a relatively short period of time, which resulted in lowering the percentage of Nobiin matches with *all* other Nubian languages.

Thus, for instance, if we assume (or, better still, somehow manage to prove) that Nobiin borrowed 6% of the Swadesh wordlist (i.e., 6 words on the 100-item list) from this third source, exclusion of these words from lexicostatistical calculation would generally normalize the matrix, increasing the overall percentage for the K/D–Nobiin and Nobiin–Midob pairs, but not for the K/D–Midob pair.

The tricky part in investigating this situation is determining the status of those Nobiin words on the Swadesh list that it does not share with K/D. If the phylogenetic structure of the entire Nubian group is such that Nobiin represents the very first branch to be split off from the main body of the tree, as in Bechhaus-Gerst's model (**fig. 1**), then we would expect a certain portion of the Swadesh wordlist in Nobiin to be represented by the following two groups of words:

- archaic Nobiin retentions that have been preserved in their original meaning in that subgroup only, replaced by innovations in the intermediate common ancestor of Midob, Birgid, K/D, and Hill Nubian;
- conversely, more recent Nobiin innovations that took place after the original separation of Nobiin; in this case, the Nobiin equivalent of the Swadesh meaning would also be opposed to the form reconstructible for the common ancestor of the remaining four branches, but would not reflect the original Proto-Nubian situation.

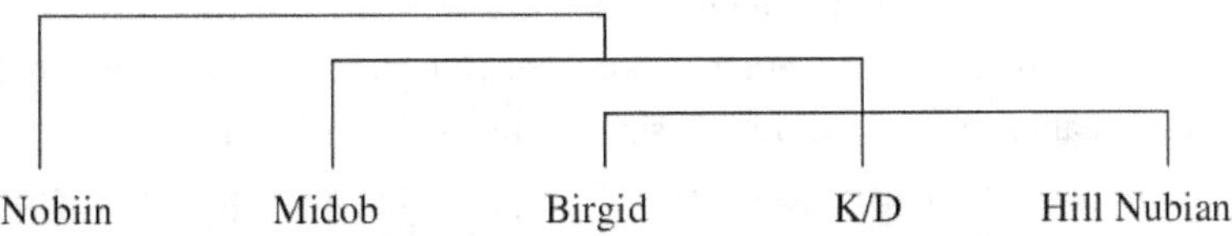

Fig. 1. The revised classification of Nubian according to Bechhaus-Gerst

Indeed, we have a large share of Nobiin basic words that set it apart from every other Nubian languages (see the more than 30 items in §/III of the list below), but how can we distinguish retentions from innovations? If the word in question has no etymological cognates in any other Nubian language, then in most cases such a distinction is impossible.[13] However, if the retention or innovation in question was not accompanied by the total elimination of the root morpheme, but rather involved a semantic shift, then investigating the situation from an etymological point of view may shed some significant light on the matter. In general, the more lexicostatistical discrepancies we find between Nobiin and the rest of Nubian where the Nobiin item has a Common Nubian etymology, the better the case for the "early separation of Nobiin" hypothesis; the more "strange" words we find in Nobiin whose etymological parallels in the other Nubian languages are highly questionable or non-existent, the stronger the case for the "pre-Nobiin substrate" hypothesis.

In order to resolve this issue, below I offer a concise and slightly condensed etymological analysis of the entire 100-item Swadesh wordlist for modern Nobiin.[14] The lexical items are classified into three groups:

› I. Lexicostatistical matches (i.e., cases where the exact same lexical root is preserved in the exact same Swadesh meaning, without semantic shifts) between Nobiin and K/D. These are further divided into subcategories I.1: common Nubian roots, also found in the same meaning in all or some other branches of Nubian beyond Nile-Nubian; and I.2: exclusive isoglosses between Nobiin and K/D that may be either retentions from Proto-Nubian, lost in all other branches, or Nile-Nubian innovations replacing more archaic words. In either case, these data have no bearing on the issue of Nobiin's uniqueness (although isoglosses in I.2 may be used to strengthen the case for Nile-Nubian).

› II. Lexicostatistical matches between Nobiin and other Nubian branches (Midob, Birgid, Hill Nubian) that exclude K/D. Upon first sight, such isoglosses might seem to weaken the Nile-Nubian connection, but in reality they are not highly significant, as the K/D equivalents of the respective meanings may simply represent recent lexical innovations that took place already after the split of Nile-Nubian.

- III. Nobiin-exclusive lexicostatistical items that have a common Nubian etymology (III.1) or do not have any parallels in any of the other attested Nubian languages (III.2). This is the most significant group of cases, with items in subgroup III.1 testifying in favor of the early separation hypothesis (particularly if the lexicostatistical meaning in Nobiin can be shown to be archaic), and items in subgroup III.2 favoring the substrate explanation. Needless to say, it is the items in this group that will be receiving the most extensive commentary.[15]

2. 100-Item Swadesh List for Nubian: The Data

2.1. I. Nobiin/Kenuzi-Dongolawi Isoglosses

2.1.1. I.1. General Nubian Isoglosses

- "ashes": N *ùbúr-tí*, K/D *ubur-ti* (= M *úfù-dì*, B *ubur-ti*, etc.).
- "belly": N *tù:*, K/D *tu:* (= M *tə̀:*, B *tu:*, etc.).
- "bird": N *kawar-ti*, K *kawir-te*, D *kawɪr-tɛ* (= M *à:béd-dí*, B *kwar-ti*, etc.).
- "bite": N *àc-*, K/D *acc-* (= M *àcc-*, Dl *aɟ*, etc.).
- "black": N *úrúm*, K/D *urumm-* (= M *údí*, B *ú:dè*, Dl *uri*, etc.). ◊ The Nile-Nubian form is an original nominal derivate (**ur-um* "darkness") from the adjectival stem **ur-* "black."
- "bone": N *gìsìr*, K *ki:d*, D *kɪhɪ:d* (= M *ə̀:dí*, B *kìzídì*, etc.). ◊ Voiced *g-* in Nile-Nubian is irregular, possibly as a result of assimilation (< **kizir*) or contamination.[16]
- "breast": N *óg*, K/D *og* (= M *ɔ́:*, B *ogi*, Dl *ɔki*, etc.).
- "claw/nail": N *sun-ti*, K *sutti*, D *sun-tɪ* (= M *súŋún-dí*, B *sun-di*, etc.).
- "cold": N *ór-kí*, K *oro:ke-l*, D *oro:fɛ-l* (= Wali *ór-kō*, Debri *worr-uŋ*, etc.).
- "die": N *dí-*, K/D *di:* (= M *tí:-*, B *ti-n-*, Dl *ti*, etc.).
- "drink": N *ní-*, K/D *ni:* (= M *tì:-*, B *ɲi:*, Dl *di*, etc.). ◊ From PN **ni-* with regular denasalization in M and Hill Nubian languages.
- "ear": N *úkkí*, K/D *ulug* (= Dl *ulɟe*, M *úlgí*, etc.). ◊ From PN **ulg-i*. The Nobiin form goes back to ON *ul(u)g-* and shows a specific phonetic development (**-lg-* > *-kk-*); the latter, however, can in no way be construed as an archaism.

› (?) "eye": N *má:ɲ* (= ON *maɲ-*), D *mɪssɪ*, K *missi* (= M *pì-dì*). ◊ A complicated case. The K/D forms perfectly correspond to M *pì-dì*, going back to PN **miC-ti*, where *-C-* is one of several consonants capable of triggering the lenition **-t-* > *-s-* in K/D. If **-C-* = **-ɲ-*, then the forms are further comparable with N *má:ɲ*, and we are either dealing with a one-time vocalic dissimilation **miɲ* > **maɲ* in N or two independent assimilations (**maɲ* > *miɲ-*) in M and K/D, respectively. Alternately, the N form may be completely unrelated to the K/D–M isogloss, in which case the word should be moved to group III.2, since a separate form like **maɲ* "eye" would have no Common Nubian etymology of its own.

› "fire": N *í:g*, K *i:g*, D *ɪ:g* (= Dl *ike*, Debri *ika*; probably also B *uzug*, M *ússí*). ◊ The forms in B and M are comparable if the original stem is to be reconstructed as **usi-gi*, with regular elimination of intervocalic **-s-* in Hill and Nile Nubian. The vocalism is still problematic, but even without the B and M forms, parallels in Hill Nubian clearly show that the Nile-Nubian items represent an inherited archaism.

› "foot": N *ó:y*, K *ossi*, D *oss(ɪ)* (= B *ose*, M *òttì*). ◊ All forms go back to PN **oy(-ti)*.

› "give": N *tè:-r*, K *ti-r*, D *tɪ-r* (= M *tì-*, B *te:-n*, Dl *ti*, etc.).

› "green": N *déssí*, K *desse* ~ *dosse*, D *dɛssɛ* (= M *tèssé*, B *te:ze*, Dl *teɟe*).

› "hand": N *èd-dì* (= ON *ey-*), K *i:*, D *ɪ:* (= M *ə̀ssì*, B *essi*, Dl *iši*, etc.). ◊ All forms go back to PN **əsi* ~ **əsi-ti*.

› "head": N *ùr*, K/D *ur* (= M *òr*, B *úr*, Dl *or*, etc.).

› "heart": N *áy* (= ON *ai-l-*), K/D *a:* (= B *ai-di*, Dl *a-l*, etc.).

› "horn": N *nì:šì*, K *nišši*, D *nɪšši* (= M *kɔ́:cí*, B *ŋis-ti*, D *dɔ-ti*). ◊ All forms go back to PN **ŋəɟi*.[17]

› "I": N *ày*, K/D *ay* (= M *ə́y*, Dl *ɛ*, etc.).

› "kill": N *fá:y-è:r*, K *be:*, D *bɛ:* (= M *pé-r-*, B *fi-la:le*).

› "knee": N *kúr-tí*, K *kur-ti*, D *kur-tɪ* (= M *ùrú-d*, B *kur-ti*, etc.).

› "know": N *ìrbé-èr* (= ON *i-* ~ *ia-r-* ~ *ie-r-*), K *iy-ir* (= M *ì:yá-*, D *i-er-*). ◊ The stem in modern Nobiin seems to be an extended form of the original stem, though the nature of the extension is not quite clear.

› "long": N *nàssí*, K *nosso*, D *noso* (= M *tàssè*, B *nizze*, Dl *dɔɟi*, etc.). ◊ Goes back to PN **nossi*, although vocalic correspondences are somewhat irregular.

› "louse": N *issi*, K *issi*, D *ɪssɪ* (= M *ì:dì*, Dl *iti-d*, etc.).

› "moon": N *ùn-áttí*, K *un-atti* ~ *an-atti*, D *un-attı* (= Dl *nɔn-ti*, Wali *ūm-tù* etc.). ◊ The Nile-Nubian root is **un-*; there are some problems with Hill Nubian forms, such as explaining the initial *n-* in Dl, but overall, there is no reason to doubt the common origin of all these items.
› "neck": N *íyyí*, K *eyye*, D *ɛyyɛ* (= Kadaru *e:*). ◊ Not clear if M *é:r* "neck" also belongs here (with a suffix?), but the Kadaru form is sufficient by itself to trace the word back to PN **eyi*.
› "not": N *-mù:n*, K/D *-mun-* (= Dl *-min*, B *-m-*, etc.). ◊ A common Nubian negative verbal stem (interestingly, not attested in M, which instead uses the suffixal morpheme *-á:-* for negation, something that could be construed as an archaism and used as a serious argument against early separation of Nobiin).
› "one": N *wè:r* ~ *wè:l*, K *we:r*, D *wɛ:r* (= M *pàr-*, B *me:l-*, Dl *be*, etc.).
› "person": N *íd* (= M *ír*, Dl *id*, etc.). ◊ The old Nubian root is largely replaced by Arabisms in K/D (K *zo:l*, D *adɛm*), but the word *ıd* is still used in D as an archaism or in various idiomatic formations.
› "rain": N *áwwí*, K *a-nn-essi* (< **aru-n-essi* "rain-water'), D *aru* (= M *áré*, B *a:le*, Dl *are*, etc.). ◊ The development **-r-* > *-w-* in N is regular before **-i*.[18]
› "red": N *gé:l*, K *ge:le*, D *gɛ:lɛ* (= M *ké:lé*, B *ke:le*, Dl *kele*, etc.).
› "sand": N *síw*, K *si:w*, D *sıu* (= Dl *šu-d*, Debri *šu-du*, etc.).
› "see": N *nè:l*, K/D *nal* (= M *kàl-*, B *ell-*, Dl *gel*, Kadaru *ŋeli*, etc.). ◊ All forms go back to PN **ŋali-*.
› "sit": (a) N *à:g-*, K/D *a:g* (= M *à:g-*, Dl *ak-i*, etc.); (b) N *tì:g-*, K *te:g*, D *tɛ:g* (= M *tə́g-*). ◊ Two roots with very close semantics, both easily reconstructible back to PN.
› "sleep": N *nè:r-*, K *ne:r*, D *nɛ:r* (= M *kèrà-*, B *ne:ri*, Dl *ɟer*, etc.). ◊ All forms go back to PN **ɲɛ:r-*.
› "star": N *wìnɟì*, K *wissi*, D *wıssı* (= M *ɔ̀ɲè-dì*, B *wa:ɲ-di*, Kadaru *wonɔ-ntu*, etc.). ◊ There are some problems with the reconstruction, but it is possible that all forms go back to PN **wiɲ-* ~ **waɲ-*; at the very least, **wiɲ-ti* "star" is definitely reconstructible for Proto-Nile-Nubian.

- "sun": N *màšà* (= ON *mašal-*), K *masil*, D *masıl* (= M *pàssàr*). ◊ The isogloss with M confirms PN status, although some phonetic peculiarities (such as the irregular *-š-* in N) as well as the attestation of the term *maša* ~ *masa* in Meroitic, where it denotes a supreme deity[19] indirectly suggest a possible areal isogloss; if so, an alternate candidate for PN "sun" would be **e:s-* > B *i:zi*, Dl *eɟ* "sun," further related to M *è:sì* "heat; midday," K *e:s* id., D *ɛ:s* "afternoon." In either case, N still aligns with K/D rather than anything else.
- you (sg.): N *ì-r*, K *e-r*, D *ɛ-r* (= M *í:-n*, B *e-di*, Dl *a*, Karko *yā*, etc.). ◊ Although all the forms are related (going back to PN **i-*), N is noticeably closer to K/D in terms of morphological structure (with the direct stem marker **-r*).
- "tongue": N *nàr*, K *ned*, D *nɛd* (= M *kàda-ŋì*, B *nat-ti*, Dl *ɟale*, Debri *ɲal-do*, etc.). ◊ All forms go back to PN **ɲal(T)-*.[20] Interestingly, the ON equivalent *tame-* (no parallels in other languages) is completely different — the only case on the list where ON differs not only from N, but from all other Nubian languages as well.
- "tooth": N *nì:d*, K *nel*, D *nɛl* (= M *kə̀d-dì*, B *ɲil-di*, Dl *ɟili*, etc.). ◊ All forms reflect PN **ɲəl-*.
- "two": N *úwwó*, K *owwi*, D *owwı* (= M *ə́d-dí*, B *ul-ug*, Dl *ore*, etc.). ◊ All forms go back to PN **awri*; the unusual cluster **-wr-* is responsible for the unusual development **-r-* > *-w-* already in Proto-Nile-Nubian (rather than just in N), and is actually seen explicitly in the extinct and very poorly attested Haraza Nubian: *auri-yah* "two."[21]
- "walk (go)": N *ɟúù-*, K/D *ɟu:* (= M *sə́-r-*, Dl *šu*, etc.). ◊ All forms go back to PN **cu:-*.
- "warm (hot)": N *ɟùg*, K/D *ɟug-ri* (= M *sù:w*). ◊ From PN **cug-*.
- "who": N *nà:y*, K *ni:*, D *nı:* (= M *kə̀:-rén*, B *ne:-ta*, Dl *de*, etc.). ◊ All forms go back to PN **ŋə(y)*.

2.1.2. I.2. Exclusive Nile-Nubian Isoglosses

- "all": N *màllé:*, K *malle:*, D *mallɛ*.
- "big": N *dàwwí*, K/D *du:-l*.
- "burn": N *ɟùgé-èr*, K/D *ɟug*.

- "egg": N *kúmbú:*, D *kumbu*. ◊ Replaced in K by the recent compound innovation *gas-katti* (where the first root probably = *ga:si* "heavy, hard, rough"), but clearly reconstructible for Nile-Nubian on the whole.
- "feather": N *šipir*,[22] D *sıbır*.
- "leaf": N *úkkí*, K/D *ulug*. ◊ Same word as "ear."
- "man": N *ògɟí-l*, K *ogiɟ*, D *ogıɟ*.
- "many": N *díyyí*, K *dig-ri:*, D *díyyí*. ◊ In ON usually attested as *di:-*, once as *dig-* (reflecting dialectal differences between N and K/D).
- "nose": N *sòrìŋ*, K *sorin*, D *sorıŋ*.
- "smoke": N *túllí*, D *tulla*. ◊ This may be a recent innovation in both languages; cf. the morphological discrepancy, the fact that the stem in N is a better match for K *tulli* "chewing tobacco," and the lack of attestation in ON. Obvious similarity with Nuer *to:l*, Dinka *tol* "smoke" suggests an old areal isogloss.
- "that": N *mán*, K/D *man*.
- "this": N *in*, K *in*, D *ın*. ◊ The subsystems of deictic pronouns in M, B, and Hill Nubian are much less cohesive than in Nile-Nubian and do not allow for reliable reconstructions of any PN items that would be different from Nile-Nubian.
- "what": N *mìn*, K *min*, D *mın*. ◊ It is quite possible that the Nile-Nubian situation here is innovative, since all other branches agree on **na(i)-* as a better equivalent for PN "what?": M *nè:-n*, B *na-ta*, Dl *na*, Karko *nái*, etc.[23]
- "woman": N *ìd-é:n*, K *e:n*, D *ɛ:n*. ◊ Technically, this is not a fully exclusive Nile-Nubian isogloss — cf. B *e:n* "woman." However, the main root for "woman" in Nubian is **il-* (ON *il-*, M *ìd-dì* < *il-ti*, Dl *eli*, Karko *îl*, etc.); **e:n* is the common Nubian word for "mother," which has, most likely, independently shifted to "woman" in general in modern Nile-Nubian languages and in B. N is particularly innovative in that respect, since it uses a compound formation: *ìd* "person" + *é:n* "mother."

2.2. II. Nobiin / Non-K/D Isoglosses

2.2.1. II.1. Potential K/D innovations

- "bark": *à:cì* (= M *àccì-dì*). ◊ Possibly < PN **aci* "bark, chaff." As opposed to K/D *gabad* (no parallels in other languages).

- "fly": *wá:y-ìr* (= B *ma:-r*). ◊ May reflect PN **way-* "to fly" (**w-* > *m-* is regular in B). However, the corresponding form in D is *war* "to jump, leap, spring," and typologically the development "jump" → "fly" is far more common than the reverse. Opposed to K *firr*, D *fırr* "to fly" with no parallels outside of Nile-Nubian.
- "liver": N *dìbè:* (= M *tèmmèɟí*). ◊ In D, the old word has been replaced by the Arabic borrowing *kıbda:d*. The isogloss between N and M allows to reconstruct PN **dib-* "liver."
- (?) "night": N *áwá* (= ON *oar-*). ◊ A rare case where K/D are clearly more innovative than N: K/D *ugu*: "night" occasionally has the additional meaning "24 hours," and further comparison with ON *uk-r-* ~ *uk-l-* "day," K *ug-re:s*, D *ug-rɛ:s*, N *ùg-ré:s*, M *ù:d* (< **ugu-d*) id. suggests that "24 hours; day-night cycle" was the original meaning. On the other hand, N *áwá* is comparable with M *ɔ̀:d* (< **awa-d*?) and could very well be the original PN equivalent.
- "skin": N *náwá* (< **nawar*, cf. pl. *nàwàr-í:*; = B *no:r*, Dl *dor*, etc.). ◊ Opposed to K *aɟin*, D *aɟın* "skin, leather."

2.2.2. II.2. Potential Synonymy in the Protolanguage

- "come": *kí-ìl* (= M *ì:-*, B *ki*). ◊ The K/D equivalent is *ta:* "to come," related to Hill Nubian forms (Dl *ta*, Debri *tɔ-rɛ*, Kadaru *ti-ri*, etc.). Old Nubian texts feature numerous instances of both *ki-* and *ta-* in the meaning "to come," with the semantic difference between them poorly understood; in any case, it is likely that both **ki-* and **ta-* have to be reconstructed for PN as synonyms (possibly suppletives), with subsequent simplification in daughter branches, meaning that neither the situation in Nobiin nor in K/D may be regarded as a straightforward innovation.

2.3. III. Nobiin-exclusive Items

2.3.1. III.1. Nobiin-exclusive Items with a Nubian Etymology

- "blood": N *dí:s* (= ON *dis-*). ◊ Related to K *des*, D *dɛs*, M *tèssì* "oil; liquid fat; butter"; the meaning in N is clearly innovative, since the original PN root for "blood" is well distributed across non-Nile-Nubian lineages (M *àggár*, B *igir*, Dl *ogor*, etc.).
- (?) "earth": N *gùr* (= ON *gul- ~ gud-*). ◊ The same word is also found in D as *gu:* "earth, ground, floor" and in K as *gu:* "field, acre; earth (surface)." According to Werner, in modern Nobiin the meaning "earth = soil" is also expressed by the same root,[24] whereas ON *iskit-* "earth; dust" > Nobiin *ìskí:d* corresponds to the narrower meaning "dust" in Werner's dictionary.[25] It is perfectly possible, however, that this is all simply a byproduct of inaccurate semantic glossing and that the situation in Nobiin is actually exactly the same as in K/D. In this case, the word has to be moved to §1.2 (or §1.1, if B *izzi-di* "earth" also belongs here).
- "hear": N *úkké-èr* (= ON *ulg-ir- ~ ulg-ar- ~ ulk-ir-*). ◊ Transparent derivation from *ulug* "ear." The old verbal root "hear" is present in K/D (K *giɉ-ir*, D *gɪɉ-ir*) and Hill Nubian (Dl *ki-er-* etc.) < PN **gi(ɉ)-*. The situation in Old Nubian/Nobiin is seemingly innovative.
- "meat": N *áríɉ*. ◊ Probably a recent innovation, since the ON equivalent for "flesh, meat" is *gad-*, with a likely etymological parallel in M *kàdì* "meat without bones." As for *áríɉ*, the shape of this word is reminiscent of an adjectival derivate (cf. *fáríɉ* "thick, heavy'), making it comparable with K *a:re*, D *a:rɛ* "inside, interior." The most common Nubian equivalent for "meat," however, is **kosi ~ *kosu* > K/D *kusu*, M *òsò-ŋí*, B *kozi*, Dl *kwaɉe*, etc.
- (?) "root": N *ɉú:*. ◊ Perhaps related to D *ɉu:* "nether stone for grinding," K *ɉu:* "hand mill" (if the original meaning was "bottom, foundation"), but the semantic link is weak. Notably, the word is not attested in ON where the equivalent for "root" is *dulist-* (no etymology). The most common form for "root" in Nubian is **ir-* (M *ír-dí*, Dl *ir-tad*, etc.).
- "say": N *í:g-ìr* (= ON *ig-ir* "tell"). ◊ Same as D *i:g* "tell, narrate"; in N, this seems to have become the main equivalent for "say." Other ON words with similar meanings include the verbs *pes-* (direct speech marker), *il-* ("speak," "tell") and *we-* (very rare, probably a K/D dialectism); the latter is the common Nubian equivalent for "say" (cf. K *we:*, D *wɛ:*, Dl *fe*, Kadaru *wei*, etc.).

- "swim": N *kúcc-ìr*. ◊ Not attested in ON; phonetically corresponds to D *kuɟ-* "to be above," *kuɟ-ur-* "to place above, set above," *kuc-cɛg-* "to mount, ride." If the etymology is correct, the semantic development can only be unidirectional ("to be on top/on the surface" → "to swim") and the meaning in N is clearly secondary. That said, the word "swim" in general is highly unstable in Nubian languages (almost every idiom has its own equivalent).
- "tree": N *kóy* (= ON *koir-*). ◊ Comparable with D *koɪd* "a k. of jujube (*Ziziphus spina-christi*)"; if the etymology is correct, a secondary generalization of the meaning to "tree (gen.)" in N would perfectly agree with the fact that a much better candidate for PN "tree" is **pər* > Dl *hor*, Dair *or*, Wali *fǿr*, K *ber* "wood," D *bɛr* "wood" (the meaning "tree" in K/D, as in N, is expressed by an innovation: K *ɟowwi*, D *ɟo:wwɪ*, formerly "*Acacia nilotica*").
- "we": N *ù:* (= ON *u-*). ◊ ON has two 1PL pronouns: *u-* and *e-r-*, the distinction between which is still a matter of debate; Browne, Werner, and others have suggested an old differentiation along the lines of inclusivity, but there is no general consensus on which of the two pronouns may have been inclusive and which one was exclusive. In any case, the two forms are in complementary distribution in modern Nile-Nubian languages: N only has *ù:*, K/D only have *a-r-*. On the external level, K/D forms are better supported (cf. M. *à:-dí*, B *a-di*), but forms cognate with N *ù:* are also occasionally found in Hill Nubian, e.g., Wali *ǒʔ*.[26] Without sidetracking into in-depth discussion, it should be acknowledged that *ù:* may well be a PN archaism retained in N.

2.3.2. III.2. Nobiin-exclusive Items without a Nubian Etymology

- "dog": N *múg* (= ON *mug-*). ◊ Not related to PN **bəl* (K *wel*, D *wɛl*, M *pà:l*, B *mɛl*, DL *bol*, etc.); no parallels in other Nubian languages.
- "dry": N *sámá*. ◊ Not related to K *soww-od*, D *soww-ɛd* "dry" or their cognates in Hill Nubian (Debri *šua-du*, etc.).

- (?) "eat": N *kàb-* (= ON *kap-*). ◊ ON shows dialectal variety: besides the more common *kap-*, there is also at least one hapax case of ON *kal-* "eat" = K/D *kal*. It is not entirely clear if the two roots are indeed unrelated: a scenario where ON *kap-*, N *kàb-* < Nile-Nubian **kal-b-* (cf. such derived stems as D *kal-bu-* pass. "be eaten," *kal-bɛːr* "eat to satisfaction") cannot be ruled out. However, it would run into additional phonetic and morphological problems. From an external point of view, only K/D *kal* < PN **kəl* has sufficient etymological backup; cf. Dl *kol*, M *ə̀l-* id. Regardless of etymologization, N *kàb-* is clearly innovative.
- "fat": N *sìlèː*. ◊ Not attested in ON; no parallels in any other languages.
- "fish": N *ángíssí*. ◊ Replaces ON *watto-*; neither of the two words has any clear parallels in K/D or any other Nubian languages. A possible, though questionable, internal etymology is "living in water" (from *aɲ-* "to live" + **essi* "water," see notes on "water" below).
- "full": N *mídd-ìr* (= ON *medd-* ~ *midd-* "to be full/ready"). ◊ Possibly from an earlier **merid-* (this form is actually attested a few times in ON sources). The item is quite unstable in the Nubian group on the whole; the PN equivalent remains obscure.
- (?) "good": N *màs*. ◊ This word does not have a Nubian etymology; however, the older equivalent *gèn* (= ON *gen-*), mainly used in the modern language in the comparative sense ("better"), is clearly cognate with D *gɛn* "good, healthy" and further with such Hill Nubian items as Dl *ken*, Debri *kɛŋ* "good," etc., going back to PN **gen-*. Were the semantic criteria to be relaxed, this item should have been moved to §/I.1.
- "hair": N *šìgír-tí*. ◊ Not attested in ON. The form is similar to K *siːr* "hair," but phonetic correspondences would be irregular (*-*g*- should not be deleted in K). On the contrary, D *dɪl-tɪ* "hair" perfectly corresponds to M *tèː-dì*, B *dill-e*, Dl *tel-ti*, etc. and is reconstructible as PN **del-* or **dɛl-*. Forms in N and K would seem to be innovations — perhaps the result of separate borrowings from a common non-Nubian source.
- "lie (down)": N *fiyy-ìr* (= ON *pi-*). ◊ No parallels in other languages.
- "mountain": N *mùlé:*. ◊ Probably a recent innovation, since the ON equivalent is *naɟ-*. No parallels in other languages. Opposed to M *ò:r*, B *kú:r*, Dl *kulí*, Karko *kúrù*, etc. < PN **kur-* (in K/D this word was replaced by borrowings from Arabic).

- "name": N *tàŋìs* (= ON *taŋis-*). ◊ No parallels in other languages. The most common Nubian equivalent for "name" is K *erri*, D *ɛrrɪ*, M *ə́rí*, B *erei*, Dl *or*, etc. < PN **əri*.
- "new": N *míríː* (= ON *miri-*). ◊ No parallels in other languages. The common Nubian root for "new" is K *eːr*, D *ɛr*, B *eːr*, Dl *er* < PN **ɛːr*.
- "road": N *dáwwí* (= ON *dawi- ~ dawu-*). ◊ Although it is likely that *dáwwí* < **dari* (see "rain" above), the word is hardly directly related to K *darub*, D *darɪb*[27] since the latter is transparently borrowed from Arabic *darb-*. A separate early borrowing into ON from the same source cannot be excluded, but it is also possible that the word has a completely different origin.
- "seed": N *kóɟìr* (= ON *koɟir-*). ◊ No parallels in other languages. The common Nubian root for "seed" is **ter-* (K *teːri*, D *tɛːrɪ*, Dl *ter-ti*).
- "small": N *kùdúːd*. ◊ No parallels in other languages, but the word is generally unstable throughout the entire family.
- "stand": N *méɲɟ-ìr*. ◊ Attested only once in ON (as *meɟɟ-*), where the usual equivalent for "stand" is *noɟ(ɟ)-*. The corresponding K/D stem is K *teːb*, D *tɛːb*, but a better candidate for PN "stand" is the isogloss between M *tèkk-ér-* and Dl *tek-er* < PN **tek-*.
- "stone": N *kìd* (= ON *kit-*). ◊ No parallels in other languages. The common Nubian root for "stone" is **kul-* (K/D *kulu*, M *ùllì*, B *kul-di*).
- "tail": N *ɟèlèw*. ◊ No parallels in other languages. The common Nubian root for "tail" is **ɛːb* (K *eːw*, D *ɛːu*, M *èːmí*, Dl *ɛb*, etc.). The old vocabulary of Lepsius still gives *aw* as an alternate equivalent,[28] meaning that *ɟèlèw* is clearly an innovation of unclear origin. (Possibly a concatenation of **ɛːb* with some different first root?).
- "water": N *ámán* (= ON *aman-*). ◊ No parallels in other languages. The common Nubian root for "water" is **əs-ti* (K *essi*, D *ɛssɪ*, M *ə́ːcí*, B *eɟi*, Dl *ɔti*, etc.). The innovative, rather than archaic, character of N *ámán* is clearly seen from the attestation of such idiomatic formations as *ès-kàlèː ~ às-kàlèː* "water wheel" and *màːɲ-éssí* "tear" (lit. "eye-water"); see also notes on the possible internal etymologization of "fish" above. The word *ámán* has frequently been compared to the phonetically identical common Berber equivalent for "water," **ama-n*,[29] but the inability to find any additional Nobiin–Berber parallels with the same degree of phonetic and semantic similarity make the comparison less reliable than one could hope for.

› "white": N *nùlù* (= ON *nulu-*). ◊ No parallels in other languages. The common Nubian root for "white" is **ar-* (K/D *ar-o*, M *àdd-é*, B *e:l-e*, Dl *ɔr-i*, etc.).

2.3.3. III.3. Nobiin-exclusive Recent Borrowings

› "cloud": N *gé:m* < Arabic *ʁayma-*. Replaces ON *niɉɉ-*, a common Nubian root (= D *niccɪ*, M *tèccì-dì*, B *na:si-di*, etc.).
› "yellow": N *asfar* < Arabic *'aṣfar*. The word in general is highly unstable in Nubian and not reconstructible for PN.

2.4. Analysis of the Data

Based on the presented data and the etymological discussion accompanying (or not accompanying) individual pieces of it, the following observations can be made:

1. Altogether, §III.2 contains twenty items that are not only lexicostatistically unique for Nobiin, but also do not appear to have any etymological cognates whatsoever in any other Nubian languages. This observation is certainly not conclusive, since it cannot be guaranteed that some of these parallels were missed in the process of analysis of existing dictionaries and wordlists, or that more extensive lexicographical research on such languages as Midob or Hill Nubian in the future will not turn out additional parallels. At present, however, it is an objective fact that the percentage of such words in the Nobiin basic lexicon significantly exceeds the corresponding percentages for any other Nubian language (even Midob, which, according to general consensus, is one of the most highly divergent branches of Nubian). Most of these words are attested already in ON, which is hardly surprising, since the majority of recent borrowings into Nobiin have been from Arabic and are quite transparent as to their origin (see §III.3).

2. Analysis of §/III.1 shows that in the majority of cases where the solitary lexicostatistical item in Nobiin does have a Common Nubian etymology, semantic comparison speaks strongly in favor of innovation, i.e., semantic shift in Nobiin: "blood" ← "fat," "hear" ← "ear," "meat" ← "inside," "say" ← "tell," "swim" ← "be on the surface," "tree" ← "jujube"; a few of these cases may be debatable, but the overall tendency is clear. This observation in itself does not contradict the possibility of early separation of Nobiin, but the near-total lack of words that could be identified as reflexes of Proto-Nubian Swadesh equivalents of the respective meanings in this particular group clearly speaks against this historical scenario.
3. It is worth mentioning that the number of isoglosses that Nobiin shares with other branches of Nubian to the exclusion of K/D (§/II.1) is extremely small, especially when compared to the number of exclusive Nile-Nubian isoglosses between Nobiin and K/D. However, this observation neither contradicts nor supports the early separation hypothesis (since we are not assuming that Nobiin should be grouped together with B, M, or Hill Nubian).

3. Conclusions

Based on this brief analysis, I suggest that rejection of the Nile-Nubian hypothesis in favor of an alternative historical scenario as proposed by Bechhaus-Gerst is not recommendable, since it runs into no less than two independent historical oddities/anomalies:

1. assumption of a huge number of basic lexical borrowings from Kenuzi–Dongolawi into Nobiin (even including such elements as demonstrative and interrogative pronouns, typically resistant to borrowing);
2. assumption of total loss of numerous Proto-Nubian basic lexical roots in all branches of Nubian except for Nobiin (19–21 possible items in §/III.2). Such conservatism would be highly suspicious; it is also directly contradicted by a few examples such as "water" (q.v.) which clearly indicate that Nobiin is innovative rather than conservative.

By contrast, the scenario that retains Nobiin within Nile-Nubian, but postulates the existence of a "pre-Nobiin" substrate or adstrate only assumes one historical oddity, similar to (1) above — the (presumably rapid) replacement of a large chunk of the Nobiin basic lexicon by words borrowed from an unknown substrate. However, it must be noted that the majority of words in §III.2 are nouns, rather than verbs or pronouns, and this makes the idea of massive borrowing more plausible than in the case of presumed borrowings from K/D into Nobiin.[30]

This conclusion is in complete agreement with the tentative identification of a "pre-Nile- Nubian substrate" in Nobiin by Claude Rilly,[31] who, based on a general distributional analysis of Nubian lexicon, claims to identify no fewer than fifty-one Nobiin lexical items derived from that substrate, most of them belonging to the sphere of basic lexicon. It remains to be ascertained if all of Rilly's fifty-one items are truly unique in Nobiin (as I have already mentioned above, some of these Nobiin isolates might eventually turn out to be retentions from Proto-Nubian if future data on Hill Nubian and Midob happens to contain etymological parallels), but the fact that Rilly and the author of this paper arrived at the same conclusion independently of each other by means of somewhat different methods looks reassuring.

If the Nile-Nubian branch is to be reinstated, and the specific features of Nobiin are to be explained by the influence of a substrate that did not affect its closest relative (K/D), this leaves us with two issues to be resolved — (a) chronology (and geography) of linguistic events, and (b) the genetic affiliation of the "pre-Nile-Nubian substrate" in question.

The aspect of chronology has previously been discussed in glottochronological terms.[32] In both of these sources the application of the glottochronological method as introduced by Morris Swadesh and later recalibrated by Sergei Starostin allowed to generate the following classification and datings (**fig. 2**):

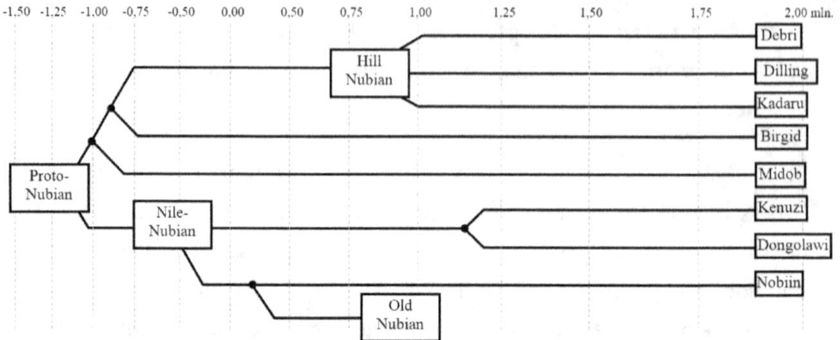

Fig. 2. Phylogenetic tree for the Nubian languages with glottochronological datings (generated by the StarlingNJ method)[33]

If we take the glottochronological figures at face value, they imply the original separation of Proto-Nile-Nubian around three to three and a half thousand years ago, and then a further split between the ancestors of modern Nobiin and K/D around two to two and a half thousand years ago. Interestingly enough, these events are chronologically correlatable with the two main events in the history of Nile-Nubian languages according to Bechhaus-Gerst, but not quite in the way that she envisions it: her "early separation of Nobiin" becomes the early separation of Nobiin and K/D, and her "later separation of K/D" becomes "final split between Nobiin and K/D." The interaction between Nobiin and the mysterious "pre-Nile-Nubian substrate" must have therefore taken place some time in the 1st millennium CE (after the split with K/D but prior to the appearance of the first written texts in Old Nubian). Nevertheless, at this point I would like to refrain from making any definitive conclusions on probable dates and migration routes, given the possibility of alternate glottochronological models.

The other issue — linguistic identification of the "pre-Nile-Nubian substrate" — is even more interesting, since its importance goes far beyond Nubian history, and its successful resolution may have direct implications for the reconstruction of the linguistic history of Africa in general. Unfortunately, at this moment one can only speculate about what that substrate might have been, or even about whether it is reasonable to speak about a single substrate or a variety of idioms that may have influenced the early independent development of Nobiin.

Thus, Rilly, having analyzed lexical (sound + meaning) similarities between his fifty-one "pre-Nile-Nubian substrate" elements and other languages spoken in the region today or in antiquity, reached the conclusion that the substrate in question may have contained two layers: one related to ancient Meroitic, and still another one coming from the same Northern branch of Eastern Sudanic languages to which Nubian itself is claimed to belong.[34] An interesting example of the former would be, e.g., the resemblance between ON *mašal* "sun" and Meroitic *ms* "sun, sun god," while the latter may be illustrated with the example of Nobiin *šìgír-tí* "hair" = Tama *sìgít* id. However, few of Rilly's other parallels are equally convincing — most of them are characterized by either significant phonetic (e.g., Nobiin *sú:* vs. Nara *sà:* "milk") or semantic (e.g., Nobiin *nó:g* "house" vs. Nara *lòg* "earth") discrepancies, not something one would really expect from contact relations that only took place no earlier than two thousand years ago. Subsequent research has not managed to alleviate that problem: cf., e.g., the attempt to derive Nobiin *nùlù* "white" from proto-Northeast Sudanic **ŋesil* "tooth,"[35] unconvincing due to multiple phonetic and semantic issues at the same time.

In *Языки Африки,* an alternate hypothesis was put forward, expanding upon an earlier observation by Robin Thelwall,[36] who, while conducting his own lexicostatistical comparison of Nubian languages with other potential branches of East Sudanic, had first noticed some specific correlations between Nobiin and Dinka (West Nilotic). Going through Nobiin data in §⁄III.2 yields at least several phonetically and semantically close matches with West Nilotic, such as:

- *túllí* "smoke" — cf. Nuer *to:l*, Dinka *tol* "smoke";
- *kìd* "stone" — cf. Luo *kidi*, Shilluk *kit*, etc. "stone";
- *ɟèlèw* "tail" — cf. Nuer *ɟual*, Dinka *yəl*, Mabaan *yilɛ*, etc. "tail."

Additionally, Nobiin *múg* "dog" is similar to East Nilotic **-ŋək-*[37] and Kalenjin **ŋo:k,*[38] assuming the possibility of assimilation (**ŋ-* > *m-* before a following labial vowel in Nobiin). These parallels, although still sparse, constitute by far the largest single group of matches between the "pre-Nile Nubian substrate" and a single linguistic family (Nilotic), making this line of future research seem promising for the future — although they neither conclusively prove the Nilotic nature of this substrate, nor eliminate the possibility of several substrate layers with different affiliation.

In any case, the main point of this paper is not so much to shed light on the origin of substrate elements in Nobiin as it is to show that pure lexicostatistics, when applied to complex cases of language relationship, may reveal anomalies that can only be resolved by means of a careful etymological analysis of the accumulated evidence. It is entirely possible that advanced character-based phylogenetic methods might offer additional insight into this problem, but ultimately it all comes down to resolving the problem by means of manual searching for cognates, albeit without forgetting about statistical grounding of the conclusions.

In this particular case, I believe that the evidence speaks strongly in favor of reinstating the Nile-Nubian clade comprising both Nobiin and Kenuzi–Dongolawi, although it must be kept in mind that a common linguistic ancestor and a common ethnic ancestor are not necessarily the same thing (e.g., the linguistic conclusion does not at all exclude the possibility that early speakers of Kenuzi–Dongolawi did shift to Proto-Nile-Nubian from some other language — not necessarily Nubian in origin itself).

4. Abbreviations

- B — Birgid;
- D — Dongolawi;
- Dl — Dilling;
- K — Kenuzi;
- K/D — Kenuzi–Dongolawi;
- M — Midob;
- N — Nobiin;
- ON — Old Nubian;
- PN — Proto-Nubian.

5. Bibliography

Armbruster, Charles H. bib/*Dongolese Nubian: A Lexicon.* Cambridge: Cambridge University Press, 1965.

Bechhaus-Gerst, Marianne. bib/"'Nile-Nubian' Reconsidered." In *Topics in Nilo-Saharan Linguistics,* edited by M. Lionel Bender. Hamburg: Helmut Buske, 1989: pp. 85–96.

Bechhaus-Gerst, Marianne. "Sprachliche und historische Rekonstruktionen im Bereich des Nubischen unter besonderer Berücksichtigung des Nilnubischen."}bib:49ab42ae-e792-4474-855c-0b2985eca9fnot found *Sprache und Geschichte in Afrika* 6 (1985): pp. 7–134.

Bechhaus-Gerst, Marianne. *Sprachwandel durch Sprachkontakt am Beispiel des Nubischen im Niltal: Möglichkeiten und Grenzen einer diachronen Soziolinguistik.* Cologne: Rüdiger Köppe, 1996.

Bechhaus-Gerst, Marianne. bib/*The (Hi)story of Nobiin: 1000 Years of Language Change.* Frankfurt am Main: Peter Lang, 2011.

Bell, Herman. bib/"Documentary Evidence on the Haraza Nubian Language." *Sudan Notes and Records* 56 (1975): pp. 1–35.

Browne, Gerald M. bib/*Old Nubian Dictionary.* Leuven: Peeters, 1996.

Greenberg, Joseph H. bib/*The Languages of Africa.* Bloomington: Indiana University Press, 1966.

Güldemann, Tom. bib/"Historical Linguistics and Genealogical Language Classification in Africa." In *The Languages and Linguistics of Africa,* edited by Tom Güldemann. Berlin: Mouton de Gruyter, 2018: pp. 58–444.

Heine, Bernd & Tania Kuteva. bib/"Convergence and Divergence in the Development of African Languages." In *Areal Diffusion and Genetic Inheritance: Problems in Comparative Linguistics,* edited by Alexandra Y. Aikhenvald and R.M.W. Dixon. Oxford: Oxford University Press, 2001: pp. 393–411.

Hofmann, Inge. bib/*Material für eine meroitische Grammatik.* Veröffentlichungen der Institute für Afrikanistik und Ägyptologie der Universität Wien 16. Vienna: Afro-Pub, 1981.

Hofmann, Inge. bib/*Nubisches Wörterverzeichnis: Nubisch-deutsches und deutsch-nubisches Wörterverzeichnis nach dem Kenzi-Material des Samuêl Alî Hisên (1863–1927).* Berlin: Dietrich Reimer Verlag, 1986.

Jakobi, Angelika. bib/"The Loss of Syllable-final Proto-Nubian Consonants." In *Insights into Nilo-Saharan Language, History and Culture,* edited by Al-Amin Abu-Manga, Leoma Gilley & Anne Storch. Cologne: Rüdiger Köppe, 2006: pp. 215–228.

Kassian, Alexei. bib/"Towards a Formal Genealogical Classification of the Lezgian Languages (North Caucasus): Testing Various Phylogenetic Methods on Lexical Data." *PLoS ONE* 10, no. 2 (2015). DOI: www/10.1371/journal.pone.0116950.

Kauczor, P. Daniel. bib/*Die Bergnubische Sprache (Dialekt von Gebel Deleṅ).* Vienna: Alfred Hölder, 1920.

Khalil, Mokhtar M. bib/*Wörterbuch der nubischen Sprache (Fadidja/Maḥas Dialekt).* Warsaw: Piotr O. Scholtz, 1996.

Krell, Amy. bib/*Rapid Appraisal Sociolinguistic Survey among Ama, Karko, and Wali Language Groups (Southern Kordofan, Sudan).* SIL International, 2012.

Lepsius, C. Richard. bib/*Nubische Grammatik. Mit einer Einleitung über die Völker und Sprachen Afrikas.* Berlin: Wilhelm Hertz, 1880.

Rilly, Claude. bib/"Language and Ethnicity in Ancient Sudan." In *The Fourth Cataract and Beyond: Proceedings of the 12th International Conference for Nubian Studies,* edited by Julie Renée Anderson and Derek A. Welsby. British Museum Publications on Egypt and Sudan, 2014: pp. 1169–1188.

Rilly, Claude. bib/*Le méroïtique et sa famille linguistique.* Leuven: Peeters, 2010.

Rottland, Franz. bib/*Die Südnilotischen Sprachen: Beschreibung, Vergleichung und Rekonstruktion.* Berlin: Dietrich Reimer Verlag, 1982.

Souag, Mostafa Lameen. bib/*Grammatical Contact in the Sahara: Arabic, Berber, and Songhay in Tabelbala and Siwa.* PhD Thesis, SOAS, University of London, 2010.

Starostin, George. bib/*Языки Африки. Опыт построения лексикостатистической классификации. Том II: Восточносуданские языки* [*Languages of Africa: An Attempt at a Lexicostatistical Classification, Vol. II: East Sudanic Languages*]. Moscow: Jazyki slavjanskoj kul'tury, 2014.

Thelwall, Robin. bib/"A Birgid Vocabulary List and Its Links with Daju." In *Gedenkschrift Gustav Nachtigall 1874–1974,* edited by Herbert Ganslmayr and Hermann Jungraithmayr. Bremen: Übersee-Museum, 1977: pp. 197–210.

Thelwall, Robin. bib/"Lexicostatistical Relations between Nubian, Daju and Dinka." In *Etudes Nubiennes, Colloque de Chantilly, 2–6 Juillet 1975,* edited by Jean Leclant and Jean Vercouttier. Cairo: IFAO, 1978: pp. 265–286.

Vasilyev, Mikhail & George Starostin. bib/"Лексикостатистическая классификация нубийских языков: к вопросу о нильско-нубийской языковой общности” ["Lexicostatistical Classification of the Nubian languages and the Issue of the Nile-Nubian Genetic Unity"]. *Journal of Language Relationship* 12 (2014): 51–72.

Voßen, Rainer. bib/*The Eastern Nilotes: Linguistic and Historical Reconstructions.* Berlin: Dietrich Reimer, 1982.

Werner, Roland. bib/*Grammatik des Nobiin (Nilnubisch). Phonologie, Tonologie und Morphologie.* Hamburg: Helmut Buske, 1987.

Werner, Roland. bib/*Tìdn-áal: A Study of Midob (Darfur Nubian).* Berlin: Dietrich Reimer, 1993.

Endnotes

1. Bechhaus-Gerst, "Nile-Nubian Reconsidered," p. 85. ↩

2. Greenberg, *The Languages of Africa,* p. 84. ↩

3. Bechhaus-Gerst, "Nile-Nubian Reconsidered"; Bechhaus-Gerst, *Sprachwandel durch Sprachkontakt am Beispiel des Nubischen im Niltal*; Bechhaus-Gerst, *The (Hi)story of Nobiin.* ↩

4. Bechhaus-Gerst, *Sprachwandel durch Sprachkontakt am Beispiel des Nubischen im Niltal,* p. 88. ↩

5. Bechhaus-Gerst, *The (Hi)story of Nobiin,* p. 22. ↩

6. E.g., Heine & Kuteva, "Convergence and Divergence in the Development of African Languages." ↩

7. E.g., Jakobi, "The Loss of Syllable-final Proto-Nubian Consonants." ↩

8. Güldemann, "Historical Linguistics and Genealogical Language Classification in Africa," p. 283. ↩

9. Rilly, *Le méroïtique et sa famille linguistique,* pp. 211–288; Rilly, "Language and Ethnicity in Ancient Sudan," pp. 1180–1183. We will return to Rilly's arguments in the final section of this paper. ↩

10. Starostin, *Языки Африки,* pp. 24–95. ↩

11. Bechhaus-Gerst, "Nile-Nubian Reconsidered" ↩

12. Starostin, *Языки Африки.* ↩

13. One possible argument in this case would be to rely on data from external comparison. Thus, if we agree that Nubian belongs to the Northern branch of the Eastern Sudanic family, with the Nara language and the Taman group as its closest relatives (Rilly, *Le méroïtique et sa famille linguistique*; Starostin, *Языки Африки*), then, in those cases where Nobiin data is opposed to the data of all other Nubian languages, it is the word that finds better etymological parallels in Nara and Tama that should be logically regarded as the Proto-Nubian equivalent. However, in order to avoid circularity or the additional problems that one runs into while investigating chronologically distant language relationship, I intentionally restrict the subject matter of this paper to internal Nubian data only. ↩

14. Reasons of volume, unfortunately, do not allow to go into sufficient details on many of the more complicated cases. A subset of 50 words, representing the most stable (on average) Swadesh items, has been analyzed in detail and published (in Russian) in Starostin, *Языки Африки,* pp. 224–295. A complete 100-item wordlist reconstructed for Proto-Nubian, with detailed notes on phonetics, semantics, and distribution, is scheduled to be added to the already available annotated 100-item wordlists for ten Nubian languages, published as part of www/ The Global Lexicostatistical Database. ↩

15. Note on the data sources: for reasons of volume, I do not include all available data in the etymologies. Nobiin (N) forms are quoted based on Werner's *Grammatik des Nobiin*; if the word is missing from Werner's relatively short glossary, additional forms may be drawn upon from either older sources, such as Lepsius's *Nubische Grammatik*, or newer ones, e.g., Khalil's *Wörterbuch der nubischen Sprache* (unfortunately, Khalil's dictionary is unusable as a lexicostatistical source due to its unwarranted omission of Arabic borrowings and conflation of various early sources). The ancient forms of Old Nubian (ON) are taken from Gerald Browne's *Old Nubian Dictionary.*

    Data on the other languages are taken from the most comprehensive published dictionaries, vocabularies, and/or wordlists and are quoted as follows: Kenuzi (K) — Hofmann, *Nubisches Wörterverzeichnis*; Dongolawi (D) — Armbruster, *Dongolese Nubian*; Midob (M) — Werner, *Tìdn-áal*; Birgid (B) — Thelwall, "A Birgid Vocabulary List"; Dilling (Dl) — Kauczor, *Die Bergnubische Sprache.* Hill Nubian data other than Dilling are used sparingly, only when it is necessary to specify the distribution of a given item; occasional forms from such languages as Kadaru, Debri, Karko, and Wali are quoted from wordlists published in Thelwall, "Lexicostatistical Relations between Nubian, Daju and Dinka" and Krell, *Rapid Appraisal Sociolinguisyic Survey among Ama, Karko, and Wali Language Groups.*

    Proto-Nubian forms are largely based on the system of correspondences that was originally laid out in Marianne Bechhaus-Gerst's reconstruction of Proto-Nubian phonology in "Sprachliche und historische Rekonstruktionen im Bereich des Nubischen unter besonderer Berücksichtigung des Nilnubischen," but with a number of emendations introduced in Starostin, *Языки Африки.* Since this study is more concerned with issues of cognate distribution than those of phonological reconstruction and phonetic interpretation, I will refrain from reproducing full tables of phonetic correspondences, but brief notes on peculiarities of reflexes of certain PN phonemes in certain Nubian languages will be given for those cases where etymological cognacy is not obvious or is disputable from the standard viewpoint of the neogrammarian paradigm. ↩

16. Bechhaus-Gerst, “Nile-Nubian Reconsidered,” p. 94 lists this as one of two examples illustrating the alleged archaicity of Old Nubian and Nobiin in retaining original PN *g-, together with ON *gouwi* “shield.” However, in both of these cases K/D also show *k-* (cf. K/D *karu* “shield”), which goes against regular correspondences for PN *g- (which should yield K/D *g-*, see “red”), meaning that it is Nobiin and not the other languages that actually have an innovation here. ↩

17. Reconstruction somewhat uncertain, but initial *ŋ- is fairly clearly indicated by the correspondences; see detailed discussion in Starostin, *Языки Африки*, pp. 56–57. ↩

18. Bechhaus-Gerst, “Nile-Nubian Reconsidered,” p. 93 counts this as an additional slice of evidence for early separation of N, but since this is an innovation rather than an archaism, there are no arguments to assert that the innovation did not take place recently (already after the separation of N from K/D). ↩

19. Hofmann, *Material für eine Meroitische Grammatik*, 86. ↩

20. See the detailed discussion on this phonetically unusual root in Starostin, *Языки Африки*, p. 80. ↩

21. Bell, “Documentary Evidence on the Haraza Nubian Language,” p. 10. ↩

22. Khalil, *Wörterbuch der nubischen Sprache*, p. 124. ↩

23. In Starostin, *Языки Африки*, p. 92 I suggest that, since the regular reflex of PN *n- in Hill Nubian is *d-*, both Nile-Nubian **min* and all the *na(i)*-like forms may go back to a unique PN stem **nwV-*; if so, the word should be moved to § I.1, but in any case this is still a common Nile-Nubian isogloss. ↩

24. Werner, *Grammatik des Nobiin*, p. 357. ↩

25. The meanings “sand; dust” are also indicated as primary for Nobiin *iskid ~ iskit* in Khalil, *Wörterbuch der nubischen Sprache*, p. 48. ↩

26. Krell, *Rapid Appraisal Sociolinguistic Survey among Ama, Karko, and Wali Language Groups*, p. 40. ↩

27. As per Bechhaus-Gerst, “Nile-Nubian Reconsidered,” p. 93. ↩

28. Lepsius, *Nubische Grammatik,* p. 274. ↩

29. Where **-n* is a productive plural marker, cf. Bechhaus-Gerst, "Sprachliche und historische Rekonstruktionen im Bereich des Nubischen unter besonderer Berücksichtigung des Nilnubischen," p. 109. ↩

30. For a good typological analogy from a relatively nearby region, cf. the contact situation between Northern Songhay languages and Berber languages as described, e.g., in Souag, *Grammatical Contact in the Sahara.* ↩

31. Rilly, *Le méroïtique et sa famille linguistique,* pp. 285–289. ↩

32. Starostin, *Языки Африки,* pp. 34–36; Vasilyey & Starostin, "Лексикостатистическая классификация нубийских языков." ↩

33. For a detailed description of the StarlingNJ distance-based method of phylogenetic classification and linguistic dating, see Kassian, "Towards a Formal Genealogical Classification of the Lezgian Languages (North Caucasus)." ↩

34. Rilly, *Le méroïtique et sa famille linguistique,* p. 285. ↩

35. Rilly, "Language and Ethnicity in Ancient Sudan," pp. 1181–1182. ↩

36. Thelwall, "Lexicostatistical Relations between Nubian, Daju and Dinka," pp. 273–274. ↩

37. Voßen, *The Eastern Nilotes,* p. 354. ↩

38. Rottland, *Die Südnilotischen Sprachen,* p. 390. ↩

article/ # Morphological Evidence for the Coherence of East Sudanic

author/ Roger M. Blench

abstract/ East Sudanic is the largest and most complex branch of Nilo-Saharan. First mooted by Greenberg in 1950, who included seven branches, it was expanded in his 1963 publication to include Ama (Nyimang) and Temein and also Kuliak, not now considered part of East Sudanic. However, demonstrating the coherence of East Sudanic and justifying an internal structure for it have remained problematic. The only significant monograph on this topic is Bender's The East Sudanic Languages, which uses largely lexical evidence. Bender proposed a subdivision into Ek and En languages, based on pronouns. Most subsequent scholars have accepted his Ek cluster, consisting of Nubian, Nara, Ama, and Taman, but the En cluster (Surmic, E. Jebel, Temein, Daju, Nilotic) is harder to substantiate. Rilly has put forward strong arguments for the inclusion of the extinct Meroitic language as coordinate with Nubian. In the light of these difficulties, the paper explores the potential for morphology to provide evidence for the coherence of East Sudanic. The paper reviews its characteristic tripartite number-marking system, consisting of singulative, plurative, and an unmarked middle term. These are associated with specific segments, the singulative in t- and plurative in k- as well as a small set of other segments, characterized by complex allomorphy. These are well preserved in some branches, fragmentary in others, and seem to have vanished completely in the Ama group, leaving only traces now fossilized in Dinik stems. The paper concludes that East Sudanic does have a common morphological system, despite its internal lexical diversity. However, this data does not provide any evidence for the unity of the En languages, and it is therefore suggested that East Sudanic be analyzed as consisting of a core of four *demonstrably related languages, and five parallel branches which have no internal hierarchy.*

keywords/ East Sudanic, Nilo-Saharan, comparative linguistics

1. Introduction

The East (formerly "Eastern") Sudanic languages, spread between Chad and Northern Tanzania, constitute a branch of Nilo-Saharan with a proposed membership of nine families, including Nilotic, the largest and most complex group. We owe the original concept of East Sudanic to Greenberg who attributed seven branches to it,[1] shown in **Table 1**, together with their modern names. Families unknown to Greenberg are added in the "Current" column.

Greenberg (1950)	Current
Nubian	Nubian + Meroitic
Beir-Didinga	Surmic
Barea	Nara
Tabi	Eastern Jebel
Merarit	Taman
Dagu	Daju
Southern	Nilotic
	Nyima
	Temein

Table 1. Greenberg's original concept of East Sudanic

Greenberg was not aware of Nyimang and Temein, and these were added later in Greenberg together with Kuliak,[2] now considered by Bender to be a separate branch of Nilo-Saharan.[3] Greenberg claimed East Sudanic was part of "Chari-Nile," a group which included Central Sudanic, Kunama, and Bertha.[4] Chari-Nile is also now not thought to be valid.[5] Somewhat confusingly, Tucker had earlier published a book entitled *The Eastern Sudanic Languages* but it is largely about

Central Sudanic, Ubangian, and Nilotic languages.[6] Prior to Greenberg, many individual languages or small groups had been described in Tucker & Bryan, but they were not combined into a larger unit.[7] Greenberg makes a large number of proposals for grammatical and lexical isomorphs, which more recent scholars have not followed up in detail.[8]

East Sudanic languages are by far the most well-known branch of Nilo-Saharan, with Nilotic and Nubian the main focal points. This is undoubtedly a reflection of the cultural prominence of the speakers and their relative accessibility. However, rather like Bantu, Nilotic represents a recent expansion and is only a fragment of the internal diversity of Eastern Sudanic. Nubian has attracted researchers because of its old manuscript attestations and epigraphic tradition. It has long been suspected that the extinct Meroitic language is part of East Sudanic,[9] but the small number of unambiguously identified lexemes made this argument difficult to sustain. However, with the work of Rilly and Rilly & De Voogt this argument can be considered secure.[10] Rilly places Meroitic as coordinate with proto-Nubian as part of his "Northern East Sudanic" family. **Map 1** shows their approximate distribution in recent times.

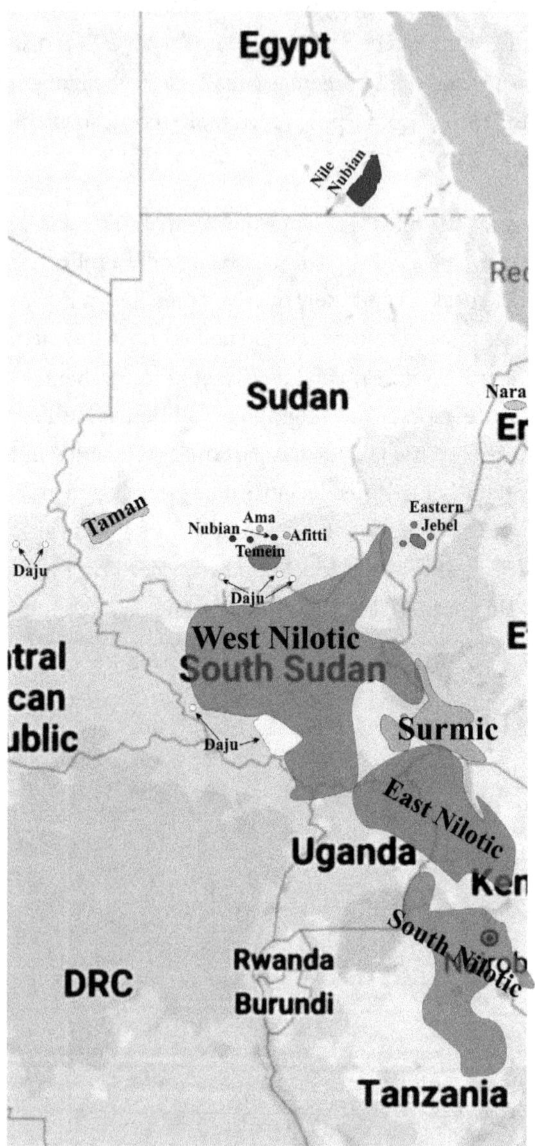

Map 1. The East Sudanic languages

The nine branches remain the accepted listing with some relatively minor reassignments. There have been few attempts to synthesise data on East Sudanic, the unpublished MSc thesis of Ross,[11] who was a student of Bender, and Bender's own studies and monograph.[12] The study by Starostin of Nubian–Nara–Tama is part of a project to re-evaluate East Sudanic as a whole from the point of view of lexicostatistics.[13] Bender gives basic phonologies representative of each branch, as well as an argument for the coherence of East Sudanic based principally on lexical evidence. This latter was locally printed in Carbondale and is best described as problematic to read for those who are not strongly motivated to penetrate its forest of acronyms and compressed citations. It has therefore had a very limited impact on Nilo-Saharan studies. However, it is full of interesting suggestions for isoglosses and presents an elaborate table of sound correspondences, so it undoubtedly merits close study. Unlike Bender's Omotic compendium,[14] it does not include original lexical forms systematically, and hence each entry needs to be rechecked against original and more current source data. It is safe to say Bender's publications did not have a resounding impact on the scholarly community.

Despite its previous acceptance, the published arguments for the coherence of East Sudanic remain weak. No unambiguous innovations, lexical or phonological, mark all branches as members. Some researchers have expressed scepticism about its unity. However, studies of East Sudanic by Dimmendaal broadly accept the classification of Bender,[15] although using very different criteria for accepting its coherence. However, Güldemann remains sceptical, arguing that internal typological differences may be evidence for convergence rather than genetic affiliation.[16] The www/Glottolog takes a far more extreme position, treating all branches as distinct families.

2. Lexical evidence

2.1. East Sudanic as a Unity

Claims for the reality of East Sudanic are largely based on lexical evidence. Bender proposes the most significant set of proposals in this area,[17] but Greenberg's original argument also includes some suggestions. Assuming the coherence of East Sudanic, the proposals for an internal structure are tenuous. Bender has argued in various places that East Sudanic has two main subdivisions, which he notates Ek and En, on the basis of the first person independent pronoun (**Table 2**).[18]

Ek	Branch	En	Branch
E1	Nubian	E2	Surmic
E3	Nara	E4	Eastern Jebel
E5	Nyima	E6	Temein(?)
E7	Taman	E8	Daju
		E9	Nilotic

Table 2. Bender's subclassification of East Sudanic

The first person singular subject pronoun in East Sudanic, first set out by Greenberg and later supplemented by Bender, forms a distinctive set (**Table 3**):

Branch	Language(s)	Form
Nubian	Nobiin	*ay*
Nara	Nara	*ag*
Nyima	Ama	*a(i)*
Taman	All	*wa, wo*
Surmic	Didinga	*a*
Surmic	Kwegu	*aan*
Eastern Jebel	Gaahmg	*aan*
Temein	Ronge	*nan*
Daju	Nyala	*aaga*
West Nilotic	Dinka	*an*
East Nilotic	Masai, Turkana, Nandi, Teso	*nanu*
South Nilotic	Pokot	*anii*

Table 3. First person singular subject pronoun in East Sudani[19]

Even this dataset does not entirely support Bender's division, since Daju appears to fall in the Ek group. The forms with a nasal largely correspond to Bender's En, while those without nasals correspond to Ek. However, on this evidence, the presence of a velar cannot be said to characterise all Ek languages.

2.2. The Ek Languages

Bender, Ehret, Rilly, and Starostin agree that at least Nubian, Nara, Tama, and perhaps Nyimang form a subgroup (Ehret's "Astaboran").[20] The lexical tables below provide a summary version of the compilations of Rilly sometimes with updated citations. **Table 4** shows the Ek forms for "drink" which seem to refer to a protoform **dii*.

Subgroup	Language	Attestation
Nara		*líí*
Nubian	Dilling	*di*
Nubian	Midob	*tìì*
Nyima	Ama	*lì*
Taman	Proto-Taman	**li(y)-*

Table 4. Ek lexical isogloss, "drink," *dii[21]

Table 5 shows a common form for "house," assuming Nubian preserves a velar lost in the other languages. The vowel is not entirely clear, but I provisionally reconstruct a mid central vowel.

Subgroup	Language	Attestation
Nubian	Midob	*kàr*
Nubian	Nyala	*aare*
Nara		*wǒl*
Nyima	Ama	*wel*
Taman	Tama	*wal*

Table 5. Ek lexical isogloss, "house," *kəl[22]

Table 6 shows a lexical isogloss for "mouth," **aŋəl*. However, the Eastern Jebel language Gaamhg also appears to be either cognate or else a loan, so this constitutes slightly imperfect evidence.

Subgroup	Language	Attestation
Nubian	Andaandi	*agil*
Nara		*aùlò*
Nyima	Ama	*ŋàl*
Taman	Abu Sharib	*awl*
E Jebel	Gaahmg	*ag*

Table 6. Ek lexical isogloss, "mouth," **aŋəl*[23]

Table 7 presents the evidence for the lexical isogloss, "two," perhaps **wari(m)* if the *-m* in Nyima is to be included.

Subgroup	Language	Attestation
Nubian	Haraza	*auri-yah*
Nubian	Old Nubian	*uwo*
Nubian	Karko	*ārè*
Nara		*ari-ga*
Nyima	Proto-Nyima	**arm-*
Taman	Proto-Taman	**wari*

Table 7. Ek lexical isogloss, "two," **wari(m)*[24]

2.3. The En Languages

Though the En languages share overlapping isoglosses, they do not share enough common material to be conclusively considered a genetic unity. Bender recognizes that the arguments for membership of Temein in his En group are sketchy. **Table 8** presents one of Bender's better common glosses.

Subgroup	Language	Attestation
Surmic	Murle	***ɓɔ****lɔ́ɔ́k*
E Jebel	Aka	***bəəb****a*
Temein	Temein	***pɔ̀p****áʈìʈ*
Daju	Liguri	*ku****ɓu****du*
E Nilotic	Lopit	*a.***bob***.io*
E Nilotic	Maa	*a.***bob***.oki*

Table 8. En lexical isogloss, "bark n.," *-bob-*

3. Morphological Evidence

In the light of these problems with the lexicon, it may be that a better case for East Sudanic can be made on the basis of morphology. Bryan had already noted the existence of a "t-k substratum" in a variety of languages across East-Central Africa.[25] These elements are affixes on nominals associated with number marking. Her argument is somewhat confused, as this feature is unlikely to be a substrate feature of some lost phylum. Most plausibly, it is a feature of Nilo-Saharan which has been borrowed *into* Afroasiatic (since it is definitely not a widespread feature of Afroasiatic). Bryan identifies the following morphological elements:

- Singulative *-t*
- Plural *-k*
- Plural *-N*

The majority of languages she uses to exemplify this principle would now be classified as East Sudanic. Greenberg calls moveable *k-* a "stage III article"[26] while Ehret calls it both an "adjective suffix" and a "noun particularizing prefix."[27] Bender, who considers it a "noun-class formative remnant,"[28] notes that it is widespread but not universal in Nilo-Saharan. Also included are some Cushitic languages, but the extension of the "substratum" is somewhat strained. The T-affix in Afroasiatic is a widespread marker of feminine gender and a deep level connection with Nilo-Saharan through semantic shift is not impossible. Bender also discusses N-affixes in Nilo-Saharan,[29] reprising observations by Tucker &

Bryan.[30] Storch also takes up the issue of N/K and T/K alternations in relation to Nilotic noun morphology.[31]

These affixes are certainly present in East Sudanic languages along with others. Many languages also permit gemination or consonant doubling. The origins of gemination in suffixes remains in doubt, but may arise from resuffixing, just as long consonants in Niger-Congo can arise from reprefixing in noun class languages. Moreover, nominals in East Sudanic can allow "affix-stacking," the addition in sequence of one or more affixes as part of historical stratification.

The paper considers each branch of East Sudanic in turn, and briefly lays out the evidence for the affix system, as well as the presence of gemination and stacking. Discussion of the membership of individual branches, and their structure is not given here, but can be consulted in standard references.[32]

4. Individual Branches

4.1. Nubian and Meroitic

Nubian demonstrates strong evidence for tripartite number marking in nouns. Jakobi & Hamdan describe Karko, which has a restricted system of suffixed singulatives, where -*Vt* and -*ɖ* are allomorphs (**Table 9**).

Gloss	SG	PL
sorghum	*wèê-t*	*wèè*
hair	*ṱēɽ-ét*	*tèèl*
bulrush millet	*ɛ̀nɖ-ɛ́t*	*ɛ̀nɖ*
tooth	*jíl-ɖ*	*jīīl*
breast	*ɔ̄l-ɖ*	*ɔ̄ɔ̄l*

Table 9. Karko singulatives[33]

However, the majority of suffixes denote plurals (**Table 10**). The majority seem to be allomorphs of the singulative suffix, thus *ɖ* ~ *Vl* ~ *Vr*, with a distinct second set, *Vɲ* ~ *Vŋ*. The suffix -*Vnd* may be a composite of the nasal and alveo-dental suffixes.

Gloss	SG	PL
body	*îl*	*īl-ḍ*
heart	*áàl*	*āl-ḍ*
star	*ōnḍ*	*ōnḍ-ôl*
milk	*éèj*	*ēj-ēl*
chicken	*kòk*	*kōk-ôr*
cat	*bùt*	*bùt-ùr*
blood	*ōg*	*ōg-ōnd*
fire	*úk*	*ūk-ūnd*
river	*ìr*	*īr-īɲ*
rope	*ə̀r*	*ə̄r-ə̄ɲ*
shield	*kə̀r*	*kə̀r-ə̀ŋ*
ostrich	*ṭùlḍ*	*ṭùlḍ-ùŋ*

Table 10. Karko plural marking[34]

Proto-Nubian may have had a fully functional tripartite system, which has now eroded leaving both singulatives and plurals, but not simultaneously. Once allomorphy is taken into account, the available affixes are very restricted. A language such as Midob has a still more reduced system, with only the alveo-dental *t* ~ *di* (**Table 11**).

Gloss	SG	PL
thing	*sáar*	*sàartì*
house	*ə̀d*	*ə̀ttì*
child	*úccí*	*ùccédí*
woman	*íddí*	*ìddédí*
cow	*tə̀ə*	*tə̀yítì*

Table 11. Midob nominal plurals[35]

The restricted corpus for Meroitic and the absence of reliable grammatical information makes it problematic to know the nature of its affix system.

However, a couple of glosses which are considered reliable almost certainly show singulatives comparable to other Nubian languages:

Gloss	Transliteration	Approx. pronunciation
sister	*kdise, kdite*	/kaɖiɕ, kaɖit/
life	*pwrite*	/bawarit/

Table 12. Meroitic glosses showing singulative marking[36]

4.2. Nara

Nominal plurals in Nara are created through suffixing and sporadic gemination of the final consonant. The six plural classes are shown in **Table 13**. There are weak correlations with semantics and these are given only as indicative:

Suffix		Gloss	SG	PL	Semantics
-ka	-K	fox	*kerfe*	*kerefka*	animals
		animal	*oof*	*oofka*	
-ta	-T	heart	*asma*	*asimta*	body parts
		meat	*nooti*	*noota*	
-a	-V	ear	*tus*	*tusa*	animals and plants
		thorn	*keer*	*keera*	
-tta	-T	blood	*kito*	*kitotta*	collectives(?)
		grass	*sum*	*sumitta*	
-CCa	-I	bride	*solobi*	*solobba*	people, animals
		goat	*bele*	*bella*	
-ʤʤa	-S	gland	*foʤi*	*foʤʤaa*	internal secretions
		milk course	*ngiʤi*	*ngiʤʤaa*	

Table 13. Nara number marking in nouns[37]

The plurals in last three classes which involve consonant doubling and change the final vowel to *-a* may simply be allomorphs of an underlying *-a* suffix. These may derive from a single rule and thus not exemplify the characteristic East Sudanic suffixes.

4.3. Nyima

Nyima covers two related languages, Nyimang and Afitti, now usually known as Ama and Dinik respectively. Both languages have retained only traces of the complex noun morphology characteristic of other East Sudanic branches. Ama nouns have a single plural-marking suffix, *-ŋi* (or *-gi* after a liquid). Even this is dropped when number can be inferred from either a numeral or a quantifier. There are a small number of suppletives for persons:

Gloss	SG	PL
person, PL people	*wodáŋ*	*wàá*
child	*wodéŋ*	*ɖúriŋ*

Table 14. Suppletive plural forms in Ama

Reduplication can be used to express collectives, e.g., *ɖàmì* "egg"; *ɖàɖàmì* "all the eggs."

Otherwise the loss of most plural marking is very marked in comparison with related branches. For Dinik, De Voogt notes number marking briefly, which he states is only applied consistently to animates. Dinik has three plural markers, -*gòr, -ná,* and *-é.*[38] A comparison of the lexicon of Dinik yields some possible evidence for fossil affixes. Dinik in particular has a wide range of nominals with -*Vk* suffixes (**Table 14**).

Gloss	Attestation
river	*kwələk*
dura sorghum	*mənək*
scorpion	*ŋwunək*
grave	*tirik*
lightning	*arsək*
salt	*ɔrdik*
spear	*mətsək*

Table 15. The fossil affix -*Vk* in Dinik[39]

Despite their lexical affinity to the Ek branch, Nyima languages have all but lost their indicative noun morphology. However, as Norton observes,[40] the characteristic *t/k* alternations are well preserved in the verbal system in the distinction between factative and progressive. **Table 16** exemplifies this alternation.

Gloss	Factative	Progressive
build	*t̪-ùg-è*	*k-ūg*
dig	*t̪-īw-ò*	*k-íw*
light (fire)	*t̪-ūɞ-ē*	*k-úɞ-ín*
build	*tugὲ*	*kwò*
chop	*tàiɔ̀*	*kaì*
dig	*tìwò*	*kìù*

Table 16. T/K marking on Ama verb stems[41]

Norton has a lengthy argument about how the nominal alternation became attached to verbs, which he summarises as follows:

> I therefore propose that this class of verbs attests the Nyima cognate of the wider Nilo-Saharan T/K alternation. This entails a chain of events in which the T/K alternation first moved from the noun (singular/plural) to the verb (singulactional/pluractional), and then shifted in meaning from verbal number to verbal aspect (factative/progressive) [...]. Seen in this light, the significance of moving T/K morphology onto verbs in the Nyima branch is that it renewed an existing system of irregular singulactional/pluractional alternations.[42]

This shift from the nominal to the verbal system suggests that Nyima need no longer be treated as the missing piece in the puzzle of East Sudanic morphology.

4.4. Taman

Descriptions of the morphology of Taman languages are very limited. Kellermann provides a summary of number marking in nouns, based on the manuscript material of Stevenson (**Table 17**):

Affix	SG	Affix	PL	Gloss
-t	*mèya-t*	-*k*	*mèya-k*	blacksmith
-t	*wìgɪ-t*	-*ɛ*	*wìgɪ-ɛ*	bird
-V	*áunyò*	-*(V)k*	*áunyò-k*	elbow
-Ø	*gaan*	-*(V)k*	*gaan-ɪk*	tree
-Ø	*wal*	-V	*wal-u*	house
-*k*	*taɽ-ak*	-V	*taɽ-o*	chief
-X	*iɲ-o*	-*(V)ɲ*	*iɲ-iɲ*	pot
-Ø	*áwór*	-*(V)ŋ*	*áwór-oŋ*	knee

Table 17. Tama nominal number-marking[43]

As with other East Sudanic languages, once allomorphy is taken into account, number-marking affixes are quite reduced. Tama has *-t, -k, -(V)N,* and an underspecified vowel. No examples of synchronic tripartite number marking are given, but the use of *-t* in the singulative and the "moveable" *-k* all point to this as formerly operative. The underspecified *V* in *-VC* suffixes suggests compounding, as in other East Sudanic languages.

4.5. Surmic

Surmic displays abundant evidence for three-term number marking. **Table 18** shows its operation in Laarim:

Gloss	SG	Generic	PL
gazelle	*boronit*	*boron-*	*boronua*
nail	*gurmaloʧ*	*gurmal-*	*gurmaleeta*

Table 18. Tripartite number marking in Laarim[44]

Yigezu & Dimmendaal focus on Baale and **Table 19** shows its number marking system and identifiable affixes. The variability in Baale is extremely high with many minor differences, so the analysis is not always certain. For example, "stomach" might represent an original *-NV* affix, eroded by the subsequent addition of the *-TV.*

Gloss	Affix	SG	Affix	PL
arm, hand	-Ø	*ayí*	-*NV*	*ayinná*
moon	-Ø	*ɲʊló*	-*KV*	*ɲɔlɔgɛ́*
man, person	-Ø	*éé*	-*TV*	*eeṯá*
goat	-Ø	*ɛ́ɛ́s*	-*TV*	*ɛ́ɛ́ta*
head	-*A*	*ɔwá*	-*TV*	*ooti*
face, forehead	-*A*	*ŋʊmmá*	-*TV*	*ŋuundí*
stomach	-*A*	*kɛŋŋá*	-*TV*	*keendi*
ear	-*NV*	*ɪtááni*	-*NV*	*ɪnná*
rope	-*S*	*mɔssáɟí*	-*N*	*mɔɔssɛ́n*

Table 19. Baale number marking and affixes[45]

From this evidence, Baale has singulars in -*(N)A*, -*S*, and -*NV* and plurals with -*KV*, -*TV*, and -*N*.

4.6. Eastern Jebel

To judge by the data in Bender,[46] Aka has a richer system of number marking than Gaahmg. Extracting the affixes from the system of number-marking, the following (at least) occur (**Table 20**):

Gloss	Affix	SG	Affix	PL
tongue	-Ø	*kala*	-A, -T	*kala.ati*
knee	-Ø	*kʊsu*	-N	*kʊsuu.ŋi*
belly	-Ø	*ɛllɛ*	-T	*ɛllɛ.ti*
ear	-Ø	*sigii*	-T	*sigii.de*
fish	-Ø	*ʔʊʊgu*	-T	*ʔʊʊgu.ði*
dog	-Ø	*kɛle*	-V	*kɛle.i*
bone	-K	*gamoo.ka*	-N	*gamoo.ɲi*
egg	-K	*ʔʊmuu.ke*	-T	*ʊʊmʊ.ti*
horn	-K	*kɔsʊl.ge*	-V	*kɔsʊʊl.i*
cloud	-V	*aabuga*	-T	*aabug.adi*

Table 20. Examples of Aka number marking on nouns[47]

As with Gaamhg, nouns can have zero marking, singulatives a velar or underspecified vowel, with plural affixes *-Ti, -Ni,* or a single vowel. Some plural suffixes, such as *-aTi,* probably combine two affixes, a pattern found elsewhere in East Sudanic.

4.7. Temein

Temein consists of three languages, Temein, Keiga Jirru, and These.[48] Surface forms for number marking in Temein are highly diverse and not easy to predict, even though the basic elements are relatively few. Temein languages operate a three-way system of number-marking with an unmarked form plus singulatives and pluratives, also known as "replacive."[49] However, the erosion of this system has meant that nouns where three terms occur synchronically are relatively rare. **Table 21** shows some examples of these:

Language	Gloss	SG	Unmarked	PL
Temein	dura	*mórɪŋɪnt̪ɛt̪* (one grain)	*mórɪŋɪs* (head of grain)	*mórɪŋ* (dura plant)
Keiga Jirru	meat	*bɪlanḍàk* (one piece)	*ɪnḍàk*	*kɪnḍaḍìk*
Keiga Jirru	medicine	*móreḍàk*		*komórò* (roots)
These	fat (n.)	*nányéḍə̀k*	*nányàʔ*	*kɪnányàʔ*

Table 21. Tripartite number marking in the Temein cluster

Number marking in Temein displays typical Nilo-Saharan characteristics, although these are combined in ways that are difficult to predict for individual nouns. The most common elements are:

- "Moveable k-" (with an underspecified vowel), prefixed, suffixed or both, where prefixed *kV-* is a typical strategy for Arabic loanwords
- Addition of final *-NI*
- Addition of final *-a[ʔ]*
- Singulative marking with *-It̪*, *-Is*
- Vowel lengthening and unpredictable changes in vowel quality
- Changes in ATR quality of the vowel
- Suppletion is present although not always easy to identify due to vowel changes and shortening

4.7.1. Prefix *k-*

In the Temein cluster *k-* is strongly associated with plurals and can occur before, after, and at both ends of a word. The underspecified vowel often results in a copy of the stem vowel, though not in every case. The vowel can disappear when the stem begins with an approximant. *Table 22* shows surface forms in Temein:

Gloss	Unmarked	PL
belly	*óòm*	*kómɪk*
big	*ḿbù*	*kɪmbɪk*
hill, stone	*kúrɛṱ*	*kukúrɛṱ*
shield	*wór*	*kwòráʔ*

Table 22. Temein -*Vk, kV-* nominal affixes

This affix has an allomorph -*Vk* that can mark singulative as in These (**Table 23**):

Gloss	SG	Unmarked
firewood	*márɛnyɪk*	*márɛŋ*
ear	*ŋwánɪk*	*kwɛɛŋ*
eye	*náánɪk*	*kɛnyɪŋ*
fish	*kɛlɛḓak*	*káála*

Table 23. These -*Vk* singulative affix

In the case of the singulative for "fish," it appears that it has already been marked once as a singulative with -*ṱ* and the -*Vk* has been subsequently affixed.

4.7.2. Final -*NI*

Less common is -*NI* or -*IN* in final position. Temein examples are shown in **Table 24**:

Gloss	Unmarked	PL
friend	*wórɪnyà*	*kórɪnyànì*
hanging frame	*sɛsɪlàŋ*	*sɛsɪlàŋì*
moon	*kóù*	*kikówɪn*

Table 24. Temein -IN, -NI plural affix

The following affixes can thus be attributed to Temein, -*T*, -*K*, -*N*, -*S*, -*V*. Temein shows no evidence for consonant gemination.

4.8. Daju

Daju languages also show evidence for the characteristic three-way number-marking contrast of Nilo-Saharan, albeit realised in a fragmentary way in many languages. Stevenson describes the three-way contrast in Shatt Tebeldia:

> Many nouns have three forms, representing mass or collective / unit / units. [...] The suffix is then replaced by another, or a further suffix is added, to denote the plural of the unit. [...][50]

This is shown for two glosses in **Table 25**:

Gloss	SG	Unmarked	PL (countable)
egg	*gilis-ic*	*gilis*	*gilis-u*
worm	*ox-uic*	*ox*	*ox-uij-iny*

Shatt and Laggori at least have considerable diversity of surface affixes marking number, either singulative or plural with suffixes as well as *replacing word endings.[51] Boyeldieu describes the number marking in Shatt Damman in some detail (**Table 26**).

Category	SG	PL
SG/pl. alternation	*-V*	*-u*
	-x	*-ɲ*
	-c	*-ɲ, -ic/-iɲ, -d(d)ic/-d(d)iɲ*
	-ic	*-u*
	-(ɨ)c	*-ta/-d(d)a*
PL only		*-iɲ*
		-u
		-ta/-d(d)a
		-ti/-d(d)i
		-tiɲ
		-dɨk
SG only	*-ic*	
	-tic/-d(d)ic	
	-c	
	-sɨnic/-zɨnɨc	

Table 26. Number-marking suffixes in Shatt Damman[52]

Boyeldieu also lists a significant number of irregular forms. There are three classes of noun, those with alternation, and those with singulatives and those with plurals. It appears there are now no examples of three-way contrast. Despite the surface variety, allomorphy suggests there are five underlying affixes, *-N, -T, -K, -y,* and *-V* where *V* is a high back vowel. In addition, the *-x* suffix may an allophone of an underlying fricative, i.e., *-S* (*s ~ z*), which would give Daju a complete set of East Sudanic affixes. Some singulative suffixes, such as *-zɨnɨc,* illustrate multiple compounding. There are, however, no examples of gemination.

The alternating nominal suffixes of Dar Daju described by Aviles present a far simpler set.[53] Every noun has one of four singular suffixes. Aviles calls these “classificatory” although they have no obvious semantic association. These alternate with four plural suffixes, although these all appear to be allomorphs of *-ge* (**Table 27**).

Class	Gloss	SG
1	elder	*ɟam-ne*
2	liver	*cacaw-ce*
3	mouth	*uk-e*
4	car	*watiɾ-i*

Table 27. Singulative suffixes in Dar Daju[54]

The singulative suffixes -*NV*, -*ʧV*, and -*V* (where *V* is a front vowel) can be attributed to Dar Daju.

4.9. Nilotic

4.9.1. West Nilotic

The principal overview of noun morphology in West Nilotic is presented by Storch. Western Nilotic also has an emergent classifier system, described in some detail in Storch but omitted here. **Table 28** summarizes the affixes of West Nilotic:

Semantics	Mayak	Mabaan	Jumjum	Dinka	Nuer
general	-*(V)k*	-*k(ã)*	-*kV*	-*k*, -*V*	
general	-*(V)n*	-*Ciṉ*	-*ni*	-*N*, -*V*	-*ní*, -*V̱*
round, mass, small		-*ăṉ*			
body		-*kù*			-*c*
space					(*-*N*?)
unspecified		-*λ*			-*y*
unspecified	-*iṯ*	-*ṯăn*		-*ṯ*	-*ṯ*
abstract	-*ḓín*				

Semantics	Anywa	Päri	Shilluk	Lüwo	Thuri
general	-k, -Ci, Cè	-ki, -ke	*-k	-kʌ̀	-k
general	-Ciʔ, -Cèʔ	-Neʔ	-V(N)	-V, -ɛ, -NVɛ́	-Ni, -in, -Nɛ́, -ɛ́n
round, mass, small	-i	-e	(.̀), (̀)	-ɛ́	-ɛ́
body	-Ci	-ì		-ì	-ì
space					
unspecified			[.̀]		
unspecified	-t, -Cè	-rí, -te	-Vdi	-t̪	-d̪i
abstract					

Semantics	Belanda Bor	S. Lwoo	Labwor
general		-k(V), -ke	-gV
general		-ni, -n(í)n, -ne	-ni, -né
round, mass, small		-e	-é, -i
body		-i	-i
space			
unspecified			
unspecified		*-ti, -(t)àʔ	-(C)áʔ
abstract			

Table 28. Number marking affixes in West Nilotic[55]

If we presume the same processes of allomorphy as elsewhere in East Sudanic, the number marking affixes of Proto-West Nilotic can be summarized more briefly:

- Underlying affixes: *-KV, -TV, -NV, -V*
- Compound affixes: *-TVN, -VTV, -VNV*

4.9.2. East Nilotic

The only survey of East Nilotic lexicon remains Voßen's,[56] and this can provide an impression of number marking morphology, although descriptions of individual languages provide more detail. For example, Kuku has unmarked nominals, with singulatives in some cases, and plurals, both suffixed. **Table 29** shows examples of the main number-marking strategies in Kuku.

Gloss	**Affix**	**SG**	**Affix**	**PL**
cattle tick	*-T(T)*	*mísír.itít*	-Ø	*másɛ̂r*
black ant	*-T*	*múkúɲ.êt*	-Ø	*múkûn*
Bari	-N + -T	*bari.nít*	-Ø	*barɪ*
hippo	-Ø	*yárɔ́*	-S + -N	*yárɔ́.ɟɪn*
school	-Ø	*sukúlu*	-K	*sukúlu.kíʔ*
nose	-Ø	*kʊmɛ́*	-S	*kʊmɛ́.sɪʔ*
cheek	-Ø	*ŋɛ́bí*	-T	*ŋɛ́bí.at*
speck	-Ø	*bɛ́rɛt*	-N	*bɛ́rɛt.án*
hedgehog	-Ø	*leɲɨpúɗut*	-T + -M	*leɲɨpúɗu(t)lɨ́n*
knife	-Ø	*wálí*	-V	*wálí.a*

Table 29. Kuku singulatives and plural markers[57]

The underlying logic of the singulatives is evident; nouns that are considered inherently plural are unmarked, with individuals marked by suffix. Thus "Bari" is a nation and the singulative applies to a Bari person. The suffixes are all allomorphs of a basic -*VT* form, except for the additional nasal, which is either a person marker or the nasal also occurring in the plural. Plural suffixes can be reduced to a dental, a velar, a nasal and an underspecified vowel. The only unusual feature is the -*sɪʔ* suffix, which may be innovative.

4.9.3. South Nilotic

There are two published reconstructions of South Nilotic.[58] Rottland includes a substantial comparative wordlist as well as discussions of number marking. Tucker & Bryan discuss number marking with respect to Pokot and Nandi-Kipsigis. Based on their illustration of Pokot, **Table 30** extracts a sample of singular/plural pairings in Pokot, which illustrate singulatives in *-V(V)N* and *-tV* and plural in *-kV.-V(V)* suffixes are also common, but it is unclear how many are allomorphs and how many are distinct roots.

Gloss	Affix	SG	Affix	PL
the calf	*-Tv*	*mɔ̀ɔ̀ɣ.tâ*	*-V*	*mòóɣ.ee?*
the duiker	*-Tv*	*cèptĭrkìc.tá̋*	*-kV*	*cèptĭrkìc.kâ̂*
the flea	*-VN + -Tv*	*kə̀mə̀tyə̀án.tɛ́ɛ́*	*-kV*	*kəmə́t.kâ̂*
the spear	*-Tv*	*ŋɔ̀t.ə́t*	*-V, -V(V)*	*ŋät.w.éè*
the lover	*-VN + -Tv*	*cȁmíín.téè*	*-V*	*cȁm.í
the barred door	*-V*	*mȁrȁn.èé?*	*-kV*	*mȁrâ̂n.kâ̂*

Table 30. Examples of Pokot number marking[59]

Pokot shows evidence for an original singulative *-V(V)N*, which has been resuffixed with *-tV(V)*.

The number system of Endo, another language of the Markweeta (Marakwet) group, is described by Zwarts. Endo has a wide range of singulative suffixes shown in **Table 31**, although once allomorphy is considered, they can probably be reduced to a rather simpler set. Zwarts argues that plurals constitute the unmarked set.

Gloss	Affix	SG	PL
cloud	*-tV*	*pool.ta*	*pool*
woman	*-ka*	*kāār.kā*	*kāār*
grasshopper	*-wa*	*taalim.wa*	*taalim*
cedar	*-wa*	*tārāāk.wā*	*taraak*
patch of grass	*-wa + -Vn*	*sīūs.wāān*	*sūūs*
medicine	*-wa + -Vn*	*saakit.yaan*	*saakit*
European	*-Vn*	*chūmp.īīn*	*chumpa*
shoe	*-V*	*kwēēr.ā*	*kwēēr*

Table 31. Endo singulative suffixes[60]

Underlyingly, therefore. Endo has the singulatives *-V(V)N*, *-tV*, *-V*, *-kV*, and an unmarked plural. Despite the surface differences, the West Nilotic system in these two examples is broadly similar.

4.10. Synthesis

A feature of East Sudanic, and indeed Nilo-Saharan more generally, is extensive allomorphy. Each affix appears under several guises, often reflecting the stem to which is suffixed. **Table 32** shows the typical allomorphs of East Sudanic nominal affixes:

Affix	Interpretation	Typical allomorphs
-T	dentals	/t/, /ʈ/, /d/, /ɖ/
-K	velars	/k/, /g/
-N	nasals	/n/, /ŋ/, /ɲ/
-S	fricatives	/s/, /ʃ/, /ʤ/
-V	non-central vowels	/i/, /u/
-A	central vowels	/a/

Table 32: Allomorphs of East Sudanic nominal affixes

Table 33 shows the presence or absence of individual affixes in each branch, together with affix-stacking and gemination, as well as the table which supports this analysis.

Branch	-T	-K	-N	-V	-S	Aff. st.	Gem.	Ref.
Nubian	+	–	+	–	–	+	–	T. 9, 10
Nara	+	+	–	+	+	–	+	T. 13
Nyima	–	?	–	–	–	–	–	T. 15, 16
Taman	+	+	+	+	–	–	–	T. 17
Surmic	+	+	+	+	+	–	–	T. 19
E Jebel	+	+	+	+	–	+	–	T. 20
Temein	+	+	+	+	+	+	–	T. 22, 23, 24
Daju	+	+	+	+	+	+	–	T. 26, 27
W Nilotic	+	+	+	+	–	+	–	T. 28
E Nilotic	+	+	+	+	+	+	+	T. 29
S Nilotic	+	+	+	+	–	+	–	T. 30, 31

Table 33. East Sudanic nominal affixes and associated

The resultant pattern is not perfect but still indicative for the structure of East Sudanic. The number-marking suffixes form complete sets in En languages, with -S attested only in Nara. This implies that all five affixes were present in proto-East Sudanic but were preferentially lost in the Ek languages. Affix-stacking, though present in Nubian, is otherwise absent in Ek languages but is likely to be a retention from proto-East Sudanic. Gemination is too sparsely distributed to draw any conclusions, but is plausibly an independent development of no classificatory significance.

5. Internal Structure of East Sudanic

The evidence presented points to a common inheritance in East Sudanic number marking strategies. The distribution of affix-stacking and complete affix sets suggest that apart from common lexemes, Ek languages are characterized by a common loss of these characters. In the light of this, **Figure 1** presents a revised internal classification of East Sudanic, grouping together the Ek languages as Northern East Sudanic, but leaving the others as independent branches.

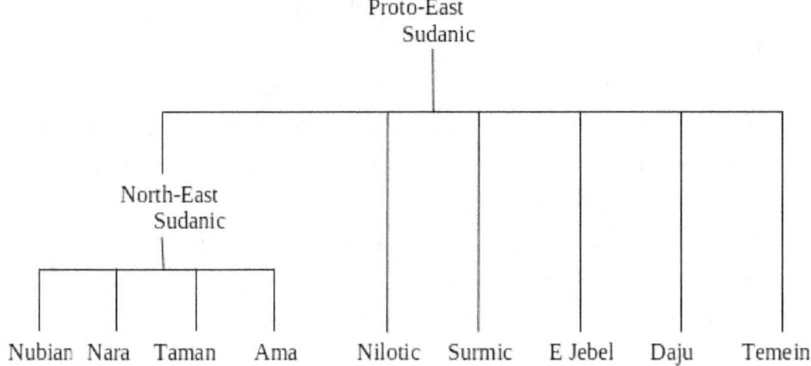

Figure 1. Proposed internal structure of East Sudanic[61]

It seems plausible that further results should be attainable from a deeper examination of the lexicon, since the effect of affix accretion and reanalysis obscures cognacy of roots.

6. East Sudanic within Nilo-Saharan

The attentive reader will have observed that many of the affixes identified in this paper have been attested outside the proposed East Sudanic. Indeed, the "t-k substratum" proposed by Tucker & Bryan is far more widespread. Particular candidates are Kuliak and Kadu, a subgroup sometimes excluded from Nilo-Saharan altogether. This section considers briefly the morphology of these two groups in relation to our understanding of East Sudanic.

I have explored this morphology in the Kadu languages while Gilley has looked into number-marking in Katcha in some detail.[62] Typically, Kadu languages have a three-term system with a singulative in *-t* and plural in *-k* and *-N*. They also have case-marking, which is only sporadically attested in East Sudanic languages and cannot be reconstructed, as well as sex-gender, which is entirely absent. This suggests that the *-T*, *-K*, and *-N* affixes can be reconstructed further back in Nilo-Saharan, but the *-V* and *-S* are distinctive to East Sudanic. The gemination found in Nara and East Nilotic is not recorded in Kadu, but may not be reconstructible to proto-East Sudanic.

The Kuliak languages, a small group in northeast Uganda which includes Ik, So, and Nyangi, were originally included by Greenberg within East Sudanic, but have long been treated as an independent branch of Nilo-Saharan. However, their lexicon has been heavily impacted both by their immediate neighbors, the Karimojong, but also by Southern Nilotic in some past era. Moreover, Lamberti has noted striking resemblances to the East Cushitic languages.[63] Heine presents an overview and reconstruction of Kuliak as it was known at the period.[64] More recently, Carlin and Schrock have provided extensive documentation of Soo and Ik (Icétôd).[65] Kuliak languages have three-term number marking, with singulative in *-T* and plurative in *-K*, *-N*, as well as allowing affix-stacking, but also have a striking nominal case-marking system not present in East Sudanic. There is no evidence for gemination.

In conclusion, East Sudanic is characterized by a series of affixes, which have developed out of a smaller set which are also present in related branches of Nilo-Saharan. Unlike Kadu, there is no trace of gender and the case marking. Case marking is also characteristic of Kuliak languages, which only have a reduced affix set. These suggest that there is a higher node within Nilo-Saharan which included these three branches, but that the East Sudanic language developed specific morphological features (or perhaps lost them at the level of the proto-language). It is striking that the lexical unity of East Sudanic is not more apparent, given the conservatism of the number-marking system.

7. Abbreviations

- A: any central vowel ±ATR;
- C: any consonant;
- I: any high front vowel ±ATR;
- K: velar consonant;
- N: any nasal consonant;
- PL: plural;
- S: any fricative consonant;
- SG: singular;
- T: any dental consonant;
- V: any vowel;
- X: any phoneme.

8. Bibliography

Alamin Mubarak, Suzan. "An Initial Description of Laggori Noun Morphology and Noun Phrase." In *Insights into Nilo-Saharan Language, History and Culture: Proceedings of the 9th Nilo-Saharan Linguistics Colloquium, Institute of African and Asian Studies, University of Khartoum, 16–19 February 2004,* edited by Al-Amin Abu-Manga, Leoma Gilley & Anne Storch. Cologne: Rüdiger Köppe, 2006: pp. 9–24.

Aviles, Arthur J. *The Phonology and Morphology of the Dar Daju Daju Language.* MA Thesis, University of North Dakota at Grand Forks, 2008.

Bell, Herman. "Documentary Evidence on the Ḥarāza Nubian." *Sudan Notes and Records* 7 (1975): pp. 1–36.

Bender, M. Lionel. *Comparative Omotic Lexicon.* Carbondale: SIU, 2003.

Bender, M. Lionel. "Genetic Subgrouping of East Sudanic." *Afrikanistische Arbeitspapiere* 45 (1996): pp. 139–150.

Bender, M. Lionel. "Proto-Koman Phonology and Lexicon." *Africa and Ubersee* 66, no. 2 (1983): pp. 259–297.

Bender, M. Lionel. "Roland Stevenson's Nyimang and Dinik Lexicon." *Afrikanistische Arbeitspapiere* 63 (2000): pp. 103–120.

Bender, M. Lionel. "The Genetic Position of Nilotic i: Independent Pronouns." In *"Mehr als nur Worte...": Afrikanistische Beiträge zum 65. Geburtstag von Franz Rottland,* edited by R. Voßen, A. Mietzner, and A. Meißner. Cologne: Rudiger Köppe, 2000: pp. 89–119.

Bender, M. Lionel. "The Eastern Jebel languages of Sudan I: Phonology." *Afrika und Übersee* 80 (1997): pp. 189–215.

Bender, M. Lionel. "The Eastern Jebel languages of Sudan II: Comparative Lexicon." *Afrika und Übersee* 81 (1998): pp. 39–64.

Bender, M. Lionel. *The East Sudanic Languages: Lexicon and Phonology.* Carbondale: Southern Illinois University, 2005.

Bender, Lionel M. bib/*The Nilo-Saharan Languages: A Comparative Essay.* 2nd edition. Munich: Lincom Europa, 1997.

Blench, Roger M. bib/"Introduction to the Temein Languages." In *Nuba Mountain Language Studies,* edited by Thilo C. Schadeberg and Roger M. Blench. Cologne: Rüdiger Köppe, 2013: pp. 485–500.

Blench, Roger M. bib/"The Kadu Languages and Their Affiliation: Between Nilo-Saharan, Niger-Congo and Afro-Asiatic." In *Insights into Nilo-Saharan Language, History and Culture: Proceedings of the 9th Nilo-Saharan Linguistics Colloquium, Institute of African and Asian Studies, University of Khartoum, 16–19 February 2004,* edited by Al-Amin Abu-Manga, Leoma Gilley, and Anne Storch. Cologne: Rüdiger Köppe, 2006: pp. 101–127.

Boyeldieu, Pascal. bib/"Dadjo-Sila." In *La qualification dans les langues africaines,* edited by Holger Tröbs, Eva Rothmaler, and Kerstin Winkelmann. Cologne: Rüdiger Köppe Verlag, 2008: pp. 57–70.

Browne, Gerald M. bib/*Old Nubian Dictionary.* Leuven: Peeters, 1996.

Bryan, Margaret. bib/"The T–K Languages: A New Substratum." *Africa* 29, no. 1 (1959): pp. 1–21. DOI: www/10.2307/1157496.

Carlin, Eithne. bib/*The So language.* Cologne: Universität zu Köln, 1993.

Cohen, Kevin B. bib/*Aspects of the Grammar of Kukú.* Munich: Lincom Europa, 2000.

Dawd, Abushush & R.J. Hayward. bib/"Nara." *Journal of the International Phonetic Association* 32, no. 2 (2002): pp. 249–255. DOI: www/10.1017/S0025100302001068.

Dimmendaal, Gerrit J. bib/"Differential Object Marking in Nilo-Saharan." *Journal of African Languages and Linguistics* 31 (2011): pp. 13–46. DOI: www/10.1515/jall.2010.003.

Dimmendaal, Gerrit J. bib/*Historical Linguistics and the Comparative Study of African Languages.* Amsterdam: John Benjamins Publishing, 2011.

Dimmendaal, Gerrit J. "Marked Nominative Systems in Eastern Sudanic and Their Historical Origin." *Afrikanistik Online* 11, no. 3 (2014): pp. 1–23. www/

https://www.afrikanistik-aegyptologie-online.de/archiv/2014/3859/fulltext/view?set_language=en.

Dimmendaal, Gerrit J. "Number Marking and Noun Categorization in Nilo-Saharan Languages." *Anthropological Linguistics* 42, no. 2 (2000): pp. 214–261.

Edgar, John T. "First Steps toward Proto-Tama." In *Proceedings of the Fourth Nilo-Saharan Conference: Bayreuth Aug. 30–Sep. 2, 1989,* edited by M. Lionel Bender. Hamburg: Helmut Buske, 1991: pp. 111–131.

Ehret, Christopher. *A Historical-Comparative Reconstruction of Nilo-Saharan.* Cologne: Rudiger Köppe, 2001.

Ehret, Christopher. *Southern Nilotic History: Linguistic Approaches to the Study of the Past.* Evanston: Northwestern University Press, 1971.

Gilley, Leoma G. "Katcha Noun Morphology." In *Nuba Mountain Language Studies,* edited by Thilo C. Schadeberg & Roger M. Blench. Cologne: Rudiger Köppe, 2013: pp. 501–522.

Greenberg, Joseph H. "Nilo-Saharan Moveable-<em>k</em> as a Stage III Article (with a Penutian Typological Parallel)." *Journal of African Languages and Linguistics* 3, no. 2 (1981): pp. 105–112. 10.1515/jall.1981.3.2.105.

Greenberg, Joseph H. "Studies in African Linguistic Classification: V. The Eastern Sudanic Family." *Southwestern Journal of Anthropology* 6, no. 2 (1950): pp. 143–160. 10.1086/soutjanth.6.2.3628639.

Greenberg, Joseph H. *The Languages of Africa.* The Hague: Mouton & Co, 1963.

Güldemann, Tom. "The Historical-Comparative Status of East Sudanic." In *Proceedings of the 14th Nilo-Saharan Linguistics Colloquium,* edited by Roger M. Blench, Petra Weschenfelder, and Georg Ziegelmeyer. Cologne: Rüdiger Köppe, forthcoming.

Hayward, Richard J. "Observations on Tone in the Higir Dialect of Nara." In *"Mehr als nur Worte...": Afrikanistische Beiträge zum 65. Geburtstag von Franz Rottland,* edited by R. Voßen, A. Mietzner, and A. Meißner. Cologne: Rudiger Köppe, 2000: pp. 247–267.

Heine, Bernd. bib/*The Kuliak Languages of Eastern Uganda.* Nairobi: East African Publishing House, 1976.

Jakobi, Angelika & Ahmed Hamdan. bib/"Number Marking on Karko Nouns." *Dotawo: A Journal of Nubian Studies* 2 (2015): pp. 271–289. DOI: www/ 10.5070/D62110017.

Joseph, Clement Lopeyok, et al. bib/*Laarim Grammar Book.* Juba: SIL-Sudan, 2012.

Kellermann, P. bib/*Eine grammatische Skizze des Tama auf der Basis der Daten von R.C. Stevenson.* MA thesis, Johann-Wolfgang-Goethe Universitat, Mainz, 2000.

Lamberti, Marcello. bib/*Kuliak and Cushitic: A Comparative Study.* Heidelberg: Carl Winter, 1988.

Norton, Russell. "Ama Verbs in Comparative Perspective." *Dotawo: A Journal of Nubian Studies* 7 (2020): article/this issue

Norton, Russell. bib/"Number in Ama Verbs." *Occasional Papers in the Study of Sudanese Languages* 10 (2012): pp. 75–94.

Rilly, Claude. bib/*Le méroïtique et sa famille linguistique.* Leuven: Peeters, 2009.

Rilly, Claude & Alex de Voogt. bib/*The Meroitic Language and Writing System.* Cambridge: Cambridge University Press, 2012.

Ross, James S. *A Preliminary Attempt at the Reconstruction of Proto-East Sudanic Phonology and Lexicon.* MA Thesis, Southern Illinois University, 1990.

Rottland, Franz. bib/*Die südnilotischen Sprachen: Beschriebung, Vergleichung und Rekonstruktion.* Berlin: Dietrich Reimer, 1982.

Schrock, Terrill B. bib/*The Ik Language: Dictionary and Grammar Sketch.* Berlin: Language Science Press, 2016.

Starostin, George. bib/"Lexicostatistical Studies in East Sudanic I: On the Genetic Unity of Nubian-Nara-Tama." *Journal of Language Relationship* [*Вопросы языкового родства*] 15, no. 2 (2017): pp. 87–113.

Stevenson, Roland C. "A Survey of the Phonetics and Grammatical Structures of the Nuba Mountain Languages, with Particular Reference to Otoro, Katcha and Nyimaŋ." *Afrika und Übersee* 40 (1956): pp. 73–84, 93–115.

Stevenson, Roland C. "A Survey of the Phonetics and Grammatical Structures of the Nuba Mountain Languages, with Particular Reference to Otoro, Katcha and Nyimaŋ." *Afrika und Übersee* 41 (1957): pp. 27–65, 117–152, 171–196.

Stirtz, Timothy M. *A Grammar of Gaahmg: A Nilo-Saharan Language of Sudan.* Utrecht: LOT, 2011.

Storch, Anne. *The Noun Morphology of Western Nilotic.* Cologne: Rudiger Köppe, 2005.

Thelwall, Robin A. "A Birgid Vocabulary List and Its Links with Daju." In *Gedenkschrift Gustav Nachtigal 1874–1974,* edited by E. Ganslmayr and H. Jungraithmayr, pp. 197–210. Bremen: Übersee Museum, 1977.

Trigger, Bruce G. "Meroitic and Eastern Sudanic: A Linguistic Relationship." *Kush* 12 (1964): 188–194.

Tucker, Archibald N. *The Eastern Sudanic Languages, Vol. I.* Oxford: Oxford University Press, 1940.

Tucker, Archibald N. & Margaret A. Bryan. *Linguistic Analyses: The Non-Bantu Languages of North-Eastern Africa.* London: Oxford University Press.

Tucker, Archibald N. & Margaret A. Bryan. *Noun Classification in Kalenjin: Nandi-Kipsigis.* London: School of Oriental and African Studies, University of London, 1964.

Tucker, Archibald N. & Margaret A. Bryan. *Noun Classification in Kalenjin: Päkot.* London: School of Oriental and African Studies, University of London, 1962.

Tucker, Archibald N. & Margaret A. Bryan. *The Non-Bantu Languages of North-Eastern Africa.* London: Oxford University Press, 1956.

Voogt, Alex de "Dual Marking and Kinship Terms in Afitti." *Studies in Language* 35, no. 4 (2011): pp. 898–911. DOI: 10.1075/sl.35.4.04dev.

Voßen, Rainer. bib/*The Eastern Nilotes: Linguistic and Historical Reconstructions.* Berlin: Dietrich Reimer, 1982.

Werner, Roland. bib/*Tìdn-áal: A Study of Midob (Darfur-Nubian).* Berlin: Dietrich Reimer, 1993.

Yigezu, Moges & Gerrit J. Dimmendaal. bib/"Notes on Baale." In *Surmic Languages and Cultures,* edited by Gerrit J. Dimmendaal and Marco Last. Cologne: Rüdiger Köppe, 1998: pp. 273–317.

Zwarts, Joost. bib/"Number in Endo-Marakwet." In *Advances in Nilo-Saharan Linguistics: Proceedings of the 8th Nilo-Saharan Linguistics Colloquium, University of Hamburg, August 22–25, 2001,* edited by Mechthild Reh and Doris L. Payne. Cologne: Rüdiger Köppe, 2007: pp. 281–294.

Endnotes

1. Greenberg, "Studies in African Linguistic Classification: V. The Eastern Sudanic Family." ↩

2. Greenberg, *The Languages of Africa.* ↩

3. Bender, *The Nilo-Saharan Languages.* ↩

4. Greenberg, *The Languages of Africa.* ↩

5. Bender, *The Nilo-Saharan Languages.* ↩

6. Tucker, *The Eastern Sudanic Languages, vol. 1.* ↩

7. Tucker & Bryan, *The Non-Bantu Languages of North-Eastern Africa.* ↩

8. Greenberg, "Studies in African Linguistic Classification: V. The Eastern Sudanic Family." ↩

9. E.g., "Meroitic and Eastern Sudanic: A Linguistic Relationship." ↩

10. Rilly, *Le méroïtique et sa famille linguistique*; Rilly & De Voogt, *The Meroitic Language and Writing System.* ↩

11. Ross, *A Preliminary Attempt at the Reconstruction of Proto-East Sudanic Phonology and Lexicon.* ↩

12. Bender, “Genetic subgrouping of East Sudanic”; Bender, *The East Sudanic Languages.* ↩

13. Starostin, “Lexicostatistical Studies in East Sudanic I”; article/Starostin, this issue. ↩

14. Bender, *Comparative Omotic Lexicon.* ↩

15. Dimmendaal, “Differential Object Marking in Nilo-Saharan"; Dimmendaal, *Historical Linguistics and the Comparative Study of African Languages*; Dimmendaal, “Marked Nominative Systems in Eastern Sudanic and Their Historical Origin.” ↩

16. Güldemann, “The Historical-Comparative Status of East Sudanic.” ↩

17. Bender, *The East Sudanic Languages.* ↩

18. Ibid.; Bender, *The Nilo-Saharan Languages.* ↩

19. Data from Bender, “The Genetic Position of Nilotic *i*” and Bender, *The East Sudanic Languages,* supplemented with more recent sources. ↩

20. Bender, *The Nilo-Saharan Languages*; Bender, *The East Sudanic Languages*; Ehret, *A Historical-Comparative Reconstruction of Nilo-Saharan*; Rilly, *Le méroïtique et sa famille linguistique*, and Starostin, “Lexicostatistical Studies in East Sudanic I.” ↩

21. Nara and Ama data from Rilly, *Le méroïtique et sa famille linguistique*; Dilling, Midob, and proto-Taman data from Starostin, “Lexicostatistical Studies in East Sudanic I.” ↩

22. Midob data from Werner, *Tìdn-áal*; Nyala data from Thelwall, “A Birgid Vocabulary List and Its Links with Daju”; Nara data from Hayward, “Observations on Tone in the Higir Dialect of Nara”; Ama data from Bender, “Roland Stevenson’s Nyimang and Dinik Lexicon”; Tama data from Edgar, “First Steps toward Proto-Tama.” ↩

23. Andaandi, Nara, and Abu Sharib data from Rilly, *Le méroïtique et sa famille linguistique*; Ama data from Bender, "Roland Stevenson's Nyimang and Dinik Lexicon"; Gaahmg data from Stirtz, *A Grammar of Gaahmg.* ↩

24. Haraza data from Bell, "Documentary Evidence on the Ḥarāza Nubian," 84; Old Nubian data from Browne, *Old Nubian Dictionary,* 138; Karko data from Jakobi & Hamdan, "Number Marking on Karko Nouns"; Nara data from Hayward, "Observations on Tone in the Higir Dialect of Nara"; Proto-Nyima data from Bender, "Roland Stevenson's Nyimang and Dinik Lexicon"; Proto-Taman data from Edgar, "First Steps toward Proto-Tama." ↩

25. Bryan, "The T–K Languages." ↩

26. Greenberg, "Nilo-Saharan Moveable-*k* as a Stage III Article." ↩

27. Ehret, *A Historical-Comparative Reconstruction of Nilo-Saharan,* pp. 176, 181. ↩

28. Bender, *The Nilo-Saharan Languages,* p. 75. ↩

29. Ibid. ↩

30. Tucker & Bryan, *Linguistic Analyses,* pp. 22–24. ↩

31. Storch, *The Noun Morphology of Western Nilotic,* p. 46. ↩

32. See Bender, *The Nilo-Saharan Languages* and the 2020 edition of www/*Ethnologue*. ↩

33. Data from Jakobi & Hamdan, "Number Marking on Karko Nouns." ↩

34. Data from Jakobi & Hamdan, "Number Marking on Karko Nouns." ↩

35. Data from Werner, *Tìdn-áal.* ↩

36. Data from Rilly, *Le méroïtique et sa famille linguistique* ↩

37. Data from Dawd & Hayward, "Nara." ↩

38. De Voogt, "Dual Marking and Kinship Terms in Afitti." ↩

39. Data from Bender, "Roland Stevenson's Nyimang and Dinik Lexicon." ↩

40. Norton, "Number in Ama Verbs"; article/Norton, this issue. ↩

41. Data from article/Norton, this issue ↩

42. article/Norton, this issue ↩

43. Data from Kellermann, *Eine grammatische Skizze des Tama auf der Basis der Daten von R.C. Stevenson.* ↩

44. Data from Joseph et al., *Laarim Grammar Book.* ↩

45. Data from Yigezu & Dimmendaal, "Notes on Baale." ↩

46. Bender, "The Eastern Jebel Languages of Sudan I"; Bender, "The Eastern Jebel Languages of Sudan II." ↩

47. Data from Bender, "Proto-Koman Phonology and Lexicon." ↩

48. Blench, "Introduction to the Temein Languages." ↩

49. See, e.g., Dimmendaal, "Number Marking and Noun Categorization in Nilo-Saharan Languages," or Blench, "Introduction to the Temein Languages." ↩

50. Stevenson, "A Survey of the Phonetics and Grammatical Structures of the Nuba Mountain Languages," 96. ↩

51. Boyeldieu, *La qualification dans les langues africaines*; Alamin Mubarak, "An Initial Description of Laggori Noun Morphology and Noun Phrase." ↩

52. Data from Boyeldieu, *La qualification dans les langues africaines.* ↩

53. Aviles, *The Phonology and Morphology of the Dar Daju Daju Language.* ↩

54. Data from Aviles, *The Phonology and Morphology of the Dar Daju Daju Language.* ↩

55. Data from Storch, *The Noun Morphology of Western Nilotic,* 385. ↩

56. Voßen, *The Eastern Nilotes.* ↩

57. Data from Cohen, *Aspects of the Grammar of Kukú.* ↩

58. Ehret, *Southern Nilotic History*; Rottland, *Die südnilotischen Sprachen.* ↩

59. Data from Tucker & Bryan, *Noun Classification in Kalenjin: Päkot*; Tucker & Bryan, *Noun Classification in Kalenjin: Nandi-Kipsigis.* ↩

60. Data adapted from Zwarts, "Number in Endo-Marakwet." ↩

61. Cf. Rilly, *Le méroïtique et sa famille linguistique,* 208. ↩

62. Blench, "The Kadu Languages and Their Affiliation"; Gilley, "Katcha Noun Morphology." ↩

63. Lamberti, *Kuliak and Cushitic.* ↩

64. Heine, *The Kuliak Languages of Eastern Uganda.* ↩

65. Carlin, *The So language*; Schrock, *The Ik Language.* ↩

www.ingramcontent.com/pod-product-compliance
Lightning Source LLC
LaVergne TN
LVHW020053110826
845155LV00022B/78

* 9 7 8 1 9 5 3 0 3 5 3 9 4 *